Tough on Kids

Tough on Kids

Rethinking Approaches to Youth Justice

Ross Gordon Green
and Kearney F. Healy

Purich Publishing Ltd.
Saskatoon, Saskatchewan
Canada

Purich Publishing Ltd.
Box 23032, Market Mall Post Office
Saskatoon, SK Canada S7J 5H3
Phone: (306) 373–5311   Fax: (306) 373–5315
Email: purich@sasktel.net
Website: www.purichpublishing.com

National Library of Canada Cataloguing in Publication Data
Green, Ross Gordon, 1955–
  Tough on kids: rethinking approaches to youth justice/Ross Gordon Green and Kearney F. Healy

Includes index.
ISBN 1-895830-22-2

  1. Juvenile justice, Administration of—Canada. 2. Juvenile delinquents—Legal status, laws, etc.—Canada. 3. Youth—Legal status, laws, etc.—Canada. I. Healy, Kearney F., 1948– II. Title.
KE9445.G73 2003   345.7'08   C2003-911007-9
KF9780.ZA2G73 2003

Cover design by NEXT Communications Inc., Saskatoon, Saskatchewan.

Editing, design, layout, and index by Roberta Mitchell Coulter, Saskatoon, Saskatchewan.

Printed in Canada by Houghton Boston, Saskatoon on acid-free paper.

The publisher acknowledges the financial assistance of the Cultural Industries Development Fund, Saskatchewan Culture, Youth and Recreation towards publication of this book.

Readers will note that words like Aboriginal, Native, and Indigenous have been capitalized in this book. In recent years, many Aboriginal people have argued that such words should be capitalized when referring to specific people, in the same manner that European and American are capitalized. We agree.
The Publishers

URLs for websites contained in this book are accurate to the time of writing to the best of the authors' knowledge.

This book is dedicated to my family, as a recognition of their love and patience which each day give me the strength and hope to carry on. As well, it is dedicated to our youthful clients, whose words and thoughts inspired this manuscript.

Ross Green

I would like to dedicate this book to my family, who have been heroic in their patience. I would especially like to thank my daughter Danara, who has shown me true courage, which she says is fear plus a prayer.

Kearney Healy

Contents

Acknowledgements

We thank our young clients and friends who took us into their confidence and showed us what really goes on in the youth criminal justice system. We also thank the victims, families, police, prosecutors, youth workers, advocates, and realists who have taught us so much.

We are indebted to the Law Foundation of Saskatchewan and to the Legal Research Institute of the University of Manitoba for financial support of our research for this book. We also extend a special thanks to Dr. Russell Smandych of the University of Manitoba for his assistance.

During our research, we received the help and support of many people across Canada: in Calgary, John Miller, Joan Bayley, Doug Borch, Gail Daniels, Cathy Lane Goodfellow, Leah Barber, Judge Karen Jordan, and Daphne Buffet; in Edmonton, Charles Seto; in Montreal, Tom and Lois Pavlasek, Jean Trepanier, Serge Charbonneau, Judge Ann-Marie Jones, Clement Laporte, and Michel Cote; in Kenora, Rupert Ross; in Toronto, Annabelle and Everett Wood, Kirk Makin, and Anthony Doob; in Ottawa, Marilou Reeve, Stephanie Robinson, and Jeff Latimer; in Saskatoon, Judge Sheila Whelan, Judge Mary Ellen Turpel-Lafond, Eugene Gamble, Judge Bria Huculak, Don Meikle, Roland Duquette, Rebecca Elder, Katharine Grier, Paul Wilkinson, Peter Prebble, Cst. Craig Nyirfa, Cst. Randy Huisman, Cst. Joceline Schriemer, Sgt. Murray Glen, Rusty Chartier, Judge Gerald Seniuk, Judge Gerald Morin of Saskatchewan Cree Court, Sarah Ninnie, Ryan, Blaine, Terry, Brendan, Jacqui Barclay, Sue Delanoy, Gene Oullette, Deb Hopkins, Tim Quigley, Allan McGuire, Grant Crookshanks, and from the Native Law Centre Professor Sa'ke'j Youngblood Henderson and Wanda McCaslin; in Winnipeg, Margaret Green, Clayton Sandy, and Justice Murray Sinclair; in Melfort, Saskatchewan, Carol Jones, Judge Barrett Halderman, Jim Richards, Jodi Hufnagel, Mike Rybinski, Peter Waldbillig, Cecil Gooliaf, Leslie Christianson, and Lorraine Sebelius; in Regina, Chief Justice Edward Bayda, Byron Werry, and Bill Jennings; in

Meadow Lake, Saskatchewan, Judge Earl Kalenith; in Nipawin, Saskatchewan, Don Watson; and in Tisdale, Saskatchewan, Ken Homeniuk and Tim Tarala. As well, we would like to thank Nils Christie of Norway.

Finally, we thank Don Purich and Karen Bolstad of Purich Publishing and editor Roberta Coulter, all of Saskatoon, for their assistance throughout this project.

"They say they don't mind being locked up, but I can tell they want to get out real bad. The so-called system won't let them out."

R.T.

Introduction

Imagine that it was necessary to build a new society. For whatever reason, possibly in response to some tragedy, we needed to lay the foundations for a fresh reorganization of our community.

Naturally, we would be concerned first with survival. We would want to ensure that we had good food, water, shelter, clothing—the basics. Then we would want to educate our young people and to encourage the use of all our personal strengths and talents in an optimistic, energetic way, to build a better life for all in our community.

And where would criminal justice, and particularly youth criminal justice, fit in? As little as possible. In our new society we would want to spend as little as possible of our scarce resources setting up formal institutions to respond to offences. Indeed, we would try hard to use informal techniques as a means of convincing each other of the importance of living together peacefully. And when these informal techniques failed, and we needed to gather together as a community to formally address the problem, we would express our anger at the offence, and at the offender for making us go this far. But in doing this we would restate our common vision, reminding the offender of his or her role in achieving a better life for everyone in the community, a community that included the offender.

But imagine a society which, for whatever reason, was not capable of convincing offenders to change and become contributing members of society. What if that same society's response had no effect on crime, or actually encouraged it? What if rather than being part of the processes that a community used to unite its people to follow a common vision of a better life for all, it was actually a powerful force to divide the community on extremely specious grounds, like race, poverty, or disabilities? What if it was a very expensive system? What if it tended to encourage minor offenders to become more serious and violent offenders?

What would you say about a society like that? Would you call for a Royal Commission? Would you call your local politicians? Would you sink into despair? Would you ask how did we get to this state of affairs? Would you turn your eyes away?

Few Canadians realize that we as a country jail nearly four times as many youth as we do adults, and we imprison more youth per capita than the United States, usually considered the world leader in "getting tough."[1] In *R. v. J.K.E.*, Judge Lilles of the Yukon Territorial Court described this situation in Canada as a "national disgrace."[2] And it is.

As lawyers who have practised for years in youth court, we have, between us, advocated for thousands of young people. Some have been some so youthful, so unsophisticated, so untrained, they really are still children. We've appeared with them day after day in all levels of court. We've represented young people charged with offences ranging from the most minor shoplifting to the most serious homicide. We've spent thousands of hours listening to their stories, their explanations, their hurts, their lies. We've watched them angry, scared, in tears. We've been in jail with them, in court, on the street, in schools, and in their homes. We've listened to their parents, their teachers, their friends, the police who arrested them, the workers assigned to them, their victims, and the friends and families of their victims. We've listened to those who hate them and those who love them. We know their awful pain.

After listening to and representing a multitude of young people within the justice system, and after researching the most current material on youth justice around the world, we hope to show that there are ways to reduce levels of youth crime. In this book, we present these solutions, many of which appear obvious, but you may be surprised at how infrequently they are being applied.

Our views may be controversial. They run contrary to most public pronouncements on how the youth justice system should be reformed. Indeed, we expect the perceived link between punishment and custody, on the one hand, and crime reduction and safer communities, on the other, is deeply ingrained in our society. But we ask you to consider our analysis and our arguments, and decide for yourself whether our suggestions make sense.

Our views should not be taken as an attack on many honest and dedicated people working across our youth justice system. Indeed, we have great respect for many police officers, youth workers, correctional staff, defence lawyers, prosecutors, and judges who toil tirelessly within this system and show an ongoing concern for those youths caught up in its courts and jails. To be sure, there are those with whom we disagree, sometimes frequently and sometimes vocally. But our criticisms and comments in this book are aimed primarily at the philosophical underpinnings driving much of today's youth justice policy, and at the structures and strategies within our criminal justice system that represent society's response to these philosophies.

Our analysis of youth criminal justice is first and foremost led by our clients' confidence in us to tell us their secrets. They have taught us why the youth criminal justice system seems to fail so often. Throughout this book we try to provide the missing piece, the hidden key: the experience of those youth and children who trusted us enough to let us speak for them.

"Obviously, the way I grew up I always knew

eventually I was going to jail."

R.T.

Chapter One

Perspectives on Youth Crime and Justice

Consider two countries. These are next door to each other, and are separated from most of the rest of the world by ocean. They share a language that virtually everyone understands, and engage in friendly trade with enormous mutual benefits. Both countries have similar national events, holidays, and traditions. Indeed, it would be hard to tell when you're in one country or the other. Their citizens watch the same movies and TV shows, shop in the same stores, and have similar schools. The lengthy border between these countries has no forts, no barriers, no armies.

To be sure, there are some differences. For example, one country offers free medical care to its citizens and has a more restrictive form of gun control. These are not major differences and probably in the future both countries will have both of them.

On the surface, these countries are very similar. But now consider the adult justice system of each country. From 1991 to 1999, in Country 'A,' to the south, the number of people in jail dramatically increased by as much as 42 percent. By 1999 this country had 682 per 100,000 people in jail. As a result, by 1999, there were an additional 650,000 prisoners in jail (at $50,000 per year) as compared to 1991. Country 'B,' on the other hand, decided to save money and put fewer adults in jail and reduced the number of prisoners by 6 percent to 106 people per 100,000 people.

Country 'A,' which increased its percentage of adults in jail to over six times as many as in Country 'B,' also increased its police force by 11 percent so that Country 'A' had 2.3 police officers per 1,000 citizens in 1999.

Country 'B' reduced its police force by the same figure of 11 percent, to 1.8 police officers per 1,000 citizens.

So in our comparison, two almost identical countries take their justice systems in opposite directions in a dramatic fashion. Country 'A' puts many more people in jail and more police officers on the street so as to deter crime, while Country 'B' reduces its police force and the number of people in jail. What happened to the crime rates in both countries? Contrary to expectations, crime declined equally in both!

This is an actual comparison of what happened in Canada and the United States between 1991 and 1999.[1]

Two conclusions are inescapable. First, something caused crime to be reduced in both Canada and the United States. Second, it had nothing to do with deterring crime by putting more people in jail and hiring more police officers, presumably to scare away potential offenders.

In many ways this reduction in crime was predictable from a historical perspective. In England, crime rose in the late eighteenth century and early nineteenth century, largely because many people were becoming marginalized. The Industrial Revolution dislocated many people from farms and villages where their families had lived for hundreds of years and scattered them to various cities to work in factories and live in closely packed slums. Then, beginning in the second quarter of the nineteenth century, crime began an impressive decline. From 1775 to 1832, the per capita incarceration rate tripled in England and Wales, but by 1880 the incarceration rate had dropped by 20 percent. By 1930, it was around one-seventh of the incarceration rate of 1830. Other countries had similar experiences.

Why? The Victorian mentality prescribed a reaching out to the marginalized, often for religious reasons. Initiatives as diverse as Boy Scouts, the John Howard Society, and the elimination of slavery are just a few examples. In his early career, Winston Churchill, who like Dostoevsky believed that the state of civilization could be determined by examining our prisons, visited prisons and granted immediate releases. Andrew Rutherford, former assistant governor in the British Prison Service, described Churchill's attitude towards custody as "a black mark on a society's honour." Mr. Churchill, he said, "saw his task, to a very large extent, in terms of getting people out, particularly young offenders and less serious offenders."[2]

The pattern is clear. Crime levels are influenced and determined by something other than incarceration rates. This reality has been confirmed by a number of researchers and authors. For example, Toronto-based author and journalist David Cayley, in his book *The Expanding Prison: The Crisis in Crime and Punishment and the Search for Alternatives*, stated that "[i]ncarceration rates are fed by the popular belief … that punishment reduces crime, a belief seemingly immune to evidence."[3] Specifically considering the link between custody and youth crime levels, Mr. Cayley described the "largest study ever to consider the effect of expected severity of punishment on criminal behaviour," which was conducted in Bremen, Germany, and involved more than 1,500 young offenders. This study showed "the expected severity of punishment had no effect on youthful criminal behaviour" nor "had the expectation of youth prison."[4]

Similarly, world-renowned sociologist Dr. Nils Christie, in his groundbreaking work *Crime Control as Industry: Towards Gulags Western Style*, considered the relationship between prison and crime levels in Europe and the United States. While stressing the dramatic increase in U.S. incarceration rates, Dr. Christie found that "the level of imprisonment in society is not determined by crime."[5]

What, then, is the other thing that influences crime, if not the use of custody and the threat of punishment? What is it that our understanding is missing? What do we have to change?

Not much. But we have to recognize first and foremost that, in terms of scaring away crime, jail doesn't work. It is not the gold standard in response to youth crime, and never will be.

Let us now consider what does work, and what approaches and resources we are not making use of. After talking to thousands of children who went through various courts we can answer that question.

Marginalized Children—Scars and Redemption

Consider for a moment which children are incarcerated. In Saskatchewan, for example, a significant majority of children in custody are Aboriginal. Aboriginal people make up about 15 percent of Saskatchewan's population but represent three-quarters of the inmates in youth facilities.[6] This over-representation exists in many other provinces. Moreover, in other provincial jurisdictions there is significant over-representation of other racial minorities.

But race is only part of the issue. It's estimated that as much as 75 percent of the children in custody have some form of disability.[7] And what of the gross over-representation of youth from low-income families?

In many ways the cause of youth crime is simple and obvious. Youth crime is a reflection of the lives of young people. The children in custody have a common connection: they exist on the margins of our society.

We are not for a moment singling out the province of Saskatchewan for special criticism. Consider the words of Chief Judge Barry Stuart of the Yukon Territorial Court who, in *R. v. Elias*,[8] described the many marginalized people imprisoned there.

> Our jails are overflowing with people who suffer from substance abuse, have few employable skills, are mentally challenged, are significantly disconnected from mainstream society, and whose lives are character- ized by little, if any, support from family or community. In the Yukon, estimates suggest that at least half of the offenders through our courts are mentally challenged as a consequence of FAS, FAE or early life trauma. Many have been to jail so often, they have become institution- alized. Most have lost the connections to community and family that induce constructive lifestyles. These are the people who fill our jails.[9]

We question whether it makes sense to continue to isolate these chil- dren from the mainstream of society, reflecting systemic discrimination on the basis of race, poverty, disability, and other factors. Perhaps work- ing with children so they can live successfully within our society would be a more realistic way to reduce youth crime. Isn't that what works with your own children?

Despite the chaotic backgrounds and circumstances of many youth brought before our courts, those who wish to maintain the present system use a particularly powerful, if at times unconscious, tool. They claim that these children have been so scarred by awful experiences at home, on the streets, and in schools that they are different from you and me and our children, and therefore the same rules don't apply. While it is sad, they claim, there is no option but to put these youth in custody, for the protec- tion of the public. And as a result, troubled and high-risk youth are la- belled, and that label is "criminal."

This may sound like the argument we've already covered. But recog- nize the difference: it acknowledges past harms done to the child, and concludes that therefore the child is different, so different that only cus- tody can change them. Yet no one seriously suggests that custody improves people.

Most troubled and marginalized children and youth have been scarred by their experiences. But to say that having had these experiences makes these children somehow different from our own is dangerous. In effect, what appears at first to be empathy further segregates and marginalizes these children.

Labelling others as different can have a devastating effect. World-renowned sociologist Nils Christie described his days as a student in Norway. He was asked by a professor to examine Norway's involvement in Hitler's program of *Nacht und Nebel* (Night and Fog). Norway was ordered to put in prisons and guard many Yugoslavians. Fifty Norwegian guards were found guilty of mistreating and even killing some of these unfortunate Yugoslavians. Christie eventually ended up talking with nearly all of the fifty guards as well as guards who had not mistreated the prisoners. He stated that none of the killers were monsters; in his words "…they were decent, ordinary people." But the conditions in the prisons were so bad—70 percent of the prisoners died in one year—that the prisoners were dehumanized; it was very difficult to keep clean, and diarrhoea, lice, loss of bladder control, infections, and misery were common. The difference between the abusive guards, including the killers, and the nonabusive guards was that the abusive guards saw the dirt, the disease, and the misery as indications that the prisoners were not like themselves. The nonabusive guards were appalled that people like themselves would have to live in such terrible conditions.[10]

In their book *The Rope, the Chair, and the Needle: Capital Punishment in Texas, 1923–1990*, James Markwart, Sheldon Ekland-Olson, and Jonathon Sorenson stated that in the first two decades after the U.S. Supreme Court opened the door to state executions, the southern U.S. states accounted for over 80 percent of the total executions because of a southern cultural tradition of exclusion, of dehumanizing certain people. They point out that as state executions went up, lynchings went down. Lynchings were the self-help tool that white Southerners resorted to when they were frightened by "them," the blacks. As a result, the state came to adopt the same methods of labelling and segregating certain people, as individual southerners had in the past.[11]

In a Canadian context, the argument that a lack of community resources forces judges and lawyers to opt for existing options within the justice system—including custody—makes short-term logical sense. We often feel the frustrations of an imbalance between need and resources. But the irony is that the cumulative effect of opting for custody, in face of unavailable resources, further exacerbates the situation, as custody is one of the most expensive of options. Spending more money on incarceration, however unavoidable it is claimed to be, over time likely cuts off the budgetary means of developing new community resources for troubled and marginalized youth.[12]

Scientific American magazine recently reported that as a result of a new research technique, meta-analysis, it is now clear that "in general, punishment is not effective and may actually increase crime rates."[13] Furthermore, programs for youth that by their nature tend to be inclusive, such as mentoring and skills instruction, "attained high success rates in preventing crimes." This research is not part of daily discussion in the youth criminal justice system, which is now clearly working with incorrect assumptions about youth. The relationship between marginalization and exclusion and reducing harmful acts is not examined.

We recognize that most new approaches that can be adopted within the youth justice system will require a reallocation of funds. They will also require a retreat from the widely held notion that getting tough, by inflicting punishment and pain on young offenders, will give us a safer society. We hope we can become a catalyst in bringing about these changes, or at least in beginning the public debate on these issues.

In contrast, consider the justice system in Iceland. Icelandic courts generally hand out lighter sentences than in neighbouring countries. Two researchers, Helgi Gunnlaugsson and Kristrun Kristinsdottir, discovered that the more severe the sentence, the more likely the person is to reoffend. Community work and education were found to be more powerful tools in reducing recidivism.[14] Once again we return to the obvious: like the rest of us, people charged with criminal offences are less likely to commit new offences if they are integrated into the community and are educated so as to succeed and contribute to the values of their community.

Of the thousands of children who have confided in us, most feel marginalized, excluded, and disenfranchised. For such youth, hopelessness is real. The belief that they may some day have a decent home, a good job, money to buy clothes, food, a car is so remote from their reality that only consistent, patient, and creative teaching can change it. These youth do not see a clear or even a fuzzy path to their own personal successes. And that is the difference between youth who are marginalized and mainstream youth. Mainstream youth can imagine and are normally confident that they will succeed, somehow, in ordinary society. Marginalized youth do not see a path to successfully ending their marginalization and often believe that the mainstream society wants to continue to marginalize them.

Tough on Crime = Tough on Kids

A person needs only to pick up a newspaper or switch on a radio or television to hear someone—likely a politician—talking about "getting tough" on youth crime. Advocates of this view believe that a more punitive approach is required to reduce youth crime and provide safer communities.

Fundamentally, we reject this punitive view. A compassionate society should not and cannot tolerate a strategy of inflicting pain on its troubled youth. In response, we argue that bringing children into the mainstream of our society and teaching them the skills to operate successfully within our community will reduce crime.

As an example of the futility of using incarceration as a key strategy in reducing crime, a recent report funded by the Solicitor General of Canada considered 111 studies involving over 442,000 offenders.[15] This report examined the relationship between various punishments and recidivism, and found "that harsher criminal justice sanctions had no deterrent effect on recidivism" and, to the contrary, "punishment produced a slight (3%) increase in recidivism." These research findings "were consistent across subgroups of offenders (adult/youth, male/female, white/minority)." In comparison to community sanctions, "imprisonment was associated with an increase in recidivism," and longer prison sentences "were associated with higher recidivism rates." Indeed, if the custodial sentences are longer then the increase in recidivism was found to be 6 percent.

While this report dealt with both adults and youth, there is evidence of the negative effects of custody solely in the youth system. For example, one Canadian study reported that a longer youth custody sentence led to a shorter average interval before another crime was committed by the youth in question.[16] Further, a study from Columbus, Ohio showed that both recidivism and the seriousness of subsequent crimes increase with the number of times a youth was incarcerated.[17] Likewise, in Ontario, upon the introduction of the *Young Offenders Act (YOA)*, the younger an incarcerated youth, the higher the subsequent recidivism rate. At that point Ontario was spending 90 cents out of every dollar spent on youth justice on custody.[18]

Massachusetts Commissioner of Youth Services Jerome Miller closed all the youth custodial facilities in the state between 1970 and 1972 and sent all the youths home or to some place that wasn't a custodial facility. Despite enormous resistance, he tried to set up programs with community partners that would give children and youth mentors and skills so they could succeed. Perhaps predictably, he was driven out of his position of power, but Harvard University concluded that in districts where his reforms were followed youth crime was reduced by 30 percent.[19]

Elsewhere in the United States, the side by side jurisdictions of Maryland and Washington, D.C. went on different paths in the 1990s. Washington reduced the use of youth detention by 71 percent, while Maryland increased its use by 3 percent. Guards routinely beat the youth in one boot camp,[20] and seven guards in another facility were fired for assaulting youth in custody.[21] Maryland experienced a decrease in violent youth crime of only 15 percent, in comparison to Washington's reduction of 55 percent.

We recognize that some degree of institutionalization and intervention may be necessary for out-of-control and high-risk youths. And we are not for a minute doubting the value of some of the programming and treatment currently available within custodial facilities, nor of the many caring and compassionate staff employed there. Yet, at the end of the day, we believe there is ample evidence to show that, in the long run, incarcerating youth does not reduce youth crime, and does not make our communities safer. In all likelihood this strategy makes our communities more dangerous, and we must be ever cautious about its use, and overuse.[22]

The only reality and certainty for virtually all youth sentenced to custody is that they will someday be released into society. This should cause us to carefully consider the long-term effects of our justice strategies. If we truly want to protect the public, are we doing so in just the short term, or, more importantly, are we also doing so in the long term?

An article in the *Economist* magazine[23] observed that, by 2000, crime in the United States was beginning to rise again in some places. Since recidivism rates in the United States for prisoners are roughly two out of three (66 percent), and since the prison population has mushroomed in recent years and now these prisoners are being released, "violent crimes such as murder (which tend to lead the way for other crime trends) are beginning to rise again." This article surmised that the rise in crime may have been caused by prisoners leaving jail.

The Effect of Jail on Kids

The best way to predict whether or not a person will commit an offence that will end in being sentenced to custody is if the person has ever been in custody. That is, once you go, you're more likely to go back. (The second best predictor of which people will be sentenced to jail is their level of education. Once a youth has grade twelve or beyond, the less likely he or she is to go to jail.[24])

> With the majority of those that end up becoming criminals, from young offenders on up, it happens because of a lot of hurts that have happened to them in their lives, and then they end up taking it out on others. And if you don't deal with the person and their internal problems and help them overcome them, they become worse. And if you warehouse them, well, you're warehousing the problems for X-num-

bers of years and then bringing them back into society worse off, and then it doesn't change anything. It's a vicious circle.

Jim Cavanagh, former inmate and subsequently director,
Kingston Chapter of Prison Fellowship Canada[25]

"One might assert that while adults adapt to the custodial system, children and young persons are adopted *by it!*"[26] One of the many unintended problems with the use of custodial facilities is that once marginalized youth become a part of the "custody culture," they use that culture's norms upon leaving custody. Jerome Miller, former Commissioner of Youth Corrections in Massachusetts, pointed out that an average person could never understand attacking someone for their clothes or running shoes, or drive-by shootings, or joining gangs, but anyone who knows custodial life would recognize these patterns. He said violence of this type indicates power, and hence status, and indifference to the plight of the other person.[27]

Children on the margins of mainstream society are not frightened away from crime. Indeed, based on our dealings with these youth, it's clear that marginalized children tend to think of the world as ordered around power relationships. They see force—even being beaten by authority figures—as a confirmation of this dysfunctional view of society, and as condoning the tactics they have learned to use in trying to get a share of power.

As an example, in *R. v. E.T.F.*[28] a young person described being bullied during the time he was remanded for court. His description of the events in remand made clear how the culture of the criminal justice system and especially jail becomes accepted as a norm. This youth testified how the biggest bully in the youth custodial facility proudly called himself "Pen Time." He said the youth referred to another bully as "the man."

The description in *E.T.F.* of a culture of intimidation and violence in our youth justice system can also be seen in the words of one First Nation youth interviewed for this book, who spoke of his treatment at the hands of a police officer:

> When the cop and I got into the elevator as soon the door closed the cop gave me a really hard shot. I thought it was because he was mad at my dog [for barking, jumping up and interfering with the youth's arrest, until the youth took the dog downstairs in his residence]. I just took it but it made me crazy. I tell other people about it but I've never met anyone who was surprised that cop would hit me just for that.[29]

As an interesting insight into the effect of corporal punishment on young offenders came from Judge Josephine Mallaieu of St. Kitts and Nevis, who had sentenced youth as young as twelve to be beaten by a tamarind rod by the police. "I used to think it was useful but I [now] don't think it deters.... [G]iving them more licks is just hardening them even more." Judge Mallalieu told the Canadian newsletter *Lawyers Weekly*[30] that she saw about 80 to 90 youth per year—out of the St. Kitts population of 45,000—and had noticed that the children and youth who came before her "have already been brutalized at home." Indeed she was convinced that "youth crime can be traced back to a troubled family life in 99.9% of the cases." She left Canada with ideas she wanted to try, for example letting youth "work with volunteer groups so that they can learn from these people who like to help society, they can learn proper skills from them."

The stark reality of life in custody for so many youth can be seen in the comments of the Aboriginal youth referred to above, who had recently been released from a custodial centre:

> You pretty much do the same thing. All you do is stay in your room, read a book, get a phone call once in a while. That's no life at all. I don't know, they put you in a dark room pretty much. They do nothing and check up on you once in a while.... Getting drunk is pretty much all we talk about in there. They can't wait until they get out and get high. They say they don't mind being locked up, but I can tell they want to get out real bad. The so-called system won't let them out.[31]

"The Way to Live Together Most Nicely"

Professor Patricia Monture-Angus, a Mohawk woman, stated that the closest approximation of the concept of criminal law in her language was "the way to live together most nicely."[32] That's what children and youth want, and that is what we want. When did we allow those clamouring to get tough on young people, and those in charge of our youth criminal justice system, to forget this?

Speaking on the CBC *Ideas* program "Prison and its Alternatives" in 1996, Finland's Director General of Prisons K.J. Lang described how only ten or eleven boys under eighteen were in Finland's prison system at that time. Finland's population was five million.[33] In Canada in 1996/97, the total number of youth in custody was 25,278—11,772 in "secure custody" and 13,506 in "open custody."[34]

Obviously, there is no "given" way that youth justice has to be done by a country. Likewise, there is no predetermined number of youths that have to be held in criminal custody.

Many people acknowledge the current problem in the youth justice system but say alternatives are not now available, and until they are we'll have to continue putting youth in custody. Workers on the street level, such as police, youth workers, and youth advocates, who express such thoughts may simply be describing the reality of their situation. They have too little power to change the circumstances under which they work. But we live in a democracy, and we must decide if we are willing to wait for some unseen and possibly nonexistent force to cause our system to be reinvigorated. We must be proactive if our goal is to have as little youth crime as possible.

When faced with this problem, Greenland (which also has a high Aboriginal population) passed legislation that stated that no punishment should be handed out unless it could be shown that the punishment would not increase the chance that the offender will commit another crime.[35]

Earlier we pointed out that Aboriginal persons make up a disproportionate number of prisoners. Many would argue that race is a difference that allows for different treatment: for some "better" treatment, for too many others more dehumanizing treatment. However, for an Aboriginal youth to be arrested by an Aboriginal police officer, prosecuted by an Aboriginal prosecutor, sentenced by an Aboriginal judge, and ordered to report to an Aboriginal youth worker/probation officer is not much of an improvement.

We believe reforms within the youth justice system are possible, with relatively few changes. Communities can unite behind a common goal, and as a result, dramatically reduce the incidence of youth crime. In one sense we are only a step away, but it's a giant step.

Jail is not the answer. Jail—by which we mean locking up young people in secured custodial facilities—probably makes the situation worse. As well, our custodial facilities are expensive and take up much of the resources dedicated to responding to crime.

After years upon years of working with youth in the justice system, we have seen how very often incarceration—especially when used to deter crime—is counter productive. After hearing powerful people consistently describe these youths as different from us despite the reality they shed the same tears as we do and for the same reasons (loneliness, futility, depression, hopelessness), we are left with an inescapable conclusion. What is missing in society's analysis of youth crime is a simple question that should be put to every youth in the criminal justice system: What can we do to convince you to join us in using your personal talents and strengths to build a better life for yourself and our community?

At present, we don't ask, we impose. When asked what he would do differently if he became a youth worker in the justice system, an Aboriginal youth reflected a sense of frustration over not being consulted:

> I wouldn't tell them [other youth] what to do. I'd ask them what they
> wanted to do. How could they help me, how could I help you? Anyways,
> I could help you. I'll try my hardest to help, because I know how they
> feel. I wouldn't want them to go through what I went through, so I'd
> help them. Giving them the rules, or whatever, just so they mess up
> even more, and get locked up again.[36]

At best, we ask youth about their problems so we can craft orders; if
these are not followed, we arrest them, often jail them, and then tell them
it's for their own good. Indeed the only consistent "help" we offer youth is
incarceration. Help for your addiction problem? Could be months, be
patient. A special education program tailored for you because you're fourteen and only have grade three? Sorry, don't have one. Special programs to
account for brains that are damaged, often before birth? Sorry, no can do.
Help you get a job? Sorry, not our problem. No food in your house? Tell
your parents about money management. Scared of the neighbourhood
you live in? Suck it up, we've all got problems kid. But if these problems
get to be too much for you, we do have jail cells waiting, morning, noon,
and night.

From one point of view, as we stand beside the children in court with
their families and victims it all seems unreal. Like the Mad Hatter's tea
party, there is no room at the table, and no one to help. The Red Queen,
however, is always shouting "Off with his head!"

In pursuing this question, the next chapter considers the statutory
framework for youth justice in Canada. Although the statute—whether
the *Juvenile Delinquents Act*, the *Young Offenders Act*, or the newly implemented *Youth Criminal Justice Act*—does not by itself define the youth
justice philosophy accepted by our society, nor the resources made available to prevent crime and to provide alternatives for youth caught in the
criminal justice system, this legislation is nonetheless vital. It provides the
framework within which the youth justice system operates, and hence a
clear understanding of it is critical in a search for new and progressive
approaches to youth justice, and youth crime reduction.

"The judge never listened to a word my lawyers said for me. I've never been in trouble outside of the city…"

B.S.

Chapter Two

Youth Justice Legislation

The Evolution of Canadian Youth Offender Legislation

Youth justice legislation has existed in Canada since passage of the *Juvenile Delinquents Act* (*JDA*) in 1908. Prior to that statute, no separate treatment of young people occurred within the criminal justice system. "Historically, children were tried alongside adults, upon reaching the age of seven, the common law age of criminal responsibility."[1] Development of a distinct court for youthful offenders was largely a development of the twentieth century.[2]

The *JDA*, which allowed a court to find a youth aged between seven and sixteen years to be a "juvenile delinquent," represented what has been called a paternalistic view to youth justice. By imposing a *parens patriae* philosophy, the youth court came to stand in the role of parent for youths thought to be misguided and the product of improper upbringing in their family life. Youths charged under the *JDA* were not considered to be criminals, but could be found delinquent "for actions for which adults could receive no punishment, most notably truancy, running away, and sexual promiscuity."[3] Little emphasis was placed on due process, such as the right to legal representation. Rules of evidence were relaxed. The *JDA* allowed an enormous discretion to the youth court respecting both the process followed in court, and the resulting sentences for young people. One view of the philosophy espoused by this Act was described by Alberta Crown prosecutor Jonathan Hak:

The classical school of criminology posits that crime results from the deliberate choice of the offender, who freely chooses to engage in criminal activity because the perceived advantages outweigh the perceived disadvantages. Therefore, crime prevention can best be achieved by ensuring that the pain of punishment sufficiently outweighs the pleasure or gains attained, so as to make further forays into crime unattractive. However, the *JDA* did not view youthful offenders as criminals, since they were not responsible their actions. Instead, it was misdirection and misguidance by adults that led youths into a state of delinquency. As a result, responsibility for delinquency fell on the family, the community, and the society, not the offenders. This philosophy denounced resorting to punishment or deterrence, as youths were in need of protection from their environment.[4]

Alternatively, the *JDA* can be viewed as a statute that had sufficient latitude to allow troubled youth to be re-educated by courts as into accepted behaviour of that society. The *JDA* appeared at the end of the Victorian era, following a period of extremely harsh punishments for all crimes, major and minor.[5] The failure of that punitive-based theory, and the corresponding success of other approaches, no doubt led, in large part, to the highly discretionary form and content of the *JDA*.

The *JDA* was replaced by the *Young Offenders Act (YOA)* in 1984. The *YOA* heralded a new focus on making young offenders accountable for their crimes, while at the same time affording them due process protection, such as the right to legal representation, the right to consult a parent, lawyer, or other person before giving a statement, and the right to the least interference with their freedom as was "consistent with the protection of society, having regard to the needs of young persons and the interests of their families"[6]. In comparison to the *JDA*, the *YOA* brought the treatment of young offenders more into line with the process and system faced by adult offenders. As Professor Kent Roach of the University of Toronto noted, "[t]he same individualistic approach that required respect for the rights of young people could also justify punishing them as adults so long as their rights were respected."[7] Although major differences still existed between the treatment of youth and adults, especially in the sentencing process, the focus had shifted from redirecting misguided delinquents to a more formalized process of trying and punishing young offenders for specific offences.

Among the many changes brought about by the *YOA* was a redefinition of the players in youth court.

In the past when a detained juvenile appeared [under the *JDA*] before the court, she or he was usually accompanied by a probation officer or a social worker. A defence counsel might also have been present. Under the *YOA*, defence counsel and prosecutor assumed the key actor roles at this stage of the proceedings. A probation officer or social worker might also be present, but they do not play central roles. The result of this change was that there came to be more Crown prosecutors and defence lawyers participating in the youth court process since the implementation of *The Young Offenders Act*.[8]

One of the most dramatic changes a practitioner experienced in moving from the *JDA* to the *YOA* was the number of people present in court. Under the *JDA*[9] only the young person, a parent, a prosecutor, a defence lawyer, the judge, court personnel, and sometimes a social worker were present. The proceedings became quite intimate and slow. Under the *YOA*, as court opened, there was often a large crowd present. This often created a very different atmosphere from that which existed under the *JDA*, evidencing what might be described as youth versus "the authorities" dynamic.

Despite the intended goals of youth accountability and due process protection, the *YOA* came to be widely criticized for not holding young offenders accountable, and hence not being "tough enough" to make a difference. These criticisms reflected a perception that repeat and violent offenders were being overprotected, often at the expense of innocent law-abiding victims.[10] Reform Party M.P. Jack Ramsay summed up this view speaking in Parliament.

[T]he weight is still balanced in favour of the young offender in this country. The protection of society, the protection of our children, is still outweighed by the so-called rights of violent and delinquent young Canadians. All we are asking is that the scales be evened out, that the rights of the victims, the rights of our children be given priority. We ask that the protection of society outweigh the protection of violent young offenders who have no respect for the lives and rights of others.[11]

These words conjure up a dichotomy between "us" and "them": our law-abiding children versus those other criminal youth. A punitive focus towards youth justice reform was again evident among opposition M.P.s after introduction of the *Youth Criminal Justice Act*. Reform Party M.P. Gurmant Grewal told the House of Commons in 1999:

On tougher sentencing, I believe strongly that our punishment to criminals is just a slap on the wrist. Appropriate punishment creates fear. That fear acts as a deterrent to any violent crime. On the other hand, if

there is no fear, and no punishment, that acts as a motivation to commit a crime. At this time when there is not adequate punishment, that
acts as a motivation for young people to commit a crime.[12]

It is difficult to reconcile this cry for punishment with national figures
on youth crime, which show a steady decline in youth court cases since
the early 1990s. Although a large part of this decrease has been in the area
of property crime, and although regional differences exist, with the prairie provinces reporting levels of youth crime significantly higher than the
national average, the national trend has been downward. The Canadian
Centre for Justice Statistics reported that, in 1998/99, youth courts across
Canada heard 7.4 percent fewer cases than in 1992/93. Despite this decrease, this same survey showed that 74 percent of those surveyed "said
youth crime had increased in their province over the last five years."[13]

It is also difficult to determine what effect political rhetoric about "getting tough" has had on public perceptions about youth crime levels, but
the above figures clearly show a gap between fact and public perception
about youth crime levels. Moreover, it is difficult to understand how those
parliamentarians who supported a punitive "get tough" approach to youth
justice reform—who presumably had easy access to expert advice and the
available research on this issue—could have so misunderstood the relationship between crime and its causes, and so overlooked the already high
levels of youth imprisonment in this country.

When the *JDA* was replaced by the *YOA*, dramatic increases in custody
were experienced across Canada.[14] The *YOA*, which was supposed to make
things "better" or "fairer" for youth than the *JDA* and result in a reduction
in crime due to more criminal-law involvement in young lives, instead
caused an increase in arrest rates as police sought to overcome the protections within the *YOA* by increasing the number of charges.

Rather than being seen as a problem or a misguided strategy, however,
an increasing crime rate led to repeated calls for more and longer custody
sentences. "Getting tough" became the answer, for many, to the youth justice "problem," without any apparent evidence that this approach was having, or would have, a positive effect. But calls for punitive responses to
youth crime were also questioned in Parliament. Justice Minister Anne
McLellan addressed the issue of youth custody after introducing the *YCJA*.

We incarcerate youth at a rate four times that of adults and twice that
of many U.S. states. We incarcerate youth despite the fact that we know-
ingly run the risk that they will come out more hardened criminals and
we incarcerate them knowing that alternatives to custody can do a better job of ensuring that youth learn from their mistakes.[15]

As her comments indicated, "getting tough" on young offenders was not the only strategy articulated in Parliament prior to passage of the *YCJA*. Professors Russell Smandych and Bryan Hogeveen, in noting the range of views among M.P.s, described this divergence as a "double movement" in political debates about youth justice reform. On the one hand, there were parliamentarians, and in particular members of the federal Liberal party, who argued that "crime prevention and rehabilitation should be made important parts of any reformed youth justice system, along with the over-riding need for 'the protection of society.'"[16] On the other hand, most federal political parties (with the notable exception of the Bloc Quebecois and perhaps the NDP) argued that "a tougher approach" was required to "deal with more serious repeat and violent young offenders."[17]

The New *Youth Criminal Justice Act*

The *Youth Criminal Justice Act* (*YCJA*)[18] received Royal Assent in Parliament on 19 February 2002 and came into force 1 April 2003. This new Act is significantly longer than the *Young Offenders Act*, and is divided into a preamble (containing definitions and a declaration of principle) and nine parts, the most significant of which deal with extrajudicial measures (handling offending behaviour outside of court), the organization of the youth criminal justice system, judicial measures (procedures and processes to be followed in youth court), the sentencing of young people, procedures governing youth custody sentences and supervision following release, and rules governing the publication of names. The following discussion of the *YCJA* is not intended to be a comprehensive analysis of all features of this Act, but, rather, an outline of the important features of and changes contained within this legislation.

Principles and purposes

Like the *YOA*, the *YCJA* contains a general statement of principles and purposes. Section 3, in defining this Act's applicable principles, sets out the goals, strategies, and key characteristics of the youth justice system. Many of these factors and principles are similar to those contained in the *YOA*, such as addressing the underlying circumstances and causes of offending behaviour, the need for accountability by offenders, the importance of crime prevention and protecting society, the recognition of procedural fairness for young persons, and the need to rehabilitate and reintegrate young offenders. But despite these similarities, new considerations appear in the *YCJA*'s general statement of principles.

One such addition is the importance placed on timeliness. Section 3 states that the youth justice system should emphasise "timely intervention that reinforces the link between the offending behaviour and its consequences" and "the promptness and speed with which persons responsible for enforcing this Act must act, given young persons' perception of time."[19] These provisions are meant to remind youth court practitioners that court processes are to educate or convince youth that their criminal actions need to be re-evaluated. This requirement for timeliness suggests the critical importance of youth being engaged in a conversation regarding their crime and its consequences, a goal that harshness will do little to facilitate.

Another feature without an apparent parallel in the *YOA* is that measures taken against young persons under the *YCJA* should "respect gender, ethnic, cultural and linguistic differences and respond to the needs of aboriginal young persons and of young persons with special requirements."[20] Our experience tells us if our society as a whole followed this principle, or even if the structures in our youth justice system focused on and stressed this as a guiding criteria, marked decreases in youth crime would follow.

The principles set out in the *YOA* contained no specific reference to victims. The corresponding section in the *YCJA* states that measures taken against young offenders should "encourage the repair of harm done to victims and the community."[21] Section 3(1)(d) contains a special reference to the rights of victims, within the youth justice system, providing that:

(ii) victims should be treated with courtesy, compassion and respect for their dignity and privacy and should suffer the minimum degree of inconvenience as a result of their involvement with the youth criminal justice system, [and]

(iii) victims should be provided with information about the proceedings and given an opportunity to participate and be heard, ...

Although the provision of information is one way of assisting victims within the youth justice system,[22] the new conferencing provisions (in section 19) should also enhance the ability of victims to participate directly. Conferencing is a key element of the *YCJA*, with section 19(1) stating that "a youth justice court judge, the provincial director, a police officer, a justice of the peace, a prosecutor or a youth worker may convene ... a conference for the purpose of making a decision required to be made under this Act." Conferences can consider "conditions for appropriate extra-judicial measures, conditions for judicial interim release, sentences, including the review of sentences, and reintegration plans." This is a new means of constructive involvement by victims, both in terms of helping them to deal with (and be compensated for) what has happened to them, but also in terms of helping them to understand the limits of what can be achieved through the criminal process. From many years of appearing in court, and hearing countless victims express their frustration about the justice system, it is obvious to us that many victims come to court with unrealistic expectations about what can be possibly be achieved. One of the benefits of a more restorative approach to justice is that victims can be heard, and can play a part in forming a response to the crime.

This new focus on the rights of victims may, from one vantage point, appear to bring the peacemaking functioning of courts into conflict with the desire of victims to seek a public affirmation of the harm done to them. Indeed, the notion that more jail equals more justice for victims seems to have become deeply ingrained in our society, reflecting the oft-stated view that any right or benefit bestowed upon an offender means, by definition, that something is being taken away from the victim. Contrary to this win/lose philosophy, however, the introduction of the victim's honest and heartfelt description of the effects of crime can be an extremely positive step, and one that allows for excellent opportunities for learning and finding meaning in apparently senseless criminal acts for both the offender and victim.

A frequently heard criticism of the statement of principles in the *YOA* was that it contained "a number of potentially conflicting, inconsistent, and unprioritised principles."[23] Although the new general statement of principles in the *YCJA* contains more guidance than did its counterpart in the *YOA*, these general principles still retain the often conflicting goals of accountability, on the hand, and rehabilitation, on the other. To some extent, these ambiguities are addressed in two other areas of the *YCJA*, which now sets the principles and objectives of extrajudicial measures (in sections 4 and 5) and the purpose and principles of sentencing (in section 38).

Many of the youth we have represented feel they were not listened to in the justice system. A young Aboriginal woman who had numerous dealing with police and courts echoed this sentiment:

> With myself, they don't involve you in the decisions that affect you, and most of the time they tell you what to do. Like you have probation, you have to be home at a certain time, or you have to go to school or you have to talk to this person or its mediation and they make you feel like you're not important and that everything you do is wrong. Even yourself, your well-being, like who you are is wrong. Like you're not impor-

tant. You're actually not worth anything. It's how a lot of them approach you. Cops, the court system and youth workers and jail. You're just treated like an animal, like you're just there.[24]

These concerns about not actively participating in the system are intertwined with feelings that officials within the justice system do not hear about the good things youth have done. As one Aboriginal youth explained:

> The courts should know the good side, not just a folder of bad stuff. Obviously the judge is going to think you're fucking up all the time. The judge doesn't really know what you can do, what your hobbies are, or the times you tried to help or comfort people. All the judge knows is bad stuff.[25]

The *YCJA* now contains a provision that "young persons have rights and freedoms in their own right, such as a right to be heard in the course of and to participate in the processes, other than the decision to prosecute, that lead to decisions that affect them."[26] We hope that this will encourage courts to ensure the active participation of youth—especially marginalized youth—within a system characterized by timely bail and pre-sentence reports (including both structured plans for the youths involved and a statement of the impact of the youth's actions on the victims involved). Following this approach, these provisions would be seen as a direction from Parliament to use every technique and resource available, to immediately engage marginalized youth. Accordingly, strategies focused on accountability and rehabilitation can be seen as joined, rather than divergent, in attempting to reduce the number of marginalized youth caught within the justice system.

Extrajudicial measures—new front-end options

The *YOA* contained only a statement (in section 3) that, where not inconsistent with protection of the public, taking either no measures or nonjudicial measures should be considered for young persons who committed offences. The declaration of principles respecting extrajudicial measures in the *YCJA* are much broader.

In section 4, extrajudicial measures are said to be:

- often the most appropriate and effective way to address youth crime;

- able to allow for effective and timely interventions focused on correcting offending behaviour;

- presumed to be adequate to hold a young person accountable for his or her offending behaviour if the young person has committed a nonviolent offence and has not previously been found guilty of an offence; and

- used if they are adequate to hold a young person accountable for his or her offending behaviour and, if the use of extrajudicial measures is consistent with the principles set out in this section, nothing in this Act precludes their use in respect of a young person who: (i) has previously been dealt with by the use of extrajudicial measures, or (ii) has previously been found guilty of an offence.

Section 5 states that extrajudicial measures should be designed to:

- provide an effective and timely response to offending behaviour outside the bounds of judicial measures;

- encourage young persons to acknowledge and repair the harm caused to the victim and the community;

- encourage families of young persons—including extended families where appropriate—and the community to become involved in the design and implementation of those measures;

- provide an opportunity for victims to participate in decisions related to the measures selected and to receive reparation; and

- respect the rights and freedoms of young persons and be proportionate to the seriousness of the offence.

Alternative measure programs were the only alternative to court proceedings defined in the *YOA*, and were restricted to cases where the Attorney General of a province had authorized a specific program and a class of persons eligible for alternative measures, and where the person given this authority (usually a prosecutor) was satisfied that these measures would be appropriate having regard to the needs of the young person and the interests of society. The *YOA* also required informed consent by the young person, including an understanding of his or her legal rights, a case on which the Crown could properly proceed, and an acceptance of responsibility for the offence by the young person.

The *YCJA* now formally sets out a number of alternatives other than laying charges. Section 6(1) compels a police officer, faced with a young person alleged to have committed an offence and before "starting judicial proceedings or taking any other measures under this Act," to:

consider whether it would be sufficient, having regard to the principles set out in section 4, to take no further action, warn the young person, administer a caution, if a program has been established under section

7, or, with the consent of the young person, refer the young person to a program or agency in the community that may assist the young person not to commit offences.

Although these options—taking no action, warning a young person, or referring them to a community program or agency—were previously within the discretion of police officers under the *YOA*, the formalization of these alternatives in the *YCJA* appears to lend priority to considering approaches other than proceeding to youth court. The need for greater consideration of front-end options can be seen in the reality that the "following offences make up over 50% of youth court cases: theft under $5000, possession of stolen property, failing to appear in court, failure to comply with a disposition (usually breach of probation), and minor assault."[27] Keeping less serious and first-time offenders out of the court system will leave more of the system's scarce resources available to deal with more serious offences.

A further front-end option contained in the *YCJA* is the caution. Section 7 provides that the Attorney General of each province may establish a program authorizing the police or prosecutors "to administer cautions to young persons instead of starting judicial proceedings." The definition and prominence of front-end options in the *YCJA* parallels similar developments in New Zealand and England, which are discussed later in this book.

Alternative measures—programs designed to deal with offences outside of youth court—were a prominent feature in the *YOA*. The *YCJA* now refers to these as extrajudicial sanctions. Sections 10 through 12 establish a system for extrajudicial sanctions that may be used if a young person "cannot be adequately dealt with by a warning, caution or referral mentioned in section 6, 7 or 8 because of the seriousness of the offence, the nature and number of previous offences committed by the young person or any other aggravating circumstances." An extrajudicial sanction may be used *only* if

- it is part of a program of sanctions authorized by each provincial government;

- the person authorized to make use of the extrajudicial sanction is satisfied that it would be appropriate, having regard to the needs of the young person and the interests of society;

- the young person, having been informed of the extrajudicial sanction, fully and freely consents to be subject to it;

- the young person has been advised of the right to legal counsel and has been given a reasonable opportunity to obtain such counsel;

- the young person accepts responsibility for the offence allegedly committed;

- there is, in the opinion of the Attorney General, sufficient evidence to proceed with the prosecution of the offence; and

- the prosecution of the offence is not in any way barred at law.

Much of the extrajudicial sanction process in the *YCJA* reflects similar provisions for alternative measures in the *YOA*. However, new notice provisions require (in section 11) that "the person who administers the program under which the sanction is used shall inform a parent of the young person of the sanction," and (in section 12) that "a police officer, the Attorney General, the provincial director or any organization established by a province to provide assistance to victims shall, on request, inform the victim of the identity of the young person and how the offence has been dealt with."

The sentencing of young persons

The *YOA* contained no separate statement of purpose guiding the sentencing of young offenders. The *YCJA* now states, in section 38(1), that the purpose of sentencing is to "hold a young person accountable for an offence through the imposition of just sanctions that have meaningful consequences for the young person and that promote his or her rehabilitation and reintegration into society, thereby contributing to the long-term protection of the public." It appears, given this link between reintegration and public protection, that Parliament intended the successful integration of youth into mainstream societal activities as the most, and perhaps the only, effective technique towards reducing crime and achieving more peaceful communities. Our experience with marginalized youth tells us that this link is indisputable. However, rehabilitation and reintegration—in effect a goal of bringing youth back into the mainstream—often requires individualized plans for young people, taking into consideration the unique reasons for their marginalization. As Leo Tolstoy once stated, "All happy families are alike; each unhappy family is unhappy in its own way."[28] Consideration of the unique factors that have contributed to bringing an offender before a youth court makes the sentencing process a key element in any attempt towards changing and improving our youth justice system.

Major changes were made to the *Criminal Code* sentencing provisions (for adults) in 1996. These amendments included a set of broad-ranging and sometimes contradictory sentencing principles. The *YCJA* has now adopted this approach, with a detailed set of sentencing principles contained in section 38(2):

(2) A youth justice court that imposes a youth sentence on a young person shall determine the sentence in accordance with the principles set out in section 3 and the following principles:

(a) the sentence must not result in a punishment that is greater than the punishment that would be appropriate for an adult who has been convicted of the same offence committed in similar circumstances;

(b) the sentence must be similar to the sentences imposed in the region on similar young persons found guilty of the same offence committed in similar circumstances;

(c) the sentence must be proportionate to the seriousness of the offence and the degree of responsibility of the young person for that offence;

(d) all available sanctions other than custody that are reasonable in the circumstances should be considered for all young persons, with particular attention to the circumstances of Aboriginal young persons; and

(e) subject to paragraph (c), the sentence must

(i) be the least restrictive sentence that is capable of achieving the purpose set out in subsection (1),

(ii) be the one that is most likely to rehabilitate the young person and reintegrate him or her into society, and

(iii) promote a sense of responsibility in the young person, and an acknowledgement of the harm done to victims and the community.

Under section 38(3) of the *YCJA*, the youth court, in determining a sentence shall consider:

• the degree of participation by the young person in the commission of the offence;

• the harm done to victims and whether it was intentional or reasonably foreseeable;

- any reparation made by the young person to the victim or the community;

- the time spent in detention by the young person as a result of the offence;

- the previous findings of guilt of the young person; and

- any other aggravating and mitigating circumstances related to the young person or the offence that are relevant to the purpose and principles set out in this section.

Section 42 of the *YCJA* sets out potential sentences for a young persons. Like the *YOA*, the *YCJA* allows a youth court judge to: grant a conditional or absolute discharge; fine the young person; order the young person to pay compensation, restitution or repayment to victims of his or her crime; order the young person to do either personal service for a victim or community service hours; make any order of prohibition, forfeiture, or seizure against the young person that may be made under any Act of Parliament or associated regulation;[29] or place the young person on probation for up to two years. The *YCJA*, however, now provides additional sanctions. A youth court judge can now reprimand a young person, which is a statement condemning the youth's behaviour. Subject to agreement by the provincial director, a youth may now be ordered into an intensive support and supervision program, or may be ordered—assuming the young person is a suitable candidate and that such programming would not interfere with their work or education—to attend a nonresidential program approved by the provincial director over a period not exceeding six months. For a young person convicted of an offence that is not a serious violent offence, the court can make a deferred custody and supervision order that is for a specified period not exceeding six months. This order is similar to a conditional sentence order for an adult under the *Criminal Code*.

While a youth court previously had discretion as to whether or not to place a young person on probation in addition to or as an alternative to custody, the *YCJA* now provides that any custody sentence be followed by a supervision order which is one-half as long as the period of custody. This supervision order will contain conditions defined in section 97, and the total length of a custody and supervision order is not to exceed two years or, if the young person is found guilty of an offence for which the punishment provided by the *Criminal Code* or any other Act of Parliament is imprisonment for life, three years from the date the order comes into force. These maximums are the same as contained in the *Young Of-*

fenders Act. Likewise the maximum sentences for first and second degree murder (ten and seven years respectively) remain unchanged under the *YCJA.*

The supervision order—similar to conditional supervision which formed the latter part of a sentence for murder under the *YOA*—brings the process of youth custody and release closer to that set out in the *Criminal Code,* and the associated correctional legislation for adults. An adult offender receives remission or "good time" usually equal to one-half of the time actually served in jail. After two-thirds of the total sentence, they are to be released on mandatory supervision, unless the authorities apply, in limited cases, to have them held in prison until their warrant of expiry date, the so-called "gating" or "detention hearing" process. Under section 97, a number of mandatory conditions must be included in supervision orders. In addition, the provincial director can set additional conditions "that support and address the needs of the young person, promote the reintegration of the young person into the community and offer adequate protection to the public from the risk that the young person might otherwise present."

The practice of "gating" is replicated in the *YCJA.* Section 98 provides that, within a reasonable time before the expiry of a custodial sentence, the Attorney General or the provincial director may apply to the youth court for an order that the young person remain in custody for a period not exceeding the remainder of the youth sentence. Section 104 sets out a similar process for young persons serving a custody sentence after being sentenced for first or second degree murder, attempted murder, manslaughter, or aggravated sexual assault, or after being sentenced to a new order called an intensive rehabilitation custody and supervision order.

The intensive rehabilitation custody and supervision order (sections 42(2)(r) and 42(7)) provides an option to other available youth sentences, or to an adult sentence, for a youth convicted either of first or second degree murder, attempted murder, manslaughter, or aggravated sexual assault, or for a youth convicted of a serious violent offence for which an adult is liable to imprisonment for more than two years when that youth has been previously convicted twice of serious violent offences. Such an order may be made, for the same duration as a normal custody and supervision order, if:

- this youth is suffering from a mental illness or disorder, a psychological disorder, or an emotional disturbance;

- a plan of treatment and intensive supervision has been developed for the young person, and there are reasonable grounds to believe that the plan might reduce the risk of the young person repeating the offence or committing a serious violent offence; and

- the provincial director has determined that an intensive rehabilitative custody and supervision program is available and that the young person's participation in the program is appropriate.

Section 42(8) of the *YCJA* provides that none of the powers given to a judge in sentencing (in section 42) restrict the rights of a young person regarding consent to physical or mental health treatment. This subsection has significance to the intensive rehabilitation custody and supervision order, as this is clearly a form of medical treatment which would require a youth's consent before forming part or all of a sentence. What is unclear is what constitutes informed consent by a youth, and what the implications are if consent is subsequently withdrawn.[30]

The *YOA* provided two levels of custody for young persons, open and secure. The appropriate level was to be determined at sentencing by the judge. The *YCJA*, in section 85, also requires each province to establish two levels of custody, "distinguished by the degree of restraint." The decision as to level of custody is now made by the provincial director, not the judge. A caveat to this is that section 88 allows each province, rather than adopting this new process of determining custody levels, to retain the *Young Offenders Act* process of open and secure custody determined by a judge.

Under the *YCJA* process, the provincial director, in determining the appropriate level of custody, assesses the least restrictive level that also addresses the seriousness of the offence, the needs and circumstances of the young person, the safety of other youth in custody, and the interests of society. The provincial director can change the level of custody for a youth during a custody sentence. If the original decision of the provincial director places the youth into a level of custody with more than a minimal degree of restraint, or if the provincial director moves a youth to a facility with a higher degree of restraint or increases the level of restraint for a youth within the same facility, an appeal is possible by the young person to a review board, established under section 87.

Despite calls for a more punitive response in the debate leading up to passage of this new Act, the *YCJA* actually contains language that suggests limiting the scope of custody for young offenders. This was in response to the high levels of custody across Canada under the *YOA*. In *R. v. J.K.E.*,[31] Chief Judge Lilles of the Yukon Territorial Court recounted the high rates of youth incarceration in Canada, in comparison to other countries:

Adults are incarcerated at a rate of 130 inmates per 100,000 population in Canada, less than the rate in the United States. Yet Canada incarcerates young people under the age of 18 at a much higher rate than adults, 447 per 100,000. Moreover, this is considerably higher than the corresponding youth incarceration rate of 311 per 100,000 for the United States, 86 per 100,000 for Scotland and 69 per 100,000 for England and Wales.... Further, more than one-half are incarcerated for property and process offences rather than for offences involving personal injury....[32]

Perhaps in recognition of these alarming rates, section 39 states that a youth court shall not sentence an offender to custody unless that young person has committed a violent offence, has failed to comply with non-custodial sentences, has committed an indictable offence for which an adult could be jailed for over two years while possessing a history indicating a pattern of criminality; or in exceptional cases where the young person has committed an indictable offence, the aggravating circumstances of the offence are such that the imposition of a noncustodial sentence would be inconsistent with the purpose and principles set out in section 38. It is hoped that this will restrict significantly the number of young people incarcerated for property offences. It is yet to be seen whether "system-generated" or "status" offences—which refer to breaches of court orders such as a probation orders, or failing to appear in court—will continue to result in many custodial sentences.

Addressing the issue of breaches

Based on figures published by Statistics Canada, during 1998 and 1999, 31 percent of the youth sentenced to custody in Canada were incarcerated for failing to appear in court, or breaching their original sentence disposition (usually a probation order).[33] The prohibition against custody in section 39, which includes the words "unless the young person has failed to comply with non-custodial sentences," will make crucial the judicial interpretation of these words. Given that the purpose of this section appears to be to reduce the number of young people in custody, it is hoped that this provision will be triggered only by repeated offences against the public that result in real harm. For example, a child whose lack of appropriate schooling has led in large part to violent outbursts against other youth of similar age may have learned how to control this behaviour, but may still be afraid to attend school. Should such a child be incarcerated for not attending school? We think not, but this may well be a common result, as conditions requiring school attendance are commonly included in the probation orders and undertakings imposed on youth in court.

Some may call breaches "repeat" offences, and some (perhaps wiser) may disagree. But if "repeat" has become the accepted parlance, this word may also have become a code-word that explains, to a large extent, the over-representation of Aboriginal and other marginalized children in custody. Our experience tells us that applying a jail-style response to breach charges will lead only to more marginalized youth, and to more victims. It may also lead to more cries for getting tough through incarcerating more young people.

Frustration over a multitude of court-ordered conditions may be seen in the comments of an Aboriginal youth when asked what changes he would like to make to the youth justice system:

> Probation, that's just like being locked up again. Obviously, not one person in the whole world is not going to be breach once in a while, like a curfew. Regarding probation, I wouldn't have so many rules. I'd ask the kids what they wanted: a job, school, counselling, whatever. I'd want them to do that. I wouldn't go to hard on a curfew. I wouldn't really tell them what to do, that just gets them mad. It doesn't let them do what they want. If you try this, they just say "fuck them."[34]

If a youth is charged only with breaches of probation, uncoupled with serious offences of violence, the decision on sentence should be governed by the principles of proportionality, restraint in using custody, rehabilitation, promoting a sense of offender responsibility, and acknowledging the harm to victims and communities. These are found sections 38(2)(c),(d), and (e) of the *YCJA*. Even those proclaiming an "eye for an eye" philosophy would have difficulty justifying a custody sentence for a youth returning home a few minutes after his or her curfew.

This issue of appropriate responses to breaches is an important one. Section 38 makes clear that the *YCJA* attempts to balance the effects of criminal activities on victims on the one hand with the effects of overincarceration of youth on the other. Typically, a youth may be charged initially with a property offence, or a minor assault. Often that youth will take to heart the message against doing this sort of thing in the future. However, as a result of the initial conviction, that youth now has conditions in a probation order which include a direction to "keep the peace and be of good behaviour," and other possible conditions, often including a residency requirement and a curfew.

These conditions have a broad and overreaching application, and can easily be breached—often unknowingly—by youths. For example, we expect few twelve-year-old youths—and quite conceivably many older youths and adults—would understand the legal definition and bounds of "good behaviour." Likewise, the residency requirement can provide unique compliance problems for marginalized youth. When a judge considers ordering a youth to reside at a specific place, usually the court will require an assurance that this is a good residence, with a reliable adult present to monitor the youth. As we will see later in Dr. Carol LaPrairie's analysis of the living conditions of Aboriginal people in nine cities, high mobility within a city is a characteristic of Aboriginal people. Moreover, Aboriginal families often rely on different adults caring for different children at different times. When, for example, a parent-teen conflict occurs, many children reasonably understand that a "time out" is necessary. If, however, that time out results in the parent leaving the residence, there is little that youth can do, other than going to stay with some other parent or supportive friend. Similarly, a curfew condition suffers from many of the same definition problems as a residency clause, given that the youth is required to be inside between certain hours at the original residence.

Conditions requiring youth to attend school are frequently made as part of a probation order or undertaking, yet the court has no corresponding power to require schools to provide appropriate education for that youth. Imagine a physically well-developed fifteen year old suffering from Fetal Alcohol Syndrome or Effect who has only grade three reading and math skills. The reality is that courts do not have the power to order government authorities to provide special schooling or housing, among other needs felt acutely by those in poverty.

Taken in this light, many of these conditions ask too much from the youth, and too little from the community. Some judges are hesitant about imposing such conditions, because they fear setting up a youth for failure. But most courts do make such orders, apparently in the hope that someone, in some agency or from the family, will step up and take charge.

We have observed and experienced many situations where young people, after an initial brush with the law, do get the message, and do stop committing crimes against other people. But, at the same time, these youths sometime do breach the conditions of their court order, in the absence of any other offending behaviour. We doubt Parliament could ever have intended that youth be imprisoned, and in such shocking numbers, following such a breach.

Elsewhere in this work, we considered a report from the Solicitor General of Canada which showed that incarceration increases, rather than decreases, recidivism by 6 percent. To put this into perspective, imagine the introduction of a virus which endangered the health and lives of 6 percent of a community. Surely this would be classified as an epidemic! Would not such a term be appropriate for a supposed solution that actually increased crime by such an amount? During the Reagan administration, the Rand Corporation (perhaps the most prestigious think-tank in the world) told President Reagan, in an initial report draft, that American prisons were criminogenic.[35] Jerome Miller, in *Over the Wall,* stated:

> The Rand Corporation, which gave us the term, incapacitation, has recently suggested that correctional institutions may produce criminals and that incapacitation as the major tenet of crime control is a questionable social policy. In a Justice Department study, Rand suggested that prisons probably encourage crime among their alumni. The word *criminogenic* was used in describing prisons in the first draft. It was excised from the final product at the insistence of government funders of the project, apparently because it flew in the face of administration rhetoric on the effectiveness of imprisonment.[36]

This knowledge was available when Parliament was drafting and debating the *YCJA,* and is reflected in many of the provisions of this Act, referring to the goal of reducing the levels of youth custody. It is, therefore, difficult to find a legislative intention within the *YCJA* that a child should be sent to prison for breaching such a condition when the actual criminal behaviour, originally a concern, has ceased.

The difficult aspect of this debate about breaches of youth court orders is that conditions are often treated as an unalterable part of the original punishment. How, then, can an offender's debt to society for breaching a condition ultimately be paid, if not by the ultimate sanction of custody? Speaking for the youth we represent, we wonder why this seems to become an insurmountable problem for young offenders. Other areas of the criminal justice system have seen reforms which have reduced the use of imprisonment. For example, the imprisonment of adults for failing to pay a fine has been dramatically reduced, largely through changes to *Criminal Code* provisions about the administration of fines. These changes were supported largely through a realization that jailing debtors was bad policy: clearly a free and democratic society could not tolerate the existence of debtors' prisons, where impecunious offenders ended up in jail mainly due to an inability to pay. Professor Tim Quigley pointed out that the Ontario *Provincial Offences Act*[37] required that, before any warrant for arrest be issued, that "there must be evidence that all other reasonable methods have been tried and failed or would not likely result in payment [of fines] in a reasonable time."[38] Fines are clearly punishment, but a condition requiring counselling or addictions treatment clearly serves no retributive purpose. Why, then, not use every other reasonable method in responding to, or deciding not to lay charges after, breaches?

One sign of hope that the seemingly endless parade of youths going into custody for breaches might be stemmed appears in section 102 of the *YCJA*. Under this provision, if the provincial director has reasonable grounds to believe that a young person has breached, or is about to breach, a condition of a custody and supervision order, that director may take one of two actions. The first option is to allow the youth to remain in the community under the order (on the same or different conditions). If the provincial director is satisfied that "the breach is a serious one that increases the risk of public safety," a second option is to direct that the young person be remanded pending a review of the sentence and order. The former option allows the provincial director to disregard trivial and technical breaches, or simply to change what otherwise might be unworkable conditions in a custody and supervision order. Hopefully, this section will be applied frequently and broadly.

Sentencing youth as adults

A major change in this new legislation is how and when youth are to be treated as adults. Under the *YOA*, it was possible for a young person to be transferred to adult court prior to trial, but this transfer process was often time-consuming and difficult.[39] As Professor Nicholas Bala of Queen's University observed, a problem with transfer hearings was that the judge did not "have complete information about the offence," but rather "was obliged to essentially accept the Crown's evidence," which was "usually based on hearsay at this point, about the offence."[40] The *YCJA* now prevents pretrial transfer. Rather, a young person must be tried in youth court, and only after a finding of guilt may he or she be sentenced as an adult in certain circumstances. Professor Sanjeev Anand suggested these transfer reforms have been widely misunderstood in the media. He summarized the overall effects of these changes from the *YOA*:

> The *YCJA* does only two things. It reduces the age limit for young offenders subject to presumptive transfer [for sentencing] to include 14- and 15-year olds. And it expands the list of offences for which presumptive transfer applies to include serious violent offences if the young offender has previously been found guilty of serious violent offences at least twice previously.[41]

The *YCJA* provides (in section 62) that an adult sentence shall be imposed on a young person who is found guilty of an indictable offence for which an adult is liable to imprisonment for a term of more than two years in the following cases:

(a) in the case of a presumptive offence, if the youth justice court makes an order under subsection 70(2) or paragraph 72(1)(b); or

(b) in any other case, if the youth justice court makes an order under subsection 64(5) or paragraph 72(1)(b) in relation to an offence committed after the young person attained the age of fourteen years.

Section 61 allows each province, in effect, to determine the minimum age at which presumptive offences apply. This minimum age may range from 14 years (as provided by the Act) up to sixteen years.

A presumptive offence (as defined in section 2(1)) can result when a youth, of the appropriate minimum age, is charged or convicted of first or second degree murder, attempted murder, manslaughter, or aggravated sexual assault or is charged or convicted of a "serious violent offence" for which an adult would liable to a jail term of more than two years, if there have been two previous findings that the youth has committed a serious violent offence. A "serious violent offence" is defined in section 2(1) as an offence in the commission of which a young person causes or attempts to cause serious bodily harm. "Serious" is not defined in this Act. All violence or threats of violence are serious, but clearly—as it appears incarceration does little to decrease future offender violence, and may actually increase it—Parliament must have intended a limited rather than broad application of this provision.

At the start of the sentencing hearing, following a finding of guilt or a guilty plea, the court will hold a hearing in cases where an adult sentence may result, and where the outcome is not conceded by the adverse party (whether the Crown or the young person).[42] The court's decision revolves largely around whether a youth sentence for a given offence would have sufficient length "to hold the young person accountable for his or her offending behaviour." In making this determination the judge considers "the seriousness and circumstances of the offence, and the age, maturity, character, background and previous record of the young person and any other factors that the court considers relevant." The onus of satisfying the youth justice court about the matters referred to above is with the party applying. In the case of a presumptive offence, the onus is on a youth to apply for an order that he or she be sentenced as a youth. In the case of all other offences, the onus will be on the Crown to apply for an order that the young person be sentenced as an adult.

The circumstance of Aboriginal young persons

One of the final amendments to the *YCJA* before final passage in the House of Commons was made to the principles of sentencing. Section 38(2)(d) now reads that, in addition to the principles contained in section 3, "all available sanctions other than custody that are reasonable in the circumstances should be considered for all young persons, *with particular attention to the circumstances of aboriginal young persons*" [emphasis added].

Although this section is a mirror image of section 718.2(e) in the *Criminal Code*, which became effective in 1996 for adult offenders, this amendment drew criticism from opposition members in the House of Commons. Speaking for the Canadian Alliance Party, Chuck Cadman, M.P. for Surrey North, said he personally did "not believe that race has any place in criminal law sentencing provisions, be it adult or young offender" and that a judge, in sentencing, was "already required to consider 'any other aggravating and mitigating circumstances related to the young person'" which "would normally include factors such as family and social circumstances, background and special needs, among other things."[43] It is not clear whether those M.P.s opposed to this amendment in the *YCJA* were unaware of the *Criminal Code* provision, or were simply opposed to the focus on circumstances of Aboriginal offenders earlier articulated in section 718.2(e) of the *Criminal Code*.

The effects of incarceration can clearly be seen in the words of an Aboriginal youth recently released from custody, when asked what he would change about the way that police, courts, judges, and jails treat young people:

> I wouldn't lock them up. Putting them in a tight room, and isolating them, that's pretty bad. I don't know about innocent until proven guilty. I don't go with that either because they just lock you up until you're found innocent or guilty and then I don't think they count the time while you're in there. The judge won't really know how they're treating you while you're in there. Locked up in your room all day, or you get to stay out or whatever. Sometimes when you're locked up in your room they even forget to give you a meal sometimes.[44]

In *R. v. Gladue*,[45] the Supreme Court of Canada interpreted section 718.2(e) of the *Criminal Code* which requires sentencing judges to consider "all available sanctions other than imprisonment that are reasonable in the circumstances" for all offenders "with particular attention to the circumstances of aboriginal offenders." Although the effects of this judgement continue to evolve, there have been some obvious implications for the sentencing of Aboriginal offenders. In *Gladue*, Justices Cory and

Iacobucci interpreted this subsection as mandatory in application, remedial in nature, and a "direction to sentencing judges to undertake the process of sentencing aboriginal offenders differently, in order to endeavour to achieve a truly fit and proper sentence in the particular case."[46]

Gladue was important for a number of reasons. Arguably, two stand out. First, the "circumstances of aboriginal offenders" are to be considered within the historical context of the relationship between Aboriginal people and Canadian society. It is difficult to give meaning to the "systemic and background" factors identified in *Gladue* without an understanding of Canadian history and how this has shaped the current reality faced by so many Aboriginal offenders. Second, judges must seek alternatives to jailing Aboriginal offenders, given their over-representation in our prisons and the apparent ineffectiveness of jail in reducing both recidivism and crime within Aboriginal communities. This search for alternative sentences is to utilize, wherever possible, restorative principles of justice, including healing and rehabilitation and restoration of the relationship between the offender, victim, and community. Although the *Gladue* decision has been held to apply to young persons under the *YOA* despite there being no mention of the circumstances of Aboriginal young persons in that Act, the sentencing principles in the *YCJA* leave little doubt that the *Gladue* decision will be applied to the sentencing of Aboriginal young people.

Given that custodial sentences have been widely applied to Aboriginal persons for many decades, and that incarceration has shown few beneficial and many dangerous effects, we often see youth court judges being placed in a difficult if not impossible position. On the one hand they must honour the statutory requirement of searching for all reasonable alternatives to custody, and of considering the particular circumstances of Aboriginal youth that have contributed to them coming before the court. On the other hand, they will face frequent requests for custody by the Crown— sometimes for lengthy terms—driven largely by a philosophy espousing punishment as a means of deterring crime. As we have suggested, this view lacks any empirical evidence to support its validity. Perhaps one way of attempting to break this impasse and find new alternatives for high-risk youth can come through the new conferencing provisions in the *YCJA*.

Conferencing

Section 19 of the *YCJA* allows for the formation and use of conferences. These meetings will assist in making various decisions under the Act, including: "advice on appropriate extrajudicial measures, conditions for judicial interim release, sentences, including the review of sentences, and reintegration plans." This provision says that a "youth justice court judge, the provincial director, a police officer, a justice of the peace, a prosecutor or a youth worker may convene or cause to be convened a conference for the purpose of making a decision required to be made under this Act." Although these conferences may focus on a variety of purposes and results, some of which are not necessarily restorative in nature, this section does provide considerable latitude for making use of restorative practices at different stages of the youth justice process. In a Canadian context, this provision represents a formalization of the conferencing processes a number of courts had already employed through the use of sentencing circles.

There are many potential benefits of conferencing. One is allowing voices other than judges, lawyers, and police to enter the youth justice dialogue. In the context of court organization and circle sentencing, Judge Barry Stuart of the Yukon Territorial Court—a pioneer in bringing restorative processes to Canadian courts—explained the need to look outside of *status quo* court procedures and processes in seeking new approaches to justice, and new alternatives for the participation of offenders, victims, and community members:

> For centuries, the basic organization of the court has not changed. Nothing has been done to encourage meaningful participation by the accused, the victim or by the community.... If the objective of the sentencing process is now to enhance sentencing options, to afford greater concern to the impact on victims, to shift focus from punishment to rehabilitation, and to meaningfully engage communities in sharing responsibility for sentencing decisions, it may be advantageous for the justice system to consider how court procedures and the physical arrangements within court-rooms militate against these new objectives.[47]

Police officers are named in section 19 as a party that can conduct a conference. This will not be a new experience for some officers. Police officers in Calgary, for example, have used conferencing as a tool in dealing with complaints for schools within Calgary. In 1997 to 1999, an average of thirty-five community group conferences each year were conducted by Calgary police officers. Some of these conferences involved more than one offender or suspect.[48] Cst. Leah Barber of the Youth, Education and Intervention Program of the Calgary Police Service had conducted many conferences in the schools to which she was assigned and saw the expansion of conferencing as a natural progression of policing:

I would like to see [conferencing] expanded in the next year or so to the point where we are training street officers who are interested in doing this type of thing. We do an awful lot of front line diversion anyway as a police department. We do a lot of finger wags where you say don't do it again and you do try to sort of mediate between say neighbourhood complaints.... I think conferencing allows a structured format that we can follow and even if it's spontaneously in somebody's kitchen, it's better than nothing so I can see it being an extremely useful tool in the future for the police department.[49]

In an international context, family group conferences have become a frequently used process in the youth justice systems of Australia, New Zealand, and England. These developments are considered in depth in chapter five of this book. Although conferences vary in design and delivery between these countries, there is an increasing recognition, around the world, of the value of using restorative conferencing in appropriate circumstances.

Youth justice committees

The *Young Offenders Act* allowed each province to establish youth justice committees to assist in any aspect of the administration of the *YOA*, or in any program or services for young offenders. The province could specify the method of appointment of committee members and the function of these committees, which served without pay. The *YCJA* contains a similar provision in section 18, but without any mention of whether youth justice committee members can be paid. In addition, this section details the functions which may be performed by a youth justice committee. These functions can be viewed as restorative, advisory, and educative in nature.

The restorative functions of a youth justice committee include: giving advice on appropriate extrajudicial measures for young persons, supporting victims by obtaining their concerns and facilitating reconciliation between victims and young persons, ensuring that community support is available to young persons by arranging for the use of services from within the community, and enlisting members of the community to provide short-term mentoring and supervision. When a young person is being dealt with by a child protection agency or a community group, the committee may also help to coordinate the interaction of the agency or group with the youth criminal justice system. A youth justice committee, in performing these and other duties, may act as a conference as established by section 19 of the *YCJA*.

The advisory functions of a youth justice committee are: advising the federal and provincial governments on whether the provisions of the *YCJA* that grant rights to young persons, or provide for the protection of young persons, are being complied with, and advising the federal and provincial governments on policies and procedures related to the youth criminal justice system.

Educative functions of a youth justice committee are providing information to the public in respect of this Act and the youth criminal justice system.

Child welfare implications

Many police officers, lawyers, youth workers, and judges encounter daily youth whom they believe would be more appropriately dealt with by child protection or mental health workers, rather than being processed through the criminal justice system. Yet if the necessary child protection or mental health resources are not available, or falter, many of these youths do end up in youth court, and often in custody. This leads to a perception that criminal justice has become our society's default system, taking in all those youth that fall between the cracks of other systems and resources. The *Young Offenders Act*, in section 24(1.1)(a), provided that custody should "not be used as a substitute for appropriate child protection, health or other social measures." Similarly, the *YCJA* now provides in section 29(1) that a young person shall not be detained in custody prior to sentence "as a substitute for appropriate child protection, mental health or other social measures," and in section 38 provides that custody shall not be used "as a substitute for appropriate child protection, mental health or other social measures."

A new feature of the *YCJA* is section 35, which provides that "a youth justice court may, at any stage of proceedings against a young person, refer the young person to a child welfare agency for assessment to determine whether the young person is in need of child welfare services." As noted previously, youth justice committees may play a part in facilitating the interaction between child protection systems and the criminal justice system. Presumably this implies that committees will help a young person guide his or her way through the often confusing maze of processes between these two systems.

This Act's stated purpose of not allowing the criminal justice system to be used as a replacement for child protection, mental health, or other social measures is laudable. To some extent this may be seen as an adjunct of other provisions of the *YCJA*, such as placing restrictions on committing youth to custody (in section 39) and requiring a sentence to be the least restrictive one that holds a youth accountable while promoting rehabilitation and reintegration.[50] It is hoped that these provisions will not only be symbolic, but rather will become a catalyst in keeping many troubled and needy youths out of the criminal system.

A related and crucial question, however, is whether the needed child protection and mental health services are actually available to youth. Our experience has shown many young people end up in custody because of a lack of resources, especially within the child protection and mental health systems. In particular, many of these youths find themselves in custody after breaching the condition of an undertaking or probation order, such as a residency. Yet realistically, these young people may have little choice in where they live, and little control over whether their parents or guardians provide appropriate supervision and compassionate support for them. This is especially so in marginalized high-need families. In many cases the root problem is a lack of or inappropriate services for that youth, yet the effect that garners most attention in the justice system is the resulting breach of a court order.

Despite a view expressed in both the *YOA* and *YCJA* that the criminal system should not replace appropriate child protection and mental health responses, our experience has been that, in a number of cases, social agencies rely on youth courts as part of their control mechanism. For example, if a child is ward of a province and is unruly, or runs to his or her natural family, the court is often asked by that agency to place certain conditions on the youth through the criminal process, such as residing in a residence approved by the agency. Criminal sanctions can then follow any breach of such an condition. As a result, the laudable goal of keeping youth out of the criminal system can be thwarted, or at least hindered.

Although there do not appear to be any reported court decisions on this question, an interesting situation would arise if the department or agency charged with protecting, as well as apprehending, children who are "in need of protection" concluded that a youth in criminal custody needed such protection. Our experiences in youth court clearly identify many cases in which young offenders, for a variety of reasons (such as their physical stature or the sexual nature of their charges), would be at extreme risk of being victimized if held in custody. In such cases, it is difficult to see how such young people would not be in need of protection. This scenario raises many issues about the interrelation of government services, but also questions the degree to which custodial facilities could be said to help, as opposed to endanger, a number of the young offenders sent there.

Statements to persons in authority and the publication of names

The *YOA* in section 56 contained a series of requirements to be met before a young person's statement could be admitted as evidence in a court proceeding. These requirements have been repeated in section 146 of the *YCJA*, and prevent admission of such statements unless the statement is voluntary and the person to whom the statement is made has explained, in language appropriate to the age and understanding of that young person, a number of factors. These include their right to silence, that any statement may be used against them, their right to consult a lawyer, parent, or other adult, and the right to have the person consulted present during the statement. Any waiver of these rights by a young person must be formally recorded, either on tape or on paper.

In *R. v. J.(J.T.)*,[51] the Supreme Court of Canada ruled that a statement that did not comply with the strict requirements of section 56 of the *YOA* was inadmissible, regardless of how streetwise the youth involved was. Apparently in response to this interpretation, the *YCJA* now allows a youth court, under section 146(6) to admit a statement into evidence despite a technical irregularity if satisfied that "the admission of the statement would not bring into disrepute the principle that young persons are entitled to enhanced procedural protection to ensure that they are treated fairly and their rights are protected." Under section 146(5), a court can accept as valid a waiver of rights not made in strict compliance with the Act, as long as it is satisfied that the young person was informed of his or her rights, and voluntarily waived them.

The subject of whether names of young offenders should be published has received much attention. Under the *YOA*, the names of young persons raised to adult court could be published. Likewise, under the *YCJA* (section 110(2)(a)) the names of young persons subsequently sentenced as adults can be published. But in addition, the court in section 75(3) is given a discretion of whether to allow publication of names of youths who receive youth sentences for "presumptive offences" within the meaning of section 2(1). In making this decision, the court decides whether allowing publication is "appropriate in the circumstances, taking into account the importance of rehabilitating the young person and the public interest." We hope this balancing of rehabilitative and public interest considerations will be considered in the context of those factors that bring—and often return—youth to the criminal justice system, a subject that is canvassed in the next chapter.

"I was sixteen when I was trying to exit the sex trade, but I didn't have any healthy support, and I was trying to isolate myself from my friends, from people who were unhealthy. And I didn't know where I could go for help."

S.N.

Chapter Three

Youth Crime: Causes and Responses

The Causes of Youth Crime

Having appeared for years with young people in the courts throughout Saskatchewan, we have observed many similarities between the youths who have become our clients. A significant majority are Aboriginal. Most are from the lowest economic strata in our society—clearly coming from homes in poverty—and most have faced some form of serious family dysfunction, whether in the form of parental alcohol abuse, physical, sexual or mental abuse, or family breakdown and separation from loved ones. Many are disabled, and many are or have previously been in foster care. According to a recent report from the National Youth in Care Network (NYICN), several "snapshots" conducted over the past few years in Alberta, Ontario, and Nova Scotia portraying which youth were in custody on a given day showed that "over half of the children in custody have past or present child welfare status."[1] In further considering exactly which people within society fill the justice system, Chief Judge Barry Stuart of the Yukon Territorial Court, in *R.* v. *Elias,*[2] observed that "[o]ur jails are overflowing with people who suffer from substance abuse, have few employable skills, are mentally challenged, are significantly disconnected from mainstream society, and whose lives are characterized by little, if any, support from family or community."[3]

Discussions about the underlying causes of youth crime are complex, and should not be viewed as an end in themselves, or merely an academic exercise. This discussion would be of little practical value unless it resulted in some guidance on strategies that can more successfully prevent crime and change the behaviour of delinquent youths. Much has been written on the causes of youth crime, and a variety of theories exist. Many of these are contradictory. Despite longing for some clear explanation as to why some youths offend, we are ultimately pulled between competing explanations, accepting the strengths and highlighting the weaknesses of each. As Professor Nicholas Bala of Queen's University commented, there "is no single theory or explanation for why adolescents commit crimes, or why some youths commit more violent offences or repeatedly offend."[4]

Theories of delinquency can be grouped generally into three categories: sociological, psychological, and biological.[5] Sociological theories focus on "the effects on human behaviour of macro issues such as social organizations, norms, values, race, ethnicity, and social stratification."[6] Sociologists have stressed social and environmental factors in explaining youth crime.[7] Psychological theories, on the other hand, "concentrate on the mind of the offender in order to determine the cause of his or her criminal or delinquent actions."[8] Biological explanations of delinquency have sought a connection between crime and the physical, genetic, psychophysiological, and psychopharmacological makeup of offenders.[9]

While giving psychological and biological theories their due, there is no doubt that we, as lawyers and authors, support a sociological explanation of crime. In part this may be because we both work in the legal aid system and deal daily with the most impoverished of society. We see firsthand how home and other environmental factors experienced by our clients correlate with, and increase, the chance of being charged with a criminal offence. But beyond the people we personally represent, we regularly observe who appears in youth court, and we know beyond a shadow of a doubt that this does not represent a socio-economic cross section of society. The vast majority of these accused represent the impoverished, the marginalized, and the lowest-status youths in our community. We see little hope in effecting change among offenders, and hence pursuing a safer society, without addressing the underlying environmental causes of crime.

A prominent sociological theory on delinquency was developed by the Chicago School of Sociology in the first half of the twentieth century. It was called social disorganization theory, and focused on crime and delinquency in urban areas.[10] Two sociologists from this school, Clifford Shaw and Henry McKay, argued that "urban industrial expansion undermines the traditional social controls inherent in the family, the church, and the community." This "erosion is most severe in a modern city's *transitional zone*, an area prone to crime and delinquency because of its social disorganization."[11] In effect, these sociologists argued that urbanization had resulted in communities with a "variety of competing cultures" which promoted "the breakdown of older, established value patterns."[12] This conflict of cultures resulted in the breakdown of basic institutions within society, including the family.[13] "Hence, deviance and criminal behaviour occur when the less dominant individual values and norms conflict with the more dominant values and norms."[14]

Sociologist Robert Merton of Columbia University agreed with his counterparts from Chicago that the causes of delinquency were found "outside of the individual."[15] He, however, focused on the generally accepted values and goals of society, as opposed to urbanization, as the major influence on behaviour.[16] Based on the work of French sociologist Emile Durkheim, Merton's work focused on "anomie," a term Durkheim used to describe "social behaviour that discards traditional values and norms for a new value system that has not yet been embraced by the broader society."[17] Merton theorized that the strain between commonly accepted goals in society—such as success through monetary wealth—and acceptable means of accomplishing these goals—such as employment and education—resulted in anomie, "a state of normative ambiguity."[18] Anomie was especially pronounced among the lowest socio-economic groups in society, who found their educational and employment opportunities restricted.[19]

According to Merton, this gulf between goals and means led to five types of adaption:

- *Conformity*, where individuals accept generalized goals, and believe they have the means to achieve these.

- *Ritualism*, where goals are not necessarily accepted, but the means are followed (such as a person working in a minimum wage job, despite rejection of the goal that everyone can succeed materially).

- *Innovation*, where goals are accepted but individuals are either unprepared or unable to attain these through legitimate means (such as youth wanting a CD player, but obtaining this by theft).

- *Retreatism*, where people reject both the goals and means of society, choosing not to participate (such as the street kids who are often viewed as the outcasts of society).

- *Rebellion*, where people reject society's goals and means, but substitute them with their own set of goals and means (such as street gangs).[20]

While each theory of crime has limitations, an alternate approach is simply to identify those factors which correlate to an increase, or a decrease, in youth crime, without any necessity of finding a causal link. The American Psychological Association, for example, identified a number of factors they claimed heightened a youth's risk profile for violent crime. These included "[b]iological factors, child rearing conditions, ineffective parenting, emotional or cognitive development, gender differences, sex role socialization, relation to peers, cultural milieu, social factors such as economic inequality and lack of opportunity, and media influences among others."[21] Similarly, a report on juvenile crime and justice in Northern Ireland described a "growing consensus in the literature which indicates the roots of youth crime lie, in large part, within the broad social and economic environment of the young person."[22] Based on research done by D.P. Farrington, this report identified a number of risk factors which "predispose children to later criminal activity."[23] These factors were: impulsivity and hyperactivity, low intelligence, learning disabilities, truancy and exclusion from school, inadequate parental supervision, neglect and abuse, family conflict, criminal parents, poverty and poor housing, lack of training and employment, association with delinquent peers, and drug and alcohol abuse.[24] This report found the implications of such research to be "that in order to be effective, prevention programs should target risk factors affecting all the main aspects of a child's life." Further, it said "[m]ultiple problems require multiple solutions, and in the long term multiple interventions will be more effective than initiatives with a single focus."[25]

The more one examines these risk factors, the more it explains which youth are found in custody. However, most if not all adolescents go through periods of development when they openly challenge authority. The chance to push boundaries and struggle for increasing levels of power and control is coupled in most youths with a will to take risks, even in the face of obvious danger. In doing so, most young people do commit acts which may be viewed as criminal. Yet much if not most of this activity goes unreported. Many adults look back to their childhoods, and wonder what stroke of luck prevented some of their activities from reaching the police, let alone youth court. As Professor Nicholas Bala of Queen's University commented:

> The fact that virtually all youths engage in some criminal activity also indicates that at least some level of youthful offending should probably be viewed as "normal." Although social and legal policies may reduce (or increase) levels of offending behaviour, they cannot eliminate all

youth crime. This does not mean that youth crime should not be the subject of legal response, but it is important to view the issue in context.[26]

What ultimately brings a young person in contact with the youth justice system varies widely. A CBC investigative report on young offenders considered this question, and the subsequent effect of the system on the lives of young people charged. A former young offender named Shareen summed up why she got into trouble:

> Well, with me, my mom didn't really care. I could do whatever and she didn't care. I come home late she'd beat me for it. If I washed the dishes the wrong way she would beat me for it. Come home, like and to me she never paid me attention if I was good all right so I started doing things to get myself in trouble just so I could get some attention from her so at least know that she recognized me that I was there and I see a lot of young people now who are doing that and it's not really the best way to go about it.[27]

Another former young offender named Ingrid told a similar story of abuse and explained her motivation for "acting out" and committing offences:

> What happened with me, with my background first of all. I came from an abusive home where I had love but my mother came from a culture where physical abuse was the main source of discipline. So beatings were quite regular for things that I would do wrong I would be beaten for it and I eventually left home and the problem I had when I left home was that … you have to remember when kids are coming from abusive situations they are coming from a powerless situation where they are being basically preyed upon by their parents or people that they trust. So when they get out of that situation, they are basically reclaiming their power, and they are not willing to give that up once they've reclaimed it. So when they get out there in the system, they take out all this anger that they weren't able to display before. Now they have the freedom. They feel they can do whatever they want and any authority figure that comes into their life whether it's a social worker or a police officer, a court in the system, they don't pay attention to that because they are just so built up on themselves not having to anymore listen to anybody, to being able to do what they want.[28]

In an Aboriginal context, a young Aboriginal woman who had worked in the sex trade as a young teenager talked about the many factors that bring youth into conflict with the law:

> I think there's a lot of reasons why youth do crime. And people don't

look at these reasons. They presume the youth do it because they are bad. Like kids selling drugs, or pimping or stealing. There are situations where many youth are living in poverty. They have no guidance and support, like a healthy stable family…. Myself, for example, I was sixteen when I was trying to exit the sex trade, but I didn't have any healthy support, and I was trying to isolate myself from my friends, from people who were unhealthy. And I didn't know where I could go for help. I was too afraid to trust someone. I think for two years I was trying to make myself feel better. I still carry lots of shame and guilt, and a lot of fear.[29]

Fetal Alcohol Syndrome

Enmeshed with, and at times indistinguishable from, the effects of home and surrounding environments on the chances of young people offending are the implications of parental prenatal behaviour. In the past few years, the issue of prenatal consumption of alcohol has become a focus in considering why many youths offend, and in forming strategies to assist those youth suffering the neurological effects commonly called Fetal Alcohol Syndrome (FAS) and Fetal Alcohol Effect (FAE). FAE is more commonly called partial FAS. The catch-all term Fetal Alcohol Spectrum Disorder (FASD) is also currently in use and includes FAS, alcohol-related birth defects, and alcohol-related neurodevelopmental disorder.

A person would have difficulty spending any significant time observing a Canadian youth court today without hearing the words Fetal Alcohol Syndrome or Fetal Alcohol Effect. The issue of neurological damage and cognitive impairment resulting from prenatal exposure to alcohol has become a significant focus of youth court judges, lawyers, youth court workers, and others employed within the system. Yet the attention now being paid to this issue is most shocking given its recency, leading many to speculate on the number of cognitively impaired youths who have been processed and incarcerated in the past, without any acknowledgement of, or compensation for, their disability.

In addition to prenatal exposure to alcohol, a diagnosis of FAS requires evidence of a delay in growth, a distinctive pattern of facial features, and a central nervous system (or brain) dysfunction.[30] FAE—also described as partial FAS—refers to those people who have suffered prenatal exposure to alcohol and who meet some but not all of the formal criteria for FAS.[31] Experts in this field stress that FAE "is not a 'milder' form of FAS, and people with FAE have the same risk of developmental and behavioural disabilities as those with FAS."[32] The neurological damage resulting from prenatal alcohol consumption is permanent and irreversible. The effects of FAS and FAE are wide-ranging and profound. Judge Mary Ellen Turpel-Lafond of the Provincial Court of Saskatchewan, in *R. v. W.D.*,[33] stated:

> The pre-natal brain damage which causes FAS leaves its victims with neuro-developmental abnormalities such as diminished IQ, fine and gross motor delays, learning disabilities relating to language dysfunction, verbal learning and memory deficits, and behaviour effects such as impulsivity and a failure to learn from mistakes.[34]

One group of researchers divided FAS/FAE disabilities into two categories. Primary difficulties among adults and adolescents were said to be "memory impairments, problems with judgement and abstract reasoning and poor adaptive functioning," while secondary disability characteristics "include being easily victimized, unfocussed and distractable [sic], difficulty handling money, problems learning from experience, trouble understanding consequences and perceiving social cues, poor frustration tolerance, inappropriate sexual behaviours, substance abuse, mental health problems and trouble with the law."[35]

Worldwide, the occurrence of FAS is estimated at 1.9 cases per thousand, while in the United States, rates are estimated at between one and two cases per thousand.[36] There does not appear to be a comprehensive study of FAS/FAE rates across Canada, but some studies have identified alarmingly high rates in specific Aboriginal communities. Researchers F.J. Boland, R. Burrill, M. Duwyn, and J. Karp, in reviewing studies done to date on FAS rates among Canadian Aboriginal communities, highlighted a 1989 study by D. Bray and P. Anderson[37] regarding the epidemiology of FAS among Canadian Aboriginal populations, which illustrated "high incidence rates."[38] Other studies have found FAS rates among Aboriginal communities of British Columbia and the Yukon to be dramatically higher than rates for the general population.[39]

In a criminal justice system focused largely on the deterrent effects of penal sanctions, the inability of those suffering from FAS or FAE to connect unacceptable behaviour with consequences is of paramount concern. As Judge Henning of the Provincial Court of Saskatchewan stated in *R. v. R.C.P.*, in sentencing an offender diagnosed with partial FAS who had spent much of his youth either in foster care or in custody, "[s]ocially unacceptable and criminal behaviours may result without any true appreciation of why such behaviour is not acceptable." Judge Henning went on to observe "[t]he ordinary connection between negative consequences of unacceptable behaviour and the behaviour does not exist, and so deterrent sentencing is wholly ineffective."[40]

Doctors Julianne Conry and Dianne Fast, in their ground-breaking work *Fetal Alcohol Syndrome and the Criminal Justice System*, summarized the challenges presented by FAS and FAE, both to youth courts and to society at large:

> FAS/FAE is an "invisible" disability, which is life-long. At present, FAS/FAE often goes undiagnosed among adolescents and adults. This leads to unrealistic expectations for their behaviour that may result in ridicule, blame and social stigma. As defendant, victim, or witness, the individual with FAS/FAE presents a challenge to the traditional criminal justice system.[41]

Although recently generating much attention and debate, the cognitive impairment caused by FAS and FAE has not been a long-standing focus of Canadian youth courts. As recently as 1995, Judge Cunliffe Barnett of the Provincial Court of British Columbia commented that FAS was "not well understood by most judges, lawyers, probation officers, corrections officers, social workers or other persons likely to encounter it in the context of the justice system."[42] The extent to which this disability has gone unnoticed in the past within our justice system was highlighted by Judge Mary Ellen Turpel-Lafond of the Provincial Court of Saskatchewan in *R. v. W.D.*[43] This case involved a thirteen-year-old Aboriginal boy who had been diagnosed with FAS as an infant. Despite this early medical confirmation of his condition, since the age of twelve he had appeared in youth court on twelve charges, totalling twenty-five appearances. He had received dispositions ranging from community service to probation to custody. His charges were all minor thefts and system-generated offences such as breaches of undertakings and probation. He had been represented by five different lawyers, none of whom apparently raised the issue of his fitness to stand trial, or his ability to instruct counsel. Neither had the prosecutor provided to the court any indication that this youth was disabled. In expressing her frustration over the past treatment of this youth, Judge Turpel-Lafond stated:

> It is a sad commentary on our society that a severely disabled boy, who is highly vulnerable to antisocial individuals, would end up in a youth jail so many times. One can only speculate on how this is preparing him to meet the challenges of adulthood, which in legal terms is a mere four years away, even if developmentally is many years in the future. One cannot but question what social policy is served by the use of the

hard penal machinery of the criminal justice system to deal with the most chronic mentally disabled youth of our society.[44]

The problems associated with the FAS/FAE disability are being felt widely across Canada, and are increasingly being recognized by judges. As an example, Chief Judge Barry Stuart of the Yukon Territorial Court, in *R. v. Elias*,[45] observed that "estimates suggest that at least half of the offenders through our courts are mentally challenged as a consequence of FAS, FAE or early life trauma."[46] Across western Canada, consideration of FAS/FAE is evidenced through a series of cases: *R. v. Williams*,[47] *R. v. Steeves*,[48] *R. v. D.E.K.*,[49] *R. v. George*,[50] and *R. v. T.J.*[51]

The dangers of incarcerating individuals suffering from FAS/FAE cannot be overstated. Doctors Conry and Fast identified a number of these concerns. First and foremost, those suffering from mental disabilities, including FAS/FAE, are at a significant risk of being victimized while in jail.[52] In addition, the difficulty of FAS/FAE individuals in comprehending and following institutional rules often leads to an inaccurate labelling of them as resistant and defiant.[53] But most troubling, in a criminal justice system that seems to favour prison as a means of changing behaviour, is the reality that cognitively impaired individuals are at a significant risk of negative influence through association with criminal role models. As these authors explained:

> People with FAS/FAE may benefit from the structure of "secure custody," but also in this setting can be influenced negatively by their peers because they want to fit in and be liked. They are manipulated and set up, for example, being caught with contraband. They can be sexually, physically, and emotionally victimized (and often are the scapegoat). They are not always aware of what is happening because of their desire to please.[54]

Likewise, in *R. v. M.L.*, Judge Turpel-Lafond queried:

> Will justice be served by taking a FAS disabled 12 year old girl into custody only to transform her into a more dangerous individual given the criminogenic associations she is sure to make in the facilities? It is the Court's view that community protection is not served by temporary warehousing FAS children in secure custodial facilities because, based on the material reviewed, in all likelihood they will return to the community in worse condition.[55]

Although many critics of sentencing practice have drawn a direct link between jail and protection of the public, Judge Henning of the Provincial Court of Saskatchewan suggested the opposite interpretation in *R. v. R.C.P.*

This case dealt with the sentencing of a nineteen-year-old offender suffering from partial FAS, who had spent the majority of his teenage years in custody. Judge Henning questioned what public interest would be served in returning this young adult to jail:

> Although the accused here is not a young offender, he is himself a product of that system who has reached adulthood without any positive effect from it. The condition that he suffers from must be managed by other means, not only for his benefit, but for the protection of the public. If custody was capable of solving this problem either by treatment or deterrence, such might reasonably be expected to have already occurred in this case as the accused has been in some form of care, custody, or incarceration most of the time since age five. The court as a matter of principle rejects an approach to sentencing that would incarcerate a person with limited mental functioning without any realistic possibility of treatment that would improve or deter the accused. The accused might well benefit from an institutional program, but not one such as exists in the conventional correctional system.[56]

While issues around the appropriate sentencing of FAS/FAE youth are enormous, and appear to encompass much if not most of judicial comment on this disability to date, an equally troubling enquiry is whether a person with FAS or FAE has the capacity to be charged and tried in our criminal justice system. This was the issue canvassed by Judge Turpel-Lafond in *W.D.* While casting scepticism on whether this youth had the capacity[57] to be tried, Judge Turpel-Lafond commented that

> [t]his lack of attention to the circumstances of a severely disabled youth raises a concern for the Youth Court about the administration of justice. A young person, like W.D., who, based on thorough medical testing and diagnosis, cannot even be presumed to instruct counsel, let alone understand the concepts of "guilt" or "innocence," should be treated differently given this disability.[58]

With the continued recognition of FAS/FAE comes an obvious enquiry about which strategies can be implemented to help those disabled, and in so doing to protect the long-term safety and best interests of society. This discussion may cause a rethinking of long-standing approaches to the treatment of alcohol-related illnesses and dependencies. Clearly, the conventional approach to addictions screening and treatment is likely to be ineffective with those affected by FAS/FAE. Mary Vandenbrink, a social worker specializing in alcohol-related birth defects, outlined the challenges of existing addictions practice in treating this disability:

1. Formal, accurate diagnosis of FASD is still infrequent enough that the process of identifying affected clients falls to front-line helpers, many of whom have little experience in this area.

2. Prenatal alcohol exposure can greatly impair ability to understand concepts, predict consequences, and exercise self-discipline. Treatment methods that require these skills may not work for clients with alcohol-related birth defects.

3. Affected people usually appear more competent than they really are, and are therefore subject to higher expectations than they can realistically deliver.

4. Verbal skills of most affected individuals far exceed their comprehension skills. They can readily repeat what they have heard, which masks their lack of competence in everyday living skills. Interview questions that ask for self-reports of competence may not uncover this lack of skills.

5. These clients are easily overwhelmed by group work or other situations that require dredging up the past. They are apt to take on others' issues as though they were their own, and may become depressed as a consequence. (Even without the presence of alcohol in their lives, they are prone to depression, suicidal thoughts and panic.)

6. Relapse prevention depends on the ability to monitor one's own behaviour. Clients with FASD are unable to do this. They require supervision if they are to avoid using again. Unless programs can build in or identify a source for such supervision, relapse will almost certainly occur.

7. Clients with FASD often state a desire to change and become self-sufficient, even though this may be an unrealistic goal. It is difficult for helpers to remain patient in the face of accumulating evidence of the client's inability to fulfill the requirements of everyday living.

8. Clients with FASD are prone to transience, and cannot always be relied upon to keep appointments. The windows of opportunity to help them may therefore be small and intermittent. It is important to equip them with supports to daily living as soon as possible, if any worthwhile intervention is going to take place.[59]

As clearly indicated in the above list, the range of challenges presented by FAS/FAE youth is significant. More than anything, these challenges highlight the need for agencies that provide service to such youth to be innovative, flexible, and dynamic in designing and delivering such services.

As the FAS/FAE disability is permanent and irreversible, changes to a person's living environment may be more feasible than changes to that person.[60] In *M.L.*, Judge Turpel-Lafond quoted from a report filed by a psychologist suggesting the most promising strategies for helping people with this disability:

> A general guideline for working with F.A.S. affected individuals is that they need to be taught expected behaviours in situations. Relying on consequences or punishment is not sufficient and rarely effective. Youths with F.A.S. need to rehearse pro-social behaviours in the setting in which they will be required to use them. They require training in the settings in which they are expected to function. This means that M.L. will need community based services to help her manage school, home and community issues. Services must allow her to rehearse responses and consolidate gains she makes. The initial training/programming will require a great deal of supervision. Life long supports will be necessary. Her family needs to be provided with information regarding F.A.S., be connected to an F.A.S. support group, learn how to manage their own substance abuse issues and learn how to assess and monitor their adolescent's needs in ways that help them maintain stability.[61]

Despite these concerns, there are treatment strategies for those dealing with FAS/FAE. Doctors Conry and Fast commented that

> [m]uch can be done in the way of prevention, early diagnosis and interventions, such as schooling, socializing and living arrangements. This would minimize the secondary disabilities that accompany FAS/FAE. The cost saving that would result, to the criminal justice system alone, may well justify taking such action. The human cost of failing to take such action can never be fully measured.[62]

There is little doubt those working in the youth justice system have a heightened awareness of cognitive issues such as FAS/FAE. We see evidence every day that lawyers, youth workers, and judges are considering whether youths within the system are affected by such impairment. But regardless of this laudable increase in knowledge, options and help for these young people appear scarce. We still see such children and youth in our courts and jails on a daily basis. Why aren't these young people in the care of child protection or mental heath professionals? Why are they squarely within the confines of the youth justice system?

Criminal Justice as a Default System

Although it is not generally seen as a reason for change, the youth criminal justice system as it operates in Canada is tremendously stressful and frustrating to most of the parties involved. This includes police officers, judges, defence lawyers, prosecutors, youth workers, victims, and young people. This sense of frustration is often openly expressed.

Police Chief Cal Johnson of Regina pointed out that Regina's position as Canada's leader in break and enters was the result of the living conditions of the Aboriginal people in Saskatchewan. Chief Johnson pointed to poverty, unemployment, substance abuse, and family dysfunction as some of the causes. In 2000, he told Regina's Board of Police Commissioners that unless "these problems are addressed we will continue to be in this unenviable position."[63] Similarly, Chief Charles Ramsay of the Washington, D.C. Metropolitan Police told a forum on youth and gangs:

> My first perspective of what these young people are thinking and doing when they first join gangs is that for one thing they are unemployable. They are frequently high school dropouts; they have no skills. Where are they going in life?[64]

If police officers find it difficult to face crime that is a result of social conditions imagine the distress of judges. Generally whenever the topic of youth justice becomes current in the media, judges will be blamed for being too soft on youth. Judges are left in an impossible situation. They can try to use their courts to solve problems so that there is some real chance of less future crime and thereby run the risk of condemnation from other professionals who don't wish to take so much time. They can impose harsher sentences and run the almost certain risk (statistically if not in each individual case) that they are thereby encouraging more crime. However, no matter what they do, they will be blamed by many for any increase in crime, indeed, often for any crime at all. In August of 2002, the *Globe and Mail* reported that because of relentless scrutiny, long dockets that must be rushed, and difficult sentencing decisions (among other factors, including obnoxious lawyers), Canadian judges live in torment.[65] Nowhere are these problems more obvious than in youth court.

Lawyers, both Crown prosecutors and defence counsel, are not immune from these frustrations. Generally, lawyers are three times more likely to suffer from depression compared to other professions. Compared to the general population lawyers are six times more likely to commit suicide, at a rate of 69 per 100,000.[66] Imagine yourself as a Crown prosecutor who is faced with the decision of whether to release an emaciated little girl of twelve who refuses to live at a foster home. There is no parent or relative but the social services department says she's not their problem. What will you do? Use jail?

Victims come to court expecting that the offender will be treated as befits the monster they've been led to believe the offender is. How difficult is it then to be considered surplus baggage whilst everyone concentrates on the offender? And consider the position of youth workers and youth facility workers. While some buy into the "attack probation" mentality, others agree with Winston Churchill that the whole punishment system is a black mark on our society. But then if they take up the case of a youth, work closely with that youth, bend the rules, change them, try to cheat the system to make it work, the good youth worker risks being blamed for that youth's failures. A nontraditional foster home might not be approved by the social services department, but it might also be run by a caring, committed, competent adult that could actually help more than a traditional foster parent. As social worker Mike Dunphy of Saskatoon explained in the context of an outreach program called Operation Help, which sought to help youth caught in the sex trade,

> We would do better with outreach workers dealing with non-traditional homes even though they might look like they're not up to standard. Kids would do better. Certainly, central offices don't like this stuff, but it is working.[67]

Parents of youth charged also have a difficult role. Like youth workers, the more they stand beside their child the more likely it is that they will be blamed. They'll also be blamed if they disappear, but at least that blame will be in absentia. York University sociologist Anne-Marie Ambert, author of *The Effect of Children on Parents,* said that her research revealed that 95 percent of parents of acting-out teenagers experienced high levels of stress and about 50 percent have had their health deteriorate. "Parents do not have an encouraging climate right now to raise their children properly. They live in a climate of blame."[68]

The inevitable conclusion is that the youth justice system is very stressful and frustrating for all concerned, not the least of whom is our clients. This frustration can be heard in the voice of an Aboriginal young person, in custody because a judge ruled he had breached too many conditions of his undertaking:

> The judge never listened to a word my lawyers said for me. I've never been in trouble outside of the city, my aunt and uncle would've made sure I'd go to school and stay out of trouble. They [the people encouraging this youth to join an Aboriginal gang] are right. You can't work with the white man.[69]

Public images and perceptions of young offenders as miniature Al Capones, Paul Bernardos, or Charles Mansons are widespread. The image of the emaciated twelve year old coming from a life of marginalization (while in itself an example of only one type of person found in youth court) is much closer to the truth. Ultimately the police officers quoted above are correct. Youth crime is primarily the result of social conditions. Once that is understood then positive work can be done.

In considering the many challenges faced within the youth justice system, a large part of the problem is that the youth criminal justice system is used meet a variety of disparate goals:

- providing custody facilities where youth can connect with a worker to learn new skills and then return to an environment where future crime is unlikely;

- using the frightening effects of criminal sanction as a deterrent, so that youths will not commit further crimes, and will obey the rules both of their household and of society; and

- teaching youth the overarching principle that hurting others is wrong, yet doing this with an approach that treats being out past curfew as a significant transgression.

All too often, the criminal justice system is used to solve problems that would be more appropriately solved by other systems within society. This was the problem Parliament had in mind when the *Young Offenders Act* was amended to forbid using youth custody facilities for mental health or child protection. The new *Youth Criminal Justice Act* states specifically that "a youth justice court shall not use custody as a substitute for appropriate child protection, mental health or other social measures."[70] These goals are laudable, but in our experience, they are easier said than accomplished.

"Karen," for example, was charged with several offences for which she, much later, was found to be innocent—she could not have been the one who committed the crimes. However, before that evidence became available, she showed signs of psychological or psychiatric distress. She became almost unmanageable. The hospitals would not accept her but her behaviour was so bizarre that all became concerned. Coincidentally her behaviour was also inconsistent with the conditions of the undertaking that was imposed on her when she was released. Accordingly, the solution to not being accepted to the hospital was criminal custody. She was sent to a psychiatric facility that said she was faking her symptoms. Eventually she was isolated in a cell for many weeks, in clear distress, until one judge courageously ordered that she be released, that she reside at the psychiatric ward at the hospital, and that the custodial facility take her there (they were very happy to oblige). The hospital felt that it could not refuse admittance under these terms. They then diagnosed her as having a mental disorder. They arranged for her to go back to the first psychiatric hospital, which had earlier said she was faking it. The appropriate treatment was provided, she was discharged, and years later she is still living a normal life.

This example illustrates a problem: the deinstitutionalization of psychiatric patients is now standard procedure. However, if the supports for these patients are lacking, only one institution is left: jail. The number of mentally ill persons in custody is unknown; some say as much as 20 percent. Others claim that the mentally ill and those with brain injuries that affect their behaviour are the majority of youth in some facilities. Parliament has said this should not happen, but it regularly does.

Child protection provides another example. Judges are understandably reluctant to release a child or youth without some assurance that he or she has a home to go to. The court's position is difficult, but made so because the overworked social services department knows that this child has a roof over her head, albeit in a custodial facility. As a result, the case seems less urgent. In the alternative, if the department has doubts about the home but does not wish to take the child into care, an easier alternative is to let the child stay in custody.

Consider "John," a challenging youth, not as respectful to adults as one might wish, or perhaps not convinced about the importance of some rules in the adult world. He was in a home under a court order to obey all house rules. He was using crutches because of an injury to his leg. When he got to the home after school he saw a letter to himself from his doctor, no doubt about his leg. He took the letter and went towards his room. The operator of the home saw him with his letter and told him that he could not have his letter until she gave it to him. That was a house rule. He went to his bedroom and closed the door. She called the police. He was arrested and kept in custody for several days. His matter was placed for trial months later. A few days before the trial the charge was dropped. You can imagine the thinking involved. The operator of the home says that the youth was disobeying the rules, she tells the police officer that her home is to help youth with their problems, that she needs youth in her care to follow the rules. This youth shows that he doesn't respect the rules. If people don't respect the rules, who are you going to call? That this is not a criminal act, that respect for rules needs to be taught, that her solution would likely make things worse appears obvious. It requires someone to say loudly and clearly that this is not a criminal problem.

One may argue that it is a criminal problem because the judge ordered him to obey the house rules. He disobeyed a house rule, and rules are rules even if they seem to be minor, such as not interrupting a conversation or prefacing all remarks with "I feel that" or that one is not to put the toothpaste on the left side of the sink but on the right side.

If you think this example is ridiculous, how would you feel about going to jail for ducking out of school during a break to pick up a drink across the street? One youth in Saskatoon was in open custody, which is to say he was permitted or expected to go to school during the day and to return to the custodial facility at night. The school, which was designed to reintegrate youth who had become disconnected from school, was actually a satellite classroom in a retail building in the area that contains an organic food store, a community-owned movie theatre, a jazz café, and the Fringe drama festival. In other words, this is an area where the ambience is try something new or something daring. This youth went across the street with his friends to buy a drink and returned to school. This was against the rules of the school. Because the youth didn't live at home, they phoned the open custody facility to enlist their help. It was decided that the appropriate course was to treat this as an escape from prison. The police arrested the youth and took him to closed custody, where he remained for several days. That charge, too, was dropped before trial.

There's always a good argument for doing these things if you accept certain premises. The youth criminal justice system has secure facilities, therefore if someone can use those facilities in order to solve a problem with a youth then why not? This young woman can't get psychiatric help, this young man isn't listening to the rules, this young woman doesn't have an appropriate residence, this young man can't get into an alcohol treatment facility, so why not put them in a closed custody facility? If having a youth charged relieves the pressure on an institution to extend itself to solve difficult problems then why not use the criminal system? It is not uncommon in our experience for well-trained professionals to decide that a youth's criminal offences are directly related to his or her alcohol or drug use, to observe that there is no treatment available now or in the near future, and to conclude that this youth should therefore remain in custody until something is available. Or so the argument goes.

If the role of the youth criminal justice system is to assist our communities in their rightful attempt to reduce harmful acts against persons, then the short-term advantage gained by using custody must be weighed against the long-term disadvantages. However, added to that equation must be the social question: why, if it is important that this youth get alcohol treatment, are we not providing it sooner rather than later? Clearly, it is not cheaper later. Clearly, custody itself is expensive. For marginalized youth who are told that they must remain in custody for weeks or longer to wait for alcohol treatment, the argument that the diagnosis of the need for treatment is only an excuse to actually keep them in custody becomes very persuasive. The financial and policy implications of reducing custody beds in order to provide more treatment beds are perhaps too abstract for most of our clients. But if they find out that it's cheaper for a community to provide treatment when it's required than it is to put them in custody, they may start to believe that society prefers them to be unhealthy and in jail rather than healthy and free.

It is clear that youth criminal justice has become a default system. If, for whatever reason, social service agencies are not presently able to provide appropriate housing for children or their families and that lack is causing problems, the solution to this problem is, all too often, criminal charges. Poor housing is a good example. As Dr. Carol LaPrairie's study points out (see chapter four), communities in which Aboriginal people need to move frequently are communities which overincarcerate Aboriginals. The same is true of mental health, addictions, schools, and other services. When these services are difficult for Aboriginal people to access or are set up so that Aboriginal people are engaged in temporary rather than mainstream services, the resulting vacuum will be evidenced most clearly in the custodial facilities and other areas of our default justice system.

All of the examples above involve a youth disobeying a court order. There is little doubt that community-based court orders, which contain conditions governing behaviour, are an important part in keeping some youth out of custody. But for marginalized youth, these conditions can be an enormous problem. These youth often come from chaotic, disorganized lives, and usually live in similar circumstances. Court orders, if non-custodial, are in effect a form of treatment plan. A youth is to reside somewhere, usually with a parent, go to school, meet with a youth worker, take counselling, obey a curfew, stay away from some friends if they were involved in an offence. These conditions are intended to guide a youth towards a better future, but their application may produce a very different result. For example, if a youth comes from a home where there is alcohol abuse, violence, or parent-teen conflict for any number of reasons, it may be difficult for the child to remain at home. But if they leave, they may have committed two crimes: changing residence, and not being in the court-ordered residence by curfew time. Another example is school. A youth may be physically large but not have much more than grade four or five. Ordering the youth to go to school is not the same as ordering the schools to make the appropriate accommodations for the youth.

Dr. Thomas Szasz, world-famous expert on the uses of insanity as a means of social control, argued that the causes of violence and shootings in school must include three facts: (1) that children, because they are dependants, are prisoners of parents and schools (if children are treated well one might argue with Dr. Szasz that this is irrelevant, but if treated badly his point makes sense); (2) schools are prisons because basic literacy and mathematics can be taught in six years or by the age twelve; and (3) forcing them to go to school to prepare for further education is counter-productive because their ability to make a positive choice is hindered by compulsion. Dr. Szasz's conclusion is that schools are used as institutions for social control, as de facto criminal psychiatric facilities, and that youths are sometimes labelled with psychiatric diagnosis in order to facilitate current and future social control.[71]

Take "not drinking" or "following the rules of a treatment program." Consider that this was ordered probably as a form of guidance to a youth from a chaotic background, but now it forms the basis of removing this youth from the community, and putting this young person in custody. It is not harm to others that is the concern, it is failing to follow a treatment plan that is now criminal. Once again the youth criminal justice system is being used for other purposes.

We recognize that the current system places social agencies in a dilemma. They can, on the one hand, change their programs and approaches to better match and accommodate the most marginalized and needy youth seeking their help. This may involve trying the unconventional. But they must not move too far away from the mainstream measures of effectiveness, such as the number of youth successfully put through, and presumably abiding by the rules of, their programs. These measures are no doubt the basis upon which funding resources are given. Without in any way trying to oversimplify the very difficult challenges faced by these agencies, the way their programs are formulated and enforced does affect which, and how many, youths are left to be dealt with by the criminal justice system.

Saskatchewan incarcerates more youth per capita than any other jurisdiction in Canada; estimates are that 75 percent of these are Aboriginal. In 1992, the Indian Justice Review Committee (the Linn Commission) found that, in Saskatchewan, an Aboriginal youth had a statistically better chance of going to jail then graduating from high school.[72] To what extent has our society's broad application of the criminal system worked against Aboriginal youth, by substituting the threat or reality of criminal sanction for the provision of needed services and resources?

The Linn Commission report also urged that the appropriate authorities "undertake a joint review of support services to and programs for aboriginal young offenders to ... reduce the incidence of offences against the justice system (e.g., failure to appear, failure to comply with disposition) among aboriginal youth."[73] This problem was still very serious in 2002, ten years later. Out of 2,801 charges before Saskatoon's youth docket court in the month of October of that year, 1,244 were the same charges the Indian Justice Review Committee was concerned about: 44 percent had no victims. The Solicitor General of Canada has described these as "lifestyle" offences:

> The prairie provinces have the most marginalized aboriginal populations and highest use of imprisonment for life-style related offences such as administration of justice and public order. This partly explains the disproportionate levels of imprisonment.[74]

In making sense of the many "system generated" charges that appear in court, Professor Dan MacAllair and Dr. Mike Males presented an interesting, somewhat facetious yet factually correct argument in article entitled "Curfew Enforcement and Juvenile Crime":

> In 1992, San Francisco authorities dismantled their previously vigorous curfew enforcement which had resulted in 1400 arrests in the previous 5 years. Only 3 curfew arrests were made during 1993–97. Crime plummeted. From 1992 to 1997, juvenile murders declined 36% and violent crimes reported to the police declined by 41%, the latter which was the largest crime decrease of any large California city. Therefore abolishing curfew is a crucial step to reduce youth crime and victimization.[75]

The researchers concluded that "a crime reduction strategy founded solely on law enforcement intervention has little effect" but rather said the focus should be "on prevention strategies, opportunities and interventions." They said while "this approach is likely to require a substantial infusion of public resources, the long term benefits appear more promising than panacea approaches such as curfew and status policies."[76]

That Aboriginal children are usually products of a depressed environment is discussed in chapter four. Yet in 1997, the Saskatchewan government stated "nearly 40% of all [youth] cases heard in Saskatchewan involved at least one offence against the administration of justice." This percentage was the highest in Canada. The most common of these offences (called administration offences by the government of Saskatchewan, which are included in the term "lifestyle offences" by the Solicitor General of Canada) were failing to appear in court and failing to comply with a disposition.[77] Obviously, many Aboriginal youth are in custody because they breached conditions that relate to their home life, and whose breach was directly affected by a myriad of social problems faced in that household. The report also states that these offences were "…the *most serious* charge in nearly one quarter of all cases heard in Saskatchewan Youth Court." [emphasis added]

Virtually all persons commit a criminal offence sometime in their life. That makes all the more important countervailing pressures to oppose the indiscriminate use of the criminal law. If these do not exist, it is difficult to see an end. It's as if we encourage Chief Wiggum to arrest Marge Simpson.

The need for reasoned discretion in invoking the criminal system was seen in a recent court case from British Columbia. In *R. v. Wright*,[78] a Supreme Court judge in B.C. set aside a conviction against the general manager of the Cowichan Capitals, a team in the B.C. Junior Hockey League. At the trial the general manager was found guilty of assaulting a referee and given an absolute discharge, which means he is to be treated as if he was never convicted. He was unsatisfied and appealed to the Supreme Court of B.C. The Supreme Court judge stated:

> Crown counsels' duty is to exercise discretion in the laying of the charge … where other far more appropriate measures are available to protect league officials there is no need to engage the public purse in the prosecution of a criminal offence. Caseloads are high because the exercise of discretion in the criminal justice system appears to be extremely limited.[79]

The proper exercise of discretion seems to be an obvious goal for all professionals in the justice system. Yet it is difficult for prosecutors to dismiss charges when clearly other "system-players" such as mental health, child protection, or other social agencies promote the use of youth custody facilities to support existing or replace nonexistent resources. In our experience, Crown prosecutors are usually well aware of how little help is available for marginalized youth and are willing in many cases to exercise their discretion when the needed resources are available outside of the justice system. However, we can also say that our experience tells us that almost all youth who are sentenced to custody, or are refused release and are remanded in custody to wait for their charges to be ultimately dealt with, are sent to custody because their charges include either breaches that they are being charged with, or breaches on their records. Our personal observations, if consistent with practices in the rest of the province, tell us that the majority of youth in custody in Saskatchewan are in custody partly because their breaches were used to suggest they should be in custody. It is our experience that if a youth had no record for breaching a court order, it is rare that their initial crime would have resulted in custody.

It is important to understand the situational nature of many offences. Psychologists Hartshorne and May gave schoolchildren a variety of opportunities to participate in dishonest acts. Their behaviour tended to be particularly sensitive to the settings in which opportunities to deceive were present (whether in the home, school, Sunday school, etc.). The results led Hartshorne and May to conclude that honesty and dishonesty do not derive from an overriding predisposition to behave in one way or the other; instead, behaviour was felt to be specific to the situation at hand.[80]

Remember that the marginalized situation is rooted in traumatic lives and chaotic living situations. The children and youth involved are no different than we are. Their struggle to survive and thrive is happily not ours, but you would recognize the stories as being examples of the human drama. We all commit crimes against each other. The difference between us, in terms of committing crimes, is a difference of degree.

This can be seen with a few political examples. In the recent U.S. presidential election, both candidates for presidency admitted to "youthful indiscretions" that, if they had been charged and convicted, would have resulted in a criminal record. One candidate for prime minister in Canada admitted the same (smoking marijuana). Looking back to the Watergate hearings, the following question was posed by Senator Herman Talmadge, and answered by John Mitchell, formerly the Attorney General and chief law enforcement officer of the United States:

Q. Am I to understand from your response that you placed the expediency of the next election above your responsibilities as an intimate to advise the President of the peril that surrounded him? Here was the deputy campaign director involved in crime, perjury, accessory after the fact, and you deliberately refused to tell him that. Would you state that the expediency of the election was more important than that?

A. Senator, I believe you have put it exactly correct....

In Canada, Correctional Service Canada tells us that 2.5 million Canadians have criminal records.[81] The majority of crimes are never reported;

of those reported a smaller portion actually result in charges, and not all those charged are convicted (and therefore have a record with Correctional Service Canada). Therefore, 2.5 million Canadians does not represent all those who have committed a criminal offence.

So how many people do commit crimes? Professor Thomas Gaber stated the "studies, as a whole, show that most, if not all, people break the law at one time or another."[81] He went on to say that in "a more recent study of a representative sample of 1,684 male adolescents in Montreal, University of Montreal researchers Marc LeBlanc and Marcel Frechette found that 97 percent reported having committed at least one criminal infraction during their adolescent years...."[82] These findings are consistent with other studies, described by Thomas Gaber:

> The evidence drawn from this body of research is astonishing. The studies, as a whole, show that most, if not all, people break the law at one time or another. One of the earliest studies was a survey conducted in New York City in which 1,700 adults were asked to provide information about their involvement in relation to 49 offences listed in a questionnaire. The subjects were selected so as to include only those people who did *not* have a criminal record. Ninety-nine per cent of the respondents admitted to committing at least one of the 49 offences listed. The average number of different *types* of offences committed in adulthood was 18 for the male and 11 for the female subjects.... [C]lose to 90 per cent of the men and over 80 per cent of the women in New York City, sampled in the 1947 study, committed larceny or theft at some point (at least once). Half the men committed at least one assault. Over half the men and just under half the women admitted to tax evasion. Perhaps even more astonishing was the fact that more than a quarter of the men admitted to auto theft and almost a fifth admitted to having committed at least one burglary at some point.[83]

The research by Wallerstein and Wyle in New York City provided some of the earliest clues to the effect that ordinary citizens have more than just a few skeletons in their closets.

> ...Martin Gold, in interviews with a representative sample of teenagers in Flint, Michigan, found that 83 per cent confessed to having committed at least a few delinquent acts. His conclusion was emphatic: "Studies of delinquent behavior itself, such as the Flint study, will, I believe, promote considerable change in our whole concept of juvenile delinquency. Most important, the idea of "the delinquent" should disappear altogether. For if social science demonstrates empirically that almost everyone sometimes breaks the law, but there are wide differences in

how frequently and seriously individuals do so, delinquency should then be recognized as a matter of degree."[84]

An Aboriginal youth who agreed with this proposition described his reality:

> That's true, there's all these laws and each one can get you into trouble. Obviously, the way I grew up I always knew eventually I was going to jail. I didn't know it was going to get this bad, but I'm getting myself straightened out now.[85]

If everyone committing an offence were charged, there would be few Canadians without some form of criminal record. Considering the justice system from this perspective, the main difference is that some have been caught and some haven't. If we really believe that the youth criminal justice system improves the youth with whom it works, then logically those who were caught must be somehow improved and at an advantage compared to the broader population. "Youthful indiscretions" are part of growing up for most if not all North Americans. Yet, would we ever set a requirement for a responsible position that the successful candidate must have gone through our improvement system, and have spent some time in closed custody? Of course this is absurd, and of course we know that time in a youth jail would not improve us. We know it would likely be the opposite.[86]

Former Chief Justice Antonio Lamar, quoted in *Lawyers Weekly* on 29 November 2002, said "whether somebody smoked pot at twenty has nothing to do with that person being able to be a Supreme Court justice at 50 or 56."[87]

Youth are in custody not just because of harmful acts against persons, but often because their "plan" hasn't worked. Some professionals suggest a plan for youths (such as custody) that they would never suggest for themselves or their children, largely because they know it would make things worse (see, for example, the section on the youth justice systems of Massachusetts and Pennsylvania in chapter eight).

As Justice Vickers pointed out in *R. v. Wright*, it is the responsibility of prosecutors to exercise discretion in laying charges.[88] Nowhere is this more obvious than when breaches of a youth's "plan" are alleged. The *Young Offenders Act* was amended, and the *YCJA* now emphasizes that custody is not to be used instead of appropriate child protection, mental health, and other social measures. In many cases breaches are used exactly for these purposes, drawing troubled and needy youths further into the criminal justice system, as if by default. The discretion now given to the provincial director in the *YCJA* (section 102) may help reduce this practice. That discretion allows the director, upon seeing that a young person has breached or is about to breach an order, an option of permitting a "young person to continue to serve a portion of his or her youth sentence in the community, on the same or different conditions." Especially in the case of minor and technical breaches, this section places a heavy and vital onus on the provincial director to properly apply this discretion.

In this chapter we have considered the causes of crime and, largely as a result of these causes, which children are over-represented within the criminal justice system and its custodial facilities. No group is more obviously over-represented, particularly in the prairies and the territories or northern Canada, than Aboriginal youth. The next chapter considers the often tenuous relationship between the conventional Canadian criminal justice system and Aboriginal young people.

"Most Aboriginal kids grow up with crime. We're taught early, it's our only chance. I only knew how to do crime. Now I want a job."

R.T.

Chapter Four

Aboriginal Youth and the Justice System

Aboriginal History from a Different Perspective

It is possible that on some sad days every youth in custody in Saskatch-ewan or Manitoba is of Aboriginal descent. Certainly, on many visits to youth custody facilities in the areas of Saskatchewan in which we practise law, we have seen only the faces of Aboriginal young people within these institutions. Although not to the same degree as in the prairie provinces, the over-representation of Aboriginal youth within custodial facilities else-where in Canada is an unavoidable reality.

How can this have happened? Is our only hope that time, by itself, will eventually solve the problems that Aboriginal peoples have faced within our justice system? Will we turn our eyes away, comforted by the assur-ance that these Aboriginal youth are only in custody because they have committed a crime? Or will we wonder how this situation can exist within a society we believe to be caring and compassionate?

The over-representation of Aboriginal youth within the justice system must be discussed very gently, for there is much pain, much guilt, much blame, and many victims. The historical record reveals so much abuse towards Aboriginal people that one can easily understand how, in Canada, there are now powerful forces that encourage crime within Aboriginal communities. Equally, one can understand that the use of punishment and incarceration has been an obvious and understandable response to that crime. But the long-term effects of this strategy are now becoming obvious. The startling participation rates of Aboriginal youth in our criminal system should give us cause to reconsider the processes and practices we have employed. Every day, we see more and more troubled Aboriginal young people become entangled in the expanding web of our youth justice system.

The Aboriginal peoples of Canada are incredibly diverse, both between nations and between individuals. Historically, their contacts with European settlers were varied, as were the responses to this contact by each nation. Within each Aboriginal nation, there was also great diversity. The question of what happened to the Aboriginal peoples of Canada after being confronted by European colonization is described here in terms that Aboriginal youth, brought to court for their crimes, understand. We have few clients who comprehend this historical account in its entirety. As an example, one Aboriginal youth commented:

> Before we Aboriginal people started coming out here, when we were out hunting and living in our teepees, we had no problems. It all sounds so peaceful. Sure we had some wars, but no crime, no jail, no money. No one said you had to be in your teepee by 10 p.m. What's sad is that the more money becomes important, the more problems we'll have. We're putting ourselves in this position, but then again they [people working in the justice system] are getting paid for it, for putting people in jail.[1]

Obviously, our clients understand only bits and pieces. However, in understanding the experiences of Aboriginal youth within our justice system, we suggest the following version to be an accurate, and ultimately useful, account.[2]

It would be helpful if we could think of this our own history, whatever our background. It is a story filled with vicious and mean-spirited decisions and actions. Surely, none of us would have chosen those responses, and all of us would dearly love to correct them, if we could. In considering this to be our own story, the richness of various First Nations cultural traditions may be missing, and most of the detail too, but the underlying question remains: What does this history tell us about how our society should function today, and how can the lives of Aboriginal youth within our society can be made better?

Earlier, in the introduction to this book, we imagined ourselves in some new society—possibly post-apocalyptic—rethinking of our collective goals. We foresaw a community where all citizens were encouraged to work together for the common good. As few resources as possible would be used on a formal criminal justice system, and instead we would rely on the informal process of criticizing harmful actions and stressing the value of working together.

Now let us imagine that our community has been very successful. Over the centuries our community and our descendants have produced citizens who are generally characterized by self-discipline, courage, patience, tenacity, humility, and temperance. On balance, our communities have been democratic and nurturing.

But now let us imagine strangers come to our community, apparently from a faraway place. These newcomers are very odd. They stumble around, often into danger of which they seem unaware. They are not always honest or brave or patient or tolerant or wise or humble. However, we pride ourselves on these qualities, and so we help them out. They want to be partners with us. They offer us things we've never seen before, some which are beautiful, some which are useful, some which are destructive to us and to them. Now we have lived a rich life, walking in beauty, so to speak, and these new things are interesting. But they don't answer the truly important questions, like how should we act so as to make our community proud of us. Still, they could add something to our life, and so we agree to partner with these newcomers.[3]

These strangers act in peculiar ways. For example, they capture animals which they keep in pens by the river or the lake, without much thought about how this affects these animals. Often they drink from the same water these animals pollute. Strange indeed. Their new techniques for gathering resources like furs are helpful and take less time, but soon, because we've traded that same fur, we have to go farther to collect it. Some of the strangers try to entice our young, especially with dangerous substances.[4] Yet we know how youth are, the voice of good and the voice of bad speaks loudly in their ears, leading them to acts of incredible nobility and self-sacrifice some days, and acts of great wilfulness and disrespect on others. The "anger drugs" given by these strangers too often lead our young people to mindless violence.

Somehow, these strangers never really seem to live up to the notion of partnership. Their men marry our daughters, but they rarely let their daughters marry our men.[5] The best among them remind us that they have never broken their promises (why should that be remarkable? we are partners after all) while the worst among them wish to treat us like we're not even human. Truth to tell, we're not sure about all of them. There's this thing about beating children—many of them do it to their own and are proud of it, and many of them want us to do it to our children.[6] And then there's the way these newcomers use and abuse our women.[7]

After a while disaster strikes. The food disappears. Our people are starving and dying of disease, and our young people are becoming more and more attracted to those anger-producing drugs. Rumours are starting that not so far away, relatives of these strangers are killing men, women, and children in communities like ours. The strangers living with us tell us that those are the bad relatives that did those things. But then we hear new rumours, that these strangers that we let live with us are now selling our territory to other strangers. Of course we are angry and concerned, but like honourable people we patiently request an explanation.[8]

We are told that the strangers love us, they say like children (now isn't that ironic!), and that they will come and make deals with us. They want to end the starvation of our community, the disease, they want to set up territories where we won't be bothered by their bad relatives (who are so numerous that it seems all the grains of sand on a beach is like the number of their good and bad relatives). We of course know that since the food is now gone we need new ways to feed ourselves, so we want that as part of our deal. We also know that these strangers have a system of teaching the techniques they use to do all those things they do. So naturally we want our young to have these techniques.

Finally we've seen enough. Where we've been honest they haven't always been, where we've been patient they haven't always been, and so on. We want to protect our traditions which are based on developing character rather than techniques to develop power. We intend on making technique subservient to character, and for that we need safe havens.

Our community signs agreements which give these strangers rights to most of our territory. Our wisdom tells us we must keep our side of the bargain. But new strangers come to replace the strangers we knew. While some are good people, some are not. But no one seems to care when some of these strangers do mean and hateful things. Starvation in our community doesn't always end, yet the strangers are not starving. The epidemics continue and sometimes it seems the strangers don't care. The simple ceremonies that we used to teach our youth how to be patient and courageous and self disciplined are made crimes in the strangers' world. Some ceremonies, no more dangerous than singing "Happy Birthday," have become crimes and are punished by jail terms or beatings or both.[9]

When our community becomes successful in new agricultural techniques, some strangers complain. They demand that our success be destroyed. They won't let us leave our now small territories unless we get a pass from our supervisor, a stranger who has enormous power over us. While the strangers have a court system to settle disputes, they make it illegal for us to hire a lawyer to argue our side of a dispute. This prohibition is maintained for almost three-quarters of a century after we signed our treaty with them.

Then the strangers take our children, for what they call "education." Some of us try to hide our children, travelling long distances to do so. But these strangers send police to find us, and take our children to their residential schools. But these schools are nothing like we imagined. The school authorities will not allow our children to see us for months at a time. Our children are taught by many different teachers. Some are fanatics, who tell our children that we, their parents, are the embodiment of stupidity and evil. Sometimes our babies are slapped for speaking their native tongue. We want our children to be cared for and comforted, but later we hear that many have been harshly disciplined and abused at these residential schools.[10]

In June, year after year, we go to that school to take our children back for the summer. Although our faces are lined with tears of joy, we see in their faces a wall, and sometimes behind that wall we glimpse anger and even hate for us, rejecting all we have held dear. By fifteen or sixteen our children finally return, all year, to our homes. They are filled with pain and confusion and refuse to talk about their problems to us; only wanting to escape through the "angry drugs" brought by the strangers.

Imagine that this was your history. Imagine that your children, in turn, gave birth to their own children, although they were not strong enough to care for them. Imagine that your grandchildren and your great-grandchildren experienced lives filled with pain and suffering, often characterized by venting their anger and frustration through drugs and alcohol. And imagine a society where your children and grandchildren were more likely to go to jail than finish high school.

How would you feel if this was your history?

On 23 April 1999 many eyes awaited a decision from the Supreme Court of Canada in the case of *R. v. Gladue*.[11] The Court had heard from many lawyers, had extensively considered many expert reports, and was now ready to announce what the evidence had shown, what their examination had uncovered, what seemed to be beyond reasonable debate about Aboriginal peoples and the criminal justice system. The seven judges were unanimous.

> ...[Y]ears of dislocation and economic development have translated for many aboriginal peoples, into low incomes, high unemployment, lack of opportunities and options, lack or irrelevance of education, substance abuse, loneliness and community fragmentation. These and other

factors contribute to a higher incidence of crime and incarceration ... Professor Tim Quigley ... ably describes the process ... "the unemployed, transients, the poorly educated are all better candidates for imprisonment. When the social, political and economic aspects of [Canadian] society place Aboriginal people disproportionately with the ranks of the latter [then] society literally sentences more of them to jail."[12]

If we return to the history of our imaginary community for a moment, let us remember one major point of distinction between us and the strangers: our community was based on strength of personal character and working within our community, while the strangers based much of their society on the pursuit and exercise of power. In North America, our criminal justice systems relies heavily on the threat and imposition of power. As seen in previous chapters, this strategy simply hasn't worked. Somehow, we have grown to expect that the criminal justice system can frighten people into honesty, self-restraint, tolerance, patience, humility, temperance.

On almost any court date we hear horrific tales of punishment, true stories gathered from the children and youth who happen to be our clients that day. We hear stories of adults being cruel sometimes to the point of torture: children's hands placed on red-hot elements, children given lawn chairs for beds in the basements of foster homes, children beaten, abandoned—the list could go on.

Our clients ask whether putting them in jail will make their lives better. They also wonder why the power of the justice system is being used to respond to their behaviour, caused in large part by past abuses—and misuse of power—against them. Can the system's power overcome these injustices, or can only helping these children to be successful in an adult world do that?

Some people, however, claim that pain has the power to alter us. That's the theory behind punishing criminals, and that's the morality behind the criminal law process. Following a "just deserts" philosophy, those who harm innocent people must be punished, as a deterrent to others. The problem with systematically inflicting pain on others is the conclusions drawn by offenders and victims to this approach, which is arguably another form of violence. Aboriginal children, for example, often see criminal punishments through the wide lens of cultural oppression rather than an attempt to regulate behaviour.

And so we come back to the beginning, to the various first contacts, when European settlers met Aboriginal people, offering them partnerships that would respect their culture. The over-representation of Aboriginal youth in youth custody facilities, and an examination of their lives, their communities, and their prospects tells us that the mainstream culture has not given them either a true partnership or respect. As other pages in this book show, true partnership with these youth, coupled with respect, is the most effective way to reduce youth crime, and to reduce or eliminate the overincarceration of Aboriginal youth.

Aboriginal Youth and the Criminal Justice System

The over-representation of Aboriginal youth

In Saskatchewan the vast majority of young people appearing before our courts are Aboriginal. As pointed out earlier, Aboriginal youth comprise 75 percent of young offenders being held in Saskatchewan's custodial facilities. At the same time, Aboriginal people account for only approximately 15 percent of Saskatchewan's population. The over-representation of Aboriginal youth with the justice systems of Manitoba and Alberta is similar if not more pronounced.[13] This over-representation, which extends outside of the prairie provinces to other areas of Canada, is clearly unacceptable, especially considering the projected growth of the Aboriginal population over the next decade. If the current high number of Aboriginal youth already in custody were to increase at the same rate as the overall Aboriginal population, the resulting effect would be crippling, both within the youth justice system and Canadian society as a whole.

There is no easy explanation for the over-representation of Aboriginal youth within our criminal justice system. Indeed, the causes of Aboriginal overincarceration are wide-ranging and complex. Professor Tim Quigley of the University of Saskatchewan suggested that these include: the poor socio-economic circumstances of many Aboriginals, the high percentage of Aboriginal youth within the range of age most susceptible to criminal activity, the level of policing in Aboriginal communities, the "snowball" effect of a prior criminal record, a greater likelihood of an Aboriginal accused being denied bail, and the lack of sentencing alternatives available for sentencing within the criminal law of Canada.[14] Another contributor to this situation has been significantly higher rates of cognitive impairment suffered as a result of prenatal consumption of alcohol. Fetal Alcohol Syndrome and Fetal Alcohol Effect (as discussed earlier in chapter three) have increasingly become an explanation for why so many Aboriginal youth find themselves in youth court and in custody. To be sure, FAS and FAE affect a broad cross section of groups within our society, and Aboriginal people are by no means the only ones to experience the effects of this impairment. But there is little doubt that the rates of FAS/FAE within Aboriginal communities are significant, and higher than the general population. Taken together with the over-representation of Aboriginal youth and adults in our criminal justice system, this heightens the need to identify those offenders within our system suffering from this disability, and to search for new and progressive ways of helping rather than punishing them.

In broader societal terms, our failure to address the problems faced by Aboriginal children—such as marginalization in terms of neighbourhood, schooling, housing, and employment—and instead using the power structures of the criminal justice system as our preferred response, is especially dangerous. A young Aboriginal woman described the effects of growing up as a marginalized child:

> When you live in a negative environment and you see negative all the time, there's no one to help you. When I was young I felt like no one cared for me. There was no hope. There was no encouragement, no support, no love, caring, or any positive feelings shown to me when I was growing up. It affects your whole point of view. When you're supposed to change, and go through the processes of life, like school or university or looking for a job, it makes you feel like you don't fit, you feel like you can't go ahead in life.[15]

Clearly, Aboriginal children face multiple forces beyond their control. Some of these—such as being marginalized from mainstream society and being channeled into a local communities where crime rates are most likely to be high—increase their chances of being stopped by the police, and of being charged with an offence, and of going to custody. The children and youth we represent share the anger, frustration, and fear that result from this situation. An Aboriginal youth with extensive experience with police and courts was asked about the treatment of Aboriginal youth in the justice system:

> I think people and judges probably think us Aboriginal kids are thugs, little wannabe thugs. Me, I'm pretty big, so they probably think being locked up in room shouldn't kill me. It's hard growing up Aboriginal. Most Aboriginal kids grow up with crime. We're taught early, it's our only chance. I only knew how to do crime. Now I want a job. Crime doesn't pay.[16]

It is very important not to lose sight of the fact that all children and youth—regardless of their race—want to succeed in the adult, mainstream world. Despite some cultural differences, this desire is held strongly by Aboriginal youth.

Earlier, in chapter three, we discussed theoretical explanations of youth crime. The theme of competing and conflicting cultures, as covered in the discussion of social disorganization theory, has great relevance to the history of Aboriginal peoples in Canada, and in particular, to the imposition of residential schools on Aboriginal children. This experience led to First Nations youth being caught between two cultures, their Aboriginal culture and that of the dominant European-based society.[17] Judge Murray Sinclair (now Justice Sinclair of the Manitoba Court of Queen's Bench), in discussing domestic abuse in many Aboriginal communities, linked such offending activity partly to oppressive practices of governments and other external systems, including the imposition of residential schools on Aboriginal children. These factors contributed to the inability of Aboriginal communities to shape appropriate social conduct for their members. Residential schools, in particular, imposed an institutional model on Aboriginal children that taught external rather than internal control. He believed a socialized dependence upon external control systems led to misbehaviour when these controls were removed.[18]

In his article "Welcome to Harlem on the Prairies,"[19] journalist John Stackhouse painted a shocking picture of crime and social dysfunction in the predominantly Aboriginal area of Saskatoon:

> With Canada's highest crime rate last year, many [Saskatoon] residents blame an aboriginal population that they say can't cope with the transition from isolated reserves to a multicultural city, where universal laws and independent police and courts are supposed to prevail. Many natives, on the other hand, believe that they are victims of a white majority that refuses to address their chronic social problems, except with the blunt end of a police force.

The effects of social disorganisation and community breakdown are widespread among Aboriginal people in Canada. Anastasia Schkilnyk's book *A Poison Stronger than Love: The Destruction of an Ojibway Community* examined the forced relocation of people from Grassy Narrows, Ontario to a new reserve close to an urban centre. She found "that crime was a means of escape for youth from the poor conditions of reserve life. As a result of the relocation and the loss of their traditional lifestyle, the youth of Grassy Narrows experienced anomie, or confusion about which norms of conduct to adhere to."[20] Similarly, Geoffrey York, in *The Dispossessed: Life and Death in Native Canada*,[21] told a similar story of how social and economic despair can lead young people to crime, as an escape from their situation:

For a bored teenager, a remote northern reserve like Gods Lake Narrows in northeastern Manitoba is a prison. There is nothing to do. There
are no jobs and few recreation programs. Tantalizing images of middle-
class urban life, beamed into native homes by satellite television contrast with a day-to-day life of poverty and isolation.... Tony Trout, an
alcohol and drug counsellor at Gods Lake Narrows, estimates that 30
percent of the reserve's teenagers are prepared to commit criminal offences to escape their reserve.[22]

Recalling the wide diversity among Aboriginal people, it is important
to keep in mind that their experiences have not been, and are not now
uniform. For example, let us consider the situation faced by Aboriginal
people in a number of Canadian cities. Some of these—Regina, Saskatoon,
Winnipeg, and Thunder Bay—have relatively high numbers of Aboriginal people per capita in jail. Other cities—Halifax, Montreal, and Toronto—have fewer Aboriginal people per capita in custody. What differences can be found between the two groups of cities, and in the experiences
of Aboriginal people living there? Perhaps the levels of participation by
Aboriginal people in the life of those communities will be an indicator.
Perhaps there is a correlation between custody levels and the degree to
which Aboriginal people participate in the economy of each city. Perhaps
the level of education they achieve is significant. And perhaps a correlation exists between the number of single mothers and the degree of tran-
siency among the Aboriginal populations of each city and the number of
Aboriginal people in jail in that city.

The above is not a hypothetical discussion. Dr. Carol LaPrairie, a principal researcher for Justice Canada, showed that in Halifax, Montreal, and
Toronto—the cities with lower per capita rates of Aboriginal incarceration—only 40 percent of Aboriginal persons had less than high school
education. Although still clearly too high for a modern country, this contrasts with the situation in Regina, Saskatoon, Winnipeg, and Thunder
Bay—cities with relatively higher rates of Aboriginal incarceration—where
52.3 percent of Aboriginal persons had less than grade twelve. Similarly,
in the first group of cities about 40 percent remained at one address for
five years, while in the second group only 28.7 percent remained at one
address for five years.

That unsuccessful lives lead to higher crime rates seems obvious, but
what if the essential root cause of these negative experiences lies mainly in
not being included in the everyday decisions of a community? What if a
community is not organized in a cohesive way, so as to include Aboriginal
people in deciding how the lives of all citizens can be made better? In her

study, Dr. LaPrairie drew a parallel between neighbourhood cohesiveness and the levels of crime and disorder found there.

> Recent research findings from a long term study on human develop-ment in 196 Chicago neighbourhoods (Sampson and Raudenbush 2001) found that the absence of "collective efficacy" defined as cohesion among neighbourhood residents combined with shared expectations for in-formal control of public space, was a significant factor in explaining levels of crime and disorder. In neighbourhoods where collective effi-cacy was strong, rates of violence were low regardless of social socio-demographic composition. The conclusion reached by the researchers was that increasing collective efficacy rather than reducing disorder re-duced crime.... They also concluded that reducing disorder *may* re-duce crime, but this happened indirectly by stabilizing communities and promoting collective efficacy.[23]

Although it might appear that removing offenders to custody from the most disorganized or marginalized neighbourhoods should help solve the problem of crime, that is not what our clients have told us. When their close relatives went to jail, they claim more problems have resulted, with fewer apparent solutions. This theme was illustrated by Professors Todd Clear and Dina Rose of John Jay College of Criminal Justice in New York during a presentation to the National Institute of Justice Research in Progress seminar in 1999.

> As a system that removes individuals from their neighbourhoods, in-carceration may improve the quality of community life when only a few residents are removed. In neighbourhoods that have many more offenders, however, removing these residents may disrupt the social networks that are the foundation of informal social control. Because high-incarceration neighbourhoods are socially disorganized, their ca-pacity to absorb these disruptions is limited. Thus, high levels of incar-ceration in some communities may leave them in worse condition than before because of the resulting disruptions in social organization.[24]

The youth we speak to and represent are constantly affected by these realities. They live in neighbourhoods where few can imagine a successful entry into mainstream society, and where opportunities are few. The ques-tion our clients ask us is why doesn't someone do something about this? Who should correct this situation? Should it be those marginalized by race, poverty, or disability? Or should it be the very able, and the very powerful in society? Should it be the directors of youth justice programs in government, the lawyers, the prosecutors, the judges? Should it be the politicians? These young people want to know why the powerful do little to improve their lives, and the lives of their friends, family, and neighbourhood. They ask us how sending them to custody can ever improve this situation. Answers to this question do not come easily, yet reliance on court and custody is a common response used by powerful adults to solve the problems presented by offending youth.

Professor Todd Clear of Florida State University listed many unintended consequences of incarceration, which he said resulted from the removal of large numbers of people from their home communities, and also from large public investments in the corrections industry. In his opinion these factors explain why the extraordinary increase in the use of imprisonment for twenty-five years did not create an equivalent decrease in crime in the U.S. Professor Clear said unintended social consequences of high rates of incarceration included: the reality that criminal groups replaced incarcerated members (and generally with younger ones), a depreciation of the public value of punishment because of its overuse, and familial deficits which arose through lost members in prison. He said unintended fiscal consequences of incarceration included: movement of economic value from urban to nonurban areas (where custodial facilities are usually located), creation of a corrections industrial complex,[25] reductions in funding of schools and other public places as a result of corrections spending, increased social inequality, growth in "future generation" debt, and cultural tolerance of official cruelty.[26]

We understand commonly held Aboriginal views of justice to reject punishment as the primary response to conflict. These views favour a focus on restoring the torn relationships, and on addressing the complex family and community dynamics brought about by crime. Similar approaches are advocated by supporters of restorative justice, and have been suggested by many of the clients we have represented. Observing the workings of our current justice system through a relationship-centred lens, we see how, when a caregiver is sent to jail, his or her children are more likely to be involved in criminal activity, or otherwise put in danger of personal crisis. We expect a similar effect when some other person close to that youth is incarcerated. Similar relationship dynamics and risk factors may be triggered when a parent is forced to leave home, for example as a requirement of a work for welfare program. As suggested by many Aboriginal leaders and Elders, retaining a community-wide focus on addressing and sustaining compassionate relationships should be at the cornerstone of any justice system, as it will help to ensure the long-term protection and benefit of young people in that society. Whether such a view of justice is described as Aboriginal, restorative, community-centred, or some other title, we believe it to be a more sophisticated, and potentially more equitable and productive, view upon which to base our youth justice system.

An important policy issue underlying youth justice strategy in each jurisdiction is the amount of money a province is prepared to spend on placing youths into custody. In Dr. Carol LaPrairie's study referred to earlier in this chapter, two of the cities with high rates of Aboriginal incarceration (Regina and Saskatoon) are in Saskatchewan, while one city with a relatively lower rate of Aboriginal imprisonment (Montreal) is in Quebec. Professors Anthony Doob, University of Toronto, and Jane Sprott, University of Guelph, compared the use of youth court and youth custody rates for the overall population and found the rate for Quebec was 4.6 youth in custody for every 1,000 youth, while the rate for Saskatchewan was almost *four* times as many youth, at 17.1 per 1,000 youths. In explaining this discrepancy, Professors Doob and Sprott pointed out that there are

> ... dramatic interprovincial differences that go beyond Quebec and that there are "local cultures" on how best to deal with young offenders that may bear no relationship to the behaviour of young people. In looking at interprovincial variations one must keep in mind one important fact about youth crime. Most young people commit crimes (Doob, Marino and Varma 1995). In fact, most young people in Canada do numerous things in any given year that could land them in youth court if they were caught and someone was thoughtless enough to bring them to court ... hence differences among provinces are best thought of as reflecting explicit or implicit decisions of those running the youth justice system....[27]

This underlies an important point. There is no "set" number of youths or adults that need to be imprisoned. In an interview, Jim Richards of Melfort, Saskatchewan, now retired but previously employed at a Regina youth custody facility, said that in 1950, 25 youths were in custody in Saskatchewan.[28] On 12 May 1999, 326 youths were in custody in Saskatchewan.[29] Saskatchewan's population over this half-century has increased only marginally.[30] It is true that the minimum and maximum ages under the *JDA* in 1950 was eight to sixteen years (as opposed to twelve to eighteen years under the *YOA* and subsequently the *YCJA*), and it might also be argued that in 1950 many Aboriginal youth were in the custody of the residential school system, but this is still a phenomenal increase. It has caused significant budgetary implications for the youth justice system. Indeed, budgetary decisions affecting the availability and application of resources can have a great effect on the number of youth in custody. In considering the over-representation of Aboriginal youth in the justice system, we must constantly question and reassess these policies and budgetary decisions about resources.

Once in youth court in Saskatoon three young Aboriginal males were brought in from the remand area. In court it became obvious that these youth should be released—their offences did not require them to remain in custody. It seemed, though, that there were no parents available to take them home. The judge was involved in conversation with the prosecutor and court workers to try to contact the parents. Meanwhile, the three youth were loudly and jokingly pushing each other, apparently unconcerned about their release or that they were in a solemn courtroom. Watching them, one might think that they were being disrespectful, laughing at the court. They had become loud enough to disturb the judge's conversation. He held up his hand to indicate to the prosecutor that he wanted to take a break.

The judge then leaned towards the three boys. In a soft gentle voice the judge said to the boys that he knew that they didn't belong in custody, that he knew that this wasn't much fun for them, and that everyone wanted them to be able to go home as soon as possible. He told them that his conversations with the court officials were to arrange finding their adult caregivers so that they could go home. He asked them to be patient with him. He then turned back to the court officials. When he turned away two of the three boys started to cry. That judge is now the Chief Justice of Saskatchewan Provincial Court, and perhaps those boys moved away from Saskatoon, but although we're in youth court almost every day we haven't seen any of them come back.

Possibilities for change—*R. v. Gladue* and a search for new alternatives

Professor Michael Jackson, in an article entitled "Locking Up Natives in Canada,"[31] detailed the over-representation of Aboriginal people within Canadian prisons and observed that, "[m]ore than any other group in Canada they are subject to the damaging impacts of the criminal justice system's heaviest sanctions."[32] In *R. v. Gladue*, the Supreme Court of Canada restated this concern. In describing the difficult position of Canada's Aboriginal people—which they said resulted, in part, from the negative effects of past decisions by government—and after citing a number of studies and commission reports over the years, the court said "aboriginal offenders are, as a result of these unique systematic and background factors, more adversely affected by incarceration and less likely to be 'rehabilitated' thereby...."[33]

This concern applies perhaps with greater force considering the number of Aboriginal youth in custody. As one way of addressing this concern, section 38(2)(d) of the *Youth Criminal Justice Act* now requires a court, before imposing a youth sentence, to consider the principles set out in section 3 of the Act, together with a list of principles including a requirement that "all available sanctions other than custody that are reasonable in the circumstances should be considered for all young persons, with particular attention to the circumstances of aboriginal young persons." This provision is accompanied by section 3(1)(c)(iv) of the *YCJA* which provides that measures taken against young persons under the *YCJA* should "respect gender, ethnic, cultural and linguistic differences and respond to the needs of aboriginal persons and of young people with special requirements."

The reference to "particular attention to the circumstances of Aboriginal young people" in section 38(2)(d) is a mirror image of the adult provision which has existed in the *Criminal Code* since 1996. In 1999, the Supreme Court of Canada, in *R. v. Gladue*, interpreted this *Criminal Code* section, which directs sentencing judges to consider "all available sanctions other than imprisonment that are reasonable in the circumstances" for all offenders "with particular attention to the circumstances of Aboriginal offenders." Although the Supreme Court was dealing with an adult offender's sentence appeal, the principles and interpretation from this decision clearly cried out for application to Aboriginal youth, especially considering the over-representation of Aboriginal youth within custodial facilities.

Many commentators have questioned what, if any, public good is being achieved through the current level of youth custody admissions. In *R. v. Gladue*, the Supreme Court of Canada, while considering the over-representation of Aboriginals within Canadian jails, cited with approval the following analysis by Professor Jackson who described the negative effect of prison on youthful Aboriginal offenders in Saskatchewan:

> Put another way, this means that in Saskatchewan, prison has become for young native men, the promise of a just society which high school and college represent for the rest of us. Placed in an historical context, the prison has become for many young native people the contemporary equivalent of what the Indian residential school represented for their parents.[34]

Many links have been drawn between the experience of residential schools by previous Aboriginal generations, and the current reality of Aboriginal youth. Eugene Gamble, the on reserve justice co-ordinator for the Saskatoon Tribal Council, drew this connection in reflecting on the causes of youth crime:

> First of all I think there are a lot of causes, a lot of them being historical, and going back to the colonization of reservations, and residential schools.... Many things have been taken away from us, particularly for aboriginal youth, including a structure and a culture, traditions of parenting, community based parenting, extended families, grandparents, guidance and understanding of the issues as First Nations people. [These were taken away] particularly through the residential schools and attempts by governments to assimilate First Nations People, taken away by the fact that the Church was the deciding factor in how people were going to be raised and how youth were going to be raised in the residential schools. How families were no longer important, how language was no longer important, basic parenting skills weren't taught any longer. It was every person for themselves, as opposed to a First Nation culture and traditions, a community based process. So, in the long run, the damage that was done to First Nations youth was a lack of guidance and understanding, a lack of a true community process where the survival of the community was ultimate, as opposed to being individualistic.[35]

Judge Lilles of the Yukon Territorial Court, in *J.K.E.*,[36] found the principles from *Gladue* to "apply with greater force in the sentencing of young offenders." Similarly, Judge Turpel-Lafond of the Provincial Court of Saskatchewan, in *R. v. M.L.*,[37] stated that the objectives of restorative justice articulated in *Gladue* applied equally to youth dispositions and that youth courts should "consider alternatives to custodial dispositions which would be meaningful to" Aboriginal youth. The inclusion of language in the *YCJA* nearly identical to that contained in section 218.2(e) of the *Criminal Code* leaves little doubt that the Supreme Court's reasoning in *Gladue* will apply to the sentencing of Aboriginal youth.

In considering the application of the *Gladue* decision, the discrepancy between the haves and have-nots can sometimes been seen in court. Recently a young adult Aboriginal offender with a significant youth court record appeared in custody in a rural Saskatchewan court. He was charged with possession of stolen property and had missed a court appearance. He had been arrested by the Saskatoon City Police and had been returned to this town which was near his home reserve. He had come from what could only be described as a horrific upbringing characterized by alcohol abuse and violence. He had moved from home to home during his childhood and had most recently been living on the street in Saskatoon. By contrast, also appearing in court that day was a professional man who had been charged with a firearms offence. His lawyer provided a glowing recitation of his career accomplishments and the devastating impact that being charged with this offence had on him, including his client's future plans for retirement. As these able representations about this man were put forward, the Aboriginal offender sat desolately in the front row waiting his turn. The only track record that could be cited for him was one of poverty, neglect, and abuse.

If the Supreme Court's decision in *Gladue* has any effect, it will be to emphasize the importance of considering how social and economic factors beyond the influence of individual offenders and linked to the historic treatment of Aboriginal people in Canada have contributed to the presence of this offender in court. The past, however, need not be the only consideration flowing from this decision. Hopefully, this decision will encourage lawyers, judges, police officers, youth workers, and other involved community members to search for alternatives to incarceration for the most marginalized of society's members. The general statement of principle in section 3 of the *YCJA* provides, in part, that the criminal justice system for young persons should emphasize rehabilitation and reintegration of youth into society. In doing this, it will become increasingly important that marginalized youth (including Aboriginal youth) both be allowed to participate in the process of sentencing at youth court and be allowed and encouraged to take part in mainstream activities within the community, during the course of the sentence.

Any discussion of the role of custody on delinquent and marginalized youths must not neglect one obvious and perhaps rhetorical question: How can we expect to see significant changes in behaviour when young offenders are returned from custody to the same environment they left before arrest, without any attempt at addressing the underlying problems present in that environment? A young Aboriginal woman described the difficult home circumstances of many Aboriginal youth:

> You have a family that can't provide for you, plus there's no growth involved either. If your family is unhealthy, you're just stuck there. Like for boys they do B&Es, and girls they get into sexual exploitation or prostitution because they lack opportunities to grow and expand. Instead of just the positive effect, they go to the negative effect and it just becomes a part of their lives. For myself, I started stealing when I was young. I started when I was eleven, and eventually went to prostitution. It's just that there has to be more opportunities for the development of

children and youth, to expand more and give them a chance to be a child or a youth, and for their parents and community to accept them for who they are. There's not enough out there, especially for Aboriginal youth or children.[38]

In searching for new alternatives to current practice we must guard against a narrow view when considering the causes of crime, the available community resources, and the alternatives available for troubled youth. And in doing so, we must also keep our eyes open to issues such as the neurological effects of prenatal consumption of alcohol in considering appropriate strategies for improving, rather than exacerbating, the situation of many Aboriginal young people who are brought before our courts.

Aboriginal notions of justice: questioning relationships of force

In attempting to reverse the over-representation of Aboriginal youth within our courts and custodial facilities, it is important to consider how the situation faced by Aboriginal youth within our criminal system meshes with Aboriginal notions of justice. This is not an attempt, on our part, to speak for Aboriginal people. We cannot do so. But we are obligated to speak for our clients. It is true most of these youth can be identified as Aboriginal. However, they do not speak to us as primarily as Aboriginal people. Rather, they speak as marginalized young people who suffer from the despair of being relegated to the shadowy margins of our society. These youths want a better and more peaceful life, free of crime both as offenders and as victims. How this can be achieved, we believe, hinges largely on the philosophy underlying our justice system.

Philosophical differences are often cited between British-based views and practices which underlie the conventional Canadian justice system, and those of Aboriginal peoples. Professor James (Sa'ke'j) Youngblood Henderson, Director of the Native Law Centre at the University of Saskatchewan, spoke to these differences in a 1999 address to a national convention of Canadian judges. Professor Youngblood Henderson referred to Britain's inability to successfully transfer its criminal justice system to the Indigenous people in its colonies.

> Far from being a Canadian anomaly, these conclusions are global. The failure of imposed foreign criminal jurisdiction system over Indigenous nations has haunted each British colony's legal system. In recent decades, every commonwealth country that has studied the problem has reached similar conclusion: the British legal system is not succeeding with Aboriginal peoples. The failure is function of relationships of force rather than justice.

Professor Youngblood Henderson's reference to the negative effects of relationships of force makes sense in terms of the ineffectiveness of criminal punishment. While our clients generally dislike custody, their return rate is high. In our experience, the harsher these youths are treated by justice officials, the farther they get from the mainstream. In talking to their families, the longer they are in custody, the worse they are when finally they return home. To state the obvious, our clients and their families agree that the use of punitive force to change these youths has been unsuccessful. Victims, when they learn that the person charged has previously been before the youth court, even sentenced to custody, wonder if the custody was too short, or they wonder whether custody works at all. In total, this "relationship of force" is not reducing recidivism, or making for safer communities.

Professor Youngblood Henderson was careful to say that the failure was not a failure of justice. Indeed, there is "no real cultural conflict as to the definition of [many] criminal behaviours" as "[t]heft, assault causing injury, sexual abuse [and] domestic violence" all "violate contemporary and traditional aboriginal norms just as surely as they violate non-aboriginal norms."[39] The philosophical beliefs and senses of justice among Aboriginal people are thought to have remained intact. What is seen to have failed is the way criminal law has been imposed on Indigenous people.

We can relate Professor Henderson's words to many of the Aboriginal clients we represent. On the one hand these youths genuinely do not believe in harming others. Yet on the other, they are often thrust into a situations (usually not of their making) where the force of circumstance causes their actions. A young Aboriginal woman who had frequently appeared in youth court in her early teens referred to the effect of circumstances when asked if it might be beneficial for judges to meet with young people outside of court, and learn about their lives:

> I think it would be good for the judges, to actually understand, if they saw the youth where they are living, and understand the circumstances they are facing and what environment they are living in. If they saw them in the jail system, if they actually saw them as kids, as children, as young people, they're not there because of some violent crime. They're there because of circumstances that made them do it. Just actually talk to them, and see them as a person, and not a number.[40]

A number of youth held in custody in Saskatoon in September, 2002 were asked: "Do you think it's okay to hurt others?" Sixteen out of eighteen replied no, it was not all right, including those charged with violent offences. Most thought that a negative answer was so patently obvious they doubted the question's seriousness. The remaining two answered that it was okay but did so in a manner that implied that their answers should not be trusted. In researching this book, in-depth interviews with other youth revealed a unanimous agreement that harming others was wrong, including those convicted of violent offences.

Professor Patricia Monture-Angus of the University of Saskatchewan is a respected scholar who has spoken and written widely about Aboriginal concepts of justice. She has explained how, historically, Aboriginal societies had no need of a specialized group of criminal practitioners, or specialized techniques, or even a specialized body of knowledge. This, she said, could be explained by a focus on healthy relationships, well-educated children, and high standards of character. She explained that in "the Mohawk language when we say law ... it really means 'the way to live together most nicely.'"[41] Law, she said,

> is about retaining, teaching and maintaining good relationships.... What we can reclaim is the values that created a system where the abuses did not occur. We can recover our own system of law, law that has as its centre the family and kinship relations. We must be generous with ourselves and kind as well, as we discover how to live again as healthy and disciplined individuals. We must know that the dominant system of government will also be kind and generous to us as we heal from five hundred years of oppression. We must be patient with each other as we learn to live in a decolonized way again... this means looking further than the mere creation of so-called Aboriginal or tribal courts.... Alternatives are merely that small add-ons to the existing system which stands ready with the full force of its adversarial and punishment-oriented values if the "nice" solution does not work....[42]

Professor Monture-Angus told the audience that "our law is family law" and urged those present to go "home, pick up your responsibilities and do it now." In particular, she said, "when you know of abuses from political corruption to the abuse of women and children occurring within your community or within your own family, do not turn the other way."[43]

To our clients, these notions of justice make much sense. However, implicit in much of present-day discourse regarding youth justice is a belief that the prevailing Canadian legal system, through its history to the present, has never encompassed such concepts. But western-based legal systems have encompassed these concepts for thousands of years, and western-based science supports these notions of justice, in contrast to many of the punitive-based strategies now being employed in our criminal system.

In drawing linkages and commonality between Aboriginal conceptions of justice and the variety of nonpunitive views existing in the broader society, it is worth remembering that, through human history, criminal law has often served the function of protecting powerful elites. For example, criminal law in Imperial Rome had much to do with stabilizing the Roman Empire. Nero, branding the early Christians as criminals, was acting to consolidate his power. The Romans quickly learned to employ criminal sanction as a way of protecting their empire from danger. As a result, criminal law and the application of force became inextricably linked. But just as Canadian Aboriginal voices have come to question this potentially harmful connection, so too have others across national lines, and across history.

Two examples of how such a "force-based" philosophy of control was questioned and opposed come from the Bible. The Assyrians, who ruled the first known war-based empire, considered any hint of unrest against their rule as criminal. In about 700 B.C., when the Assyrians were about to cause great destruction on the people of Jerusalem, the prophet Isaiah wrote these verses condemning as criminal the situation he saw in Jerusalem:

> Shame on you! You make unjust laws and publish burdensome decrees, depriving the poor of justice, robbing the weakest of My people of their rights, despoiling the widow and plundering the orphan, what will you do when called to account, when ruin from afar confronts you? To whom will you flee for help, and where will you leave your children, so they will not cower before the gaoler, or fall by the executioner's hand?[44]

Elsewhere in the Bible, Jesus echoed a same sentiment about how the poor and desolate should be treated. In Matthew 25:31–46 he described how God will see the actions of men and women, again as if in a court:

> "Lord, when was it we saw you hungry or thirsty or a stranger or naked or ill or in prison and did nothing for you?" and he will answer, "I will tell you this, anything you did not do for any one of these, however humble, you did not do for me." And they will go away to eternal punishment but the righteous will enter eternal life.[45]

From these biblical references, we see a clear questioning of what Professor Youngblood Henderson referred to as the relationships of force. History has shown us many examples of how a dominant group used force to stifle any dissent, and used its criminal justice system as a means of suppressing those on the margins. But whether we look to the historical precedents that underpin our criminal justice system, or to alternative justice philosophies and practices described in this book, it is possible to find conceptions of justice that are not punitive and force-based. These conceptions of justice encompass the Aboriginal views earlier described in this section, but also the views of many within the broader community. As Professor Monture-Angus put it so aptly, these all relate to how we can learn "to live together most nicely."

Actually the concept that justice means something other than learning to live together well and instead that crime equals revolt against the state is a relatively recent invention in the western world. Throughout much of recorded history, our response to theft, assault, and murder was similar to what we now describe as Aboriginal law. For example, the importance of restitution to the victim has a crucial history. The Code of Ur-Nammu, a Sumerian King in 2500 B.C., provided for restitution, even in violent offences. The Code of Hammurabi, about 1700 B.C., described restitution for property crimes. The Roman Law of the Twelve Tables, 449 B.C., required convicted thieves to pay double the value of stolen goods. Lex Salica of the Germanic King Clovis in A.D. 496 recognized restitution for crimes that included homicide, assaults, and thefts. The Laws of Ethelbert in A.D. 600 England had detailed restitution schedules.[46]

What is noteworthy in this historical account is the obvious interest in rebuilding healthy relations between victim and offender. One commentator described justice in pre-1066 England this way:

> The job is to clean the case up, to suppress or penalize the illegal behaviour and to bring the relations of the disputants back into balance, so that life may resume its normal course. This type of law-work has frequently been compared to work of the medical practitioner. It's family doctor stuff, essential to keeping the *social body* on its feet." [emphasis added][47]

In 1066, William the Conqueror became king of England and took title to all land. For a lasting example of the effect of this action, look at the title to your home or land. It doesn't say you "own" it; it says you have "an estate in fee simple," which means the Crown retains a claim to your property. King Henry I, son of William, in 1116 issued Leges Henrici, which expanded the king's justice jurisdiction to encompass what was called "the king's peace." Suddenly, response to criminality wasn't to help the victim, it was to allow the king to recover "fines." Other social implications became irrelevant. "The Norman word for such a breach of faith [with the king] was 'felony'... [and] the felon's land was escheated to his lord, however, and only his chattels [movable property] to the crown."[48] Author and lawyer Daniel Van Ness described the effect of these changes.

As a result the victim had no remedy. The criminal proceeding generated fines for the king. In felony cases, conviction meant all the offender's property reverted to his lord and to the king. The victim would have no way to recover through civil action against the impoverished offender.[49]

Mr. Van Ness noted this changed system benefited the king through an enriched treasury and, more importantly, through an increase in power.[50] The notion that responding to crime means something other than learning to live together in a way that allows for life, liberty, and the pursuit of happiness was identified in the French Revolution when ordinary people stormed and tore down the Bastille, the prison that stood as a seemingly permanent symbol of the royal power over common folk.

One of the signers of the American Declaration of Independence, Dr. Benjamin Rush, wrote an influential pamphlet in 1792. It was entitled *Considerations on the Injustice and Impolicy of Punishing Murder by Death.* To Dr. Rush, the imposition of the king in criminal proceedings was dangerous and led to morally repugnant results. He saw it as undemocratic since democracy itself implies mutual assistance and life:

> Kings consider their subjects as their property: no wonder therefore that they shed their blood with as little emotion as men shed the blood of their sheep or cattle. But the principles of republican governments speak a very different language... an execution in a republic is like a human sacrifice in religion.[51]

Chief Poundmaker, after realizing that the promises made to his people in the treaties had been broken and upon hearing that his protest against the power of the Canadian state was to result in three years of imprisonment at Stoney Mountain Prison in Winnipeg, slumped and said: "I'd rather prefer to be hung at once than to be in that place." He died shortly after his release, in despair.[52]

By using the fiction that crime is entirely a problem between the person and the state, we drift into a situation where those with the least power vis-à-vis the state—the poor, the disabled, and racial minorities—become the most represented in jail.

So long as law-enforcement agencies are subject to the will and desires of middle-class and upper-class members of the community but are free to behave as they wish without fear of reprisal toward lower-class members of the community, then the legal system will continue to function in the highly discriminating way it does now.[53]

But why should only law-enforcement agencies be blamed? Why not re-examine the entire structure of the state, from federal power to quasi-governmental regulatory bodies, to determine whether they have done what they can to reduce the marginalization of, in this case, youth? The fiction that all crime is primarily against the state allows the same state of quasi-legal bodies to inflict the death of a thousand cuts on the marginalized. Crime is used as a distraction from problems in education, addictions, employment, housing, whatever.

It is important to remember that the use of the fiction of crime being against the state was a choice. Albert Einstein discussed this point in this way:

> They [the conquerors] seized for themselves a monopoly of the land ownership and appointed a priesthood from among their own ranks. The priests in control of education, made the class division of society into a permanent institution and created a system of values by which the people were thenceforth, to a large extent unconsciously, guided in their social behaviour.[54]

Einstein's analysis was that the state and its bureaucracies must be transformed to serve, not the state itself, but individuals and society, including those without power and influence.

And what of the role of religion? Earlier in this book we discussed the southern United States and the correlation between self-help lynching of blacks and capital punishment by the state. In *The Journal of Southern Religion,* Professor Donald G. Mathews of the University of North Carolina at Chapel Hill traced the theological underpinnings of such actions. He claimed these began with Anselm, the Archbishop of Canterbury (1033–1109). Dr. Mathews said that Anselm introduced a new metaphor for the work of Christ, which was "satisfaction":

> He [Anselm] did so within the context of a society that was highly stratified and in which legal metaphors ruled. An elaborate code of "honour" sustained social solidarity. Offences against those of high rank demanded punishment or, in its place, satisfaction relative to the nature of the insult and the rank of the one offended lest the social order be unbalanced... Whereas the work of Christ was once conceived as victory over the power of evil [Satan] now it was conceived as payment to God to satisfy the debt owed by mankind for its sin. Once it was the devil who held mankind ransom, but now it was God...[55]

Dr. Mathews wrote that over the next few hundred years "satisfaction, punishment and suffering became the dominant themes of salvation." Although perhaps controversial in present-day terms, Mathews described how that theory was used to support the right to repress "the African."

This theory may also be seen as consistent with the treatment of marginalized youth within our society today. Dr. Mathews wrote:

> [F]or Southerners... the clearest statement of the theory was made by Robert Lewis Dabney whose desire to distinguish clearly between faith and faithlessness made the ideal spokesperson for the religious of the region. He basked in the language of punishment... he wrote easily of God... "in his punitive providence," of a justice that demanded punishment...[56]

This was not a theology to remain abstract, not while there were Yankees and Africans (and Unitarians), the ungodly to be dealt with. As Dr. Mathews explained:

> Dabney... appealing to the horror felt by the virtuous such as he when criminals were not punished, and he reminded Christians of the oft expressed desire of Biblical writers for "proper retribution at the hand of God." The Christian, he insisted, should find pleasure in others "suffering for sin." Christians know, Dabney thundered, that criminals must suffer "penal retribution." It was rational, just and sacred. The Christian should realize that having participated "in the judicial triumphs of the Redeemer" through grace s/he was free to participate in righteous violence...[57]

As Mathews later pointed out, God as Supreme Hangman did not make white Christians rush out to lynch black people. However this theology gave the feeling of self-righteousness that permitted extreme forms of punishment: lynching, later executions, and now an indiscriminate use of custody no matter what the evidence of its irrationality.

Many of our colleagues have argued that, in truth, everyone in the justice system knows that our work is both cruel and irrational. Some explain it as bad religion, some explain it as a conscious decision to keep the citizens distracted. We believe, as stated earlier, that public discourse about justice issues together with public policy within the criminal system has increasingly become captive to the notion increased punishment will reduce crime, and make communities safer. We believe many people in all walks of society are quite prepared to rethink this notion.

Earlier in this book, we discussed the demonization of youth as described by Dr. Bernard Schissel, which represented a theory that young offenders were being labelled in very negative terms. A divergent view of how we should view and treat our children was articulated by Professor Rita Nakashima Brock. In a way that appears consistent with widely held Aboriginal views of community and justice, Professor Brock stated:

I can imagine that someday we will regard children not as creatures to manipulate or to change but rather as messengers from a world we once knew but we have long since forgotten, who can reveal to us more about the true secrets of life, and also our own lives, than our parents were ever able to. We do not need to be told whether to be strict or permissive with our children. What we do need is to have respect for their needs, their feelings, and their individuality, as well as for our own.[58]

In considering the issue of community control of youth crime as it relates to questioning relationships of force in our current youth justice system, we can do no better than to quote *Money* magazine in May 1995: "The future that we hold in trust for our children will be shaped by our fairness to other people's children."[59] In regaining a community focus for all youth across the spectrum of society, it is important to remember that the concepts underlying Aboriginal notions of justice and restorative processes are not strange or foreign to the broader society. Indeed, as the analysis of the work of Rush and Einstein shows, there are many linkages between such historical records which form part of our collective social fabric and the philosophies espoused by current advocates of Aboriginal justice approaches and restorative justice practices. These concepts question punitive means of justice enforcement and the use of relationships of force in attempting to shape a more peaceful society. Such connections exist over time between cultures and heritages, but also across borders in today's world. The next chapter considers such linkages between the Canadian youth justice system and other international youth systems.

"I've never had a worker on the 'ins' [in custody] or 'out' actually sit with me and counsel me. On the 'ins' you're just supposed to do your time and get out. On the 'outs' they just kind of process you."

B.W.

Chapter Five

International Comparisons of Youth Justice Systems

The Youth Criminal Justice Act has brought about significant changes to the statutory framework of youth justice in Canada. One means of understanding, and making sense of, these changes is to compare developments within youth justice systems around the world. In particular, the jurisdictions of New Zealand, Australia, and England provide an informative comparison, and some clue towards the origins of many of the new provisions found in the *YCJA*. Like Canada, these countries are predominantly English-speaking and share a common, although not identical, legal history.

England

Like Canada, England has recently undergone legislative change in the area of youth justice. *The Crime and Disorder Act 1998*,[1] based on an overarching aim to "prevent youth offending," has brought a focus on reducing delays in the youth justice system, and hence allowing offenders to "see a connection between their offence and the punishment." It has also established an interdisciplinary and interagency approach called Youth Offending Teams (YOTs).[2] YOTs are designed to "deliver new and coordinated youth services" across England and represent a comprehensive approach to dealing with young offenders.[3]

This legislation is administered by the Youth Justice Board. The stated aims and objective of this board are reducing delays in the youth justice system, confronting young offenders with the consequences of their actions, "intervening to reduce the risk of re-offending, appropriate punishment, encouraging reparation to victims," and "reinforcing the responsibilities of parenting."[4] This board has focused on the link between "social factors, home factors and life patterns"[5] and the risk of offending. This relationship is likewise a focus of Canada's *Youth Criminal Justice Act*, which provides, in section 3(1)(a)(i)), that the youth justice system is intended to "prevent crime by addressing the circumstances underlying a young person's offending behaviour." In November 2001, England's Youth Justice Board explained the correlation between socio-economic issues and youth crime:

> Educational underachievement, school non-attendance, broken homes, substance abuse, lack of parental support and a failure to recognise the consequences of behaviour are some of the characteristics of children most at risk of becoming young offenders. The Youth Justice Board provides funding and support to projects which seek to address these complex and interlinking issues and thereby reduce the risks of offending. These projects cover drug and alcohol abuse, cognitive behaviour programmes, mentoring support for young people and parenting courses for the parents of young offenders or children at risk of offending.[6]

YOTs are the major instrument by which the goal of youth crime prevention is to be delivered. These teams are based in each local authority which "in cooperation with other agencies, has a duty to establish a youth offending team for its area and to produce a youth justice plan, stating how services are going to be provided and funded."[7] To December of 2001, 155 YOTs had been established across England and Wales. These YOTs include at least one of each of the following: social worker, probation officer, police officer, a person nominated by a health authority in the local authority area, and a person nominated by the local authority's chief education officer.[8]

YOTs serve as a further recognition within youth justice systems around the world that the traditional stalwarts of the criminal justice system—police, lawyers, and judges—cannot effect meaningful change by themselves. There is an increasing recognition that a pooled approach, bringing together talents and resources from a variety of departments and agencies, provides a better means and chance of changing behaviour and preventing youth crime. In emphasising this wide-ranging view, England's Youth Justice Board referred to YOTs as "one-stop shops for all young offenders" and as "the epitome of joined up management—different services jointly engaged in tackling management."[9]

The legislative tools available to YOTs in the legislation include reprimands and final warnings, parenting orders, reparation (restitution) orders, action plan orders, and detention and training orders.[10] In addition to these orders, youth court magistrates have a further option—called referral orders—which will involve local communities and victims in determining what reparations a youthful offender should make to that community and victim. As explained by the Youth Justice Board:

> With effect from April 2002 every young person appearing in court for the first time and pleading guilty will be referred to a Youth Offender Panel made up of community members assisted by the local Youth Offending Team. The magistrates will decide the length of the referral order that must be served. If the offence is serious enough to warrant a custodial sentence a referral order will not apply. Referral panels provide a more informal setting in which trained volunteers from the local community can discuss the circumstances of the offence with the young person, his or her parents and the victim, if they wish to attend. The panel will then draw up a contract detailing the reparation that the offender must make either to the victim or the community and any other action to help prevent reoffending. Failure to complete the contract will result in a return to court but completion will mean that the conviction is considered spent.[11]

Canada's new *Youth Criminal Justice Act,* in sections 6 to 9, formalizes the practice of warnings, cautions, and referrals that front-line police officers can utilize to avoid judicial proceedings with a young person. This is similar to the practices being employed in England. Professor David Farrington of Cambridge University noted that since 1985 "police forces have increasingly begun to use informal (unrecorded) warnings and to take no further action with apprehended juveniles who they believe to be guilty."[12] Since the implementation of *The Crime and Disorder Act 1998,* the practice of final warnings has replaced that of repeat cautioning of a youth. Although an "informal warning" or "telling off" on the street is still an informal option open to police who encounter a young person believed to have committed an offence, a more formal final warning may occur following an interview of the young person.[13] Under the system of final warnings, young people "have to admit their offence and it is impressed upon them that this is their final warning—any further offending results in the young person being charged and sent directly to court."[14]

The referrals to Youth Justice Panels, mentioned above, signal a greater focus on restorative processes within the youth justice system of England. The Thames Valley Police have been pioneers and vocal supporters of restorative approaches to youth justice. Inspired by the work of Senior Sergeant Terry O'Connell of New South Wales Police in Australia, the Thames Valley force began a restorative pilot project in the Aylesbury area of England. This project utilized police officers as facilitators of restorative conferences which brought together victims and offenders and, where appropriate, their families and other supporters.[15] This pilot project served as a springboard for restorative programming across the police service's jurisdiction, as explained by Superintendent Mel Lofty, head of Youth Justice and Restorative Justice for the Thames Valley Police:

> The success of the Aylesbury pilot prompted the establishment of the headquarters based Restorative Justice Consultancy as well as the "rolling out" of restorative conferencing forcewide, such that since April 1998, all cautions, reprimands and final warnings have been delivered in this way, via eleven restorative justice units distributed amongst the ten force areas, working in partnership with the consultancy. Officers are increasingly making use of community conferencing techniques as tool to resolve incidents of non-criminal or semi-criminal behaviour such as neighbourhood disputes and bullying within schools.[16]

Superintendent Lofty's remarks about the role of police in employing restorative and often informal means of settling disputes—rather than laying charges and invoking the often-harsh mechanisms of the criminal system—brings to mind the issue discussed elsewhere in this book about the overuse of youth court. His words reflect a realization that keeping youth out of the criminal system may be the most effective way of reducing crime, and protecting communities, in the long run.

Although the expansion of restorative practices in England appears encouraging, there are challenges associated with its development. Sir Charles Pollard, chief constable of the Thames Valley Police and member of the Youth Justice Board, described the "two issues currently under debate in relation to restorative justice" as surrounding "firstly, whether conferences should be facilitated by police officers; and secondly, the point in the criminal justice process at which conferences should be held."[17] The former issue brings to mind criticisms by Professor Harry Blagg of Australia regarding what he viewed to be a police-centred and -dominated approach to family group conferencing in New South Wales.

In a Canadian context, these same issues are likely to be debated following implementation of the *YCJA*. During our research on restorative conferencing in Calgary, it became obvious that two different forms of conferencing were being conducted. One was by Calgary Community Conferencing, which employed facilitators with a social work background to conduct conferences after a guilty plea and prior to sentencing of a young person. Another approach was being used by the Calgary Police Service, who used police officers to conduct restorative conferences after complaints were received about potentially criminal activity within the school system. Section 19 of the *YCJA* provides that a conference can be convened at virtually any stage in the process, from initial contact with a police officer, to contact with a youth worker or prosecutor, to appearance in court before a judge; as a result, it is expected that there will be many questions raised about how the conferencing process should best be utilized.

In recent years in England the state has become increasingly involved in issues surrounding the responsibility of parents for the actions of their youth. Under a parenting order, a youth court "may require a young offender's parents to attend regular counselling or guidance sessions ... or to comply with other conditions to help them control their children."[18] In other cases, such orders can require "parents to ensure their children attend court or school, or that the children are at home during certain hours of the day or night." These orders can be made against the parents of a youth convicted of an offence.[19] A parent can be fined for failing to comply with such an order. Before a youth court imposes a parenting order, "the court is expected to assess the effects of such an order on the offender's family circumstances."[20]

Given the strong emphasis on crime prevention being touted by government and youth justice system officials, it will be interesting to observe what changes occur in this area under the ongoing reforms. In recognizing the encouraging steps being taken with the English youth justice system, John Graham, Deputy Director of the Strategic Policy Unit, Home Office (London), sounded a word of caution about shifting resources from the convention youth criminal system to crime prevention initiatives:

> It is encouraging that much of the government's current efforts to tackle youth crime are firmly grounded in research-based evidence on the causes of crime. The key issue, however, is whether any of the considerable resources that are currently tied up in identifying and processing young offenders can be shifted to the potentially more effective strategy of preventing children from becoming offenders in the first place.[21]

Mr. Graham observed that a report in the late nineties shows how improving the effectiveness of the youth justice system (by reducing the average number of court appearances, by further diverting young people from the court system by the use of cautions and community intervention, and by replacing "pre-trial custody remands with bail support schemes") had saved a substantial amount of money, which could be used for crime prevention. In pointing to a 1996 study by the Rand Corporation in the United States which found that "parent training, graduation incentives, and delinquent supervision" were all "more cost-effective than incarceration," Mr. Graham concluded that governments "seriously interested in preventing offending should pay greater attention to evidence of this kind, rather than continue to seek the solution to juvenile crime solely within the narrow horizons of the criminal justice system."[22]

New Zealand

There are a number of similarities between New Zealand's historical relationship with the Maori people and the history of Aboriginal people in Canada. Both countries saw initial offers of partnership between European settlers and Aboriginal residents dissolve into colonization and attempts at assimilation of these indigenous inhabitants. Canadian government policy towards First Nations people, characterized in large part by the *Indian Act* regime and by residential schools for Aboriginal youth, finds some parallel in the process of attempted assimilation of Maori people in New Zealand. Catherine Love, a Maori woman and a psychologist, family therapist, researcher, and trainer from Lower Hutt, New Zealand, described this process:

> For Maori, the [assimilation] process amounted to a form of cultural genocide. Maori whanau [nuclear and extended family] were forced to send their children to schools where the speaking of Maori language was forbidden, the special and communal nature of Maori relationships with the whenua (land) was destroyed, and land passed from whanau, hapu [subtribe] and iwi [tribe] control to state and individual ownership.[23]

The post–World War II industrial expansion in New Zealand brought government policy aimed at moving large numbers of Maoris to urban centres so as to ensure a supply of unskilled and semiskilled workers. These people were further marginalized by housing policies that divided communities and families.[24] These changes resulted in an increasing presence of Maori people within the criminal justice system.

> By the late 1960s and early 1970s, most Maori had relocated from rural kinbased communities to towns and cities. Prior to this time, Maori rates of imprisonment and incarceration in psychiatric institutions were very low. As whanau struggled to maintain their mana [prestige, standing and authority] and to survive in surroundings that were largely hostile to Maori traditions and values, and as many became increas-

ingly disconnected from their cultural institutions and support systems, Maori began to figure in psychiatric, criminal conviction, and imprisonment rates. As the semi- and unskilled labour market dried up, Maori began featuring increasingly and disproportionately in the ranks of the unemployed; psychiatric institutionalization, criminal convictions, and the imprisonment rates for Maori also climbed relentlessly.[25]

In addition to increased participation rates of Maori adults within its jails and courts, New Zealand also experienced a significant over-representation of Maori youth in its justice and child protection systems. In large part responding to this, *The Children, Young Persons and their Families Act*[26] was passed in 1989. This Act, among other provisions, established the use of family group conferences in juvenile delinquency and child protection cases.[27] These conferences were styled after and intended to incorporate elements of Maori culture and restorative practice.

The problems that led to this new legislation resulted in a searching for new alternatives to existing justice practices. Author Jim Consedine suggested that the prevailing English system of criminal courts, focused on the activities of prosecutors, judges, and lawyers, "weaving their way through legal precedents and volumes of law and acts of Parliament was totally alien to Maori."[28] Most significantly, English law focused on individual responsibility and culpability, whereas "Maori law always presumed a collective or corporate responsibility for offending and restoration."[29] But this legislation was not directed only at the pressing needs of the Maori. According to Michael Doolan, southern regional manager of the New Zealand Children and Young Persons Service, other factors resulting in this shift to a restorative approach included:

- "Dissatisfaction among practitioners (reflected in the wider community) about the effectiveness of work with young offenders" resulting from insufficient resources, a lack of enthusiasm by justice workers, and programs for youth-at-risk that resulted in net-widening;

- "The growing rejection of the paternalism of the state and its professionals, and a need to redress the imbalance of power between the state and its agents and individuals and families engaged by the criminal justice system"; and

- "Sixty years of years of paternalistic welfare legislation had little impact on levels of offending behaviour. Costly therapeutic programs that congregated young offenders, particularly in residential settings, emerged as part of the problem rather than as part of the solution."[30]

Key elements of the changes to New Zealand's youth justice system involved an increased usage of police discretion through warnings and other methods of diverting offending youth from youth court, and implementation of family group conferences either as an alternative to, or in conjunction with, youth court processes.[31] Principal youth court judge Michael Brown described the effects of these legislative changes on youth court practice in New Zealand:

> Immediately significant changes occurred with much greater police diversion of offenders, far fewer young people appearing in Court or being detained in residences and prison. There has been more family involvement than ever before. Different cultural practices and the needs of victims were at last being recognized, although it must be acknowledged that there is potential for much greater improvement in that last mentioned area.[32]

Judge Brown went on to stress that the participation and support of victims was essential to the success of the restorative provisions contained in this new legislation. After stating that the "ability of the victim to have input at the family group conference ... is one of the most significant virtues of the new Youth Justice procedures" he cautioned that "victims must be sympathetically encouraged to attend these meetings and every step taken to allay any fears or apprehension they may have."[33]

Family group conferencing formed the basis of the restorative reforms to New Zealand's youth justice system. These conferences were facilitated by a youth justice coordinator. Other participants included the young person, any member of the young person's family, whanau, or hapu, support persons invited by the young person or his or her family, the young person's lawyer, social workers involved in the case, a police Youth Aid officer and the victim.[34] Professor Murray Levine of the State University of New York, in his study of family group conferencing in New Zealand, defined the purpose of a conference as holding youth accountable though making decisions about reparations to the victim, and by imposing an appropriate penalty. He stressed that, although the "group can take the youth's welfare into account,... accountability is a major purpose for the meeting."[35]

The issue of accountability is key to any restorative process. In the introductory chapter of this book, we considered how a community might be structured to avoid an overuse of the formal justice system, and in particular courts and correctional facilities. We suggested some form of community meeting with the offender and victim would be an integral component in both holding that youth accountable for his or her actions, but also ensuring that the youth remains a contributing part of the community.

The normal format and process of a family group conference was described by Professor Levine in the following terms:

> After the coordinator greets the group, orients everyone to the conference and recites the details of the offence, group members, including the victim speak. The victim might describe the impact of the offence on his or her family, and has the opportunity to express feelings about the offender. Participants including the youth and the family say what they think would be an appropriate plan or punishment. Following a statutory provision, the family and the youth withdraw to deliberate in private. After deliberating, they present their plan to the other participants who can suggest modifications. The group continues the discussion until the participants reach consensus. The police representative, the coordinator, and the youth have veto power over the final plan. If the group does not reach consensus, the case is sent to youth court.[36]

The legislative changes in New Zealand clearly signalled a major shift in youth crime policy. Key among these changes were greater diversion from the court system and family group conferencing. Professors Allison Morris and Gabrielle Maxwell of Victoria University in Wellington, in an article published in 1997, assessed the effect of these legislative changes in the following manner:

> Few juvenile offenders now appear in courts, few of these receive any type of court order and even fewer receive any kind of residential or custody order. On the other hand, about 85 per cent of the young people who took part in family group conferences agreed to carry out what we have called elsewhere "active penalties," that is to say, community work, reparation, and the like. If we add "apologies" to this, the figure comes closer to 95 per cent. But New Zealand's capacity to fundamentally reform youth justice lies in its innovative features—participation by young persons, their families, and victims, and agreements reached by them about how best to deal with the offending.[37]

The changes to the youth justice system in New Zealand have not been without criticism. Professor Levine noted, in reviewing the available studies on family group conferencing, that victims were "the least satisfied group" in these conferences.[38] He also questioned the level of follow-up after conferences, raising the spectre that victims would become disillusioned if promises made at conferences were not subsequently kept by offenders.[39]

Further criticisms came from criminology professor Juan Tauri of Victoria University in Wellington. Professor Tauri argued that the statutory changes of 1989 did not represent an adoption of a Maori justice system, but rather an indigenization of the existing justice system, involving the Maori in the delivery of existing justice services and programs, but also adopting some Maori justice philosophies and practices for the purpose of religitimizing the existing state legal system.[40] In a subsequent article, Professor Tauri argued that the introduction of family group conferences formed part of the New Zealand government's policy of biculturalism of existing government structures and programs, and described the conferencing process as "precisely the type of 'twist' in judicial policy and practice one might expect as the State moves away from an openly assimilationist policy agenda towards one directed at the biculturalisation of Government 'corporate identity.'"[41]

Catherine Love, in her critique of family group conferencing, observed that many "whannau, offenders, and victims who have experienced family group conferencing have found the process beneficial and preferable to the previous court-based system."[42] However, she expressed concerns about under-resourcing of these conferences by government in terms of "people, money and time."[43] These limitations, she said, could result in "key whannu members not attending family group conferences, ... delays in conferences being convened, and too few opportunities for conferencing—particularly for monitoring, review and reevaluation purposes."[44] She also questioned the over-reliance on professionals in these conferences, claiming their presence was "intimidating and disempowering" and outcomes of these conferences were largely predetermined by professionals who retain final decision-making power within this forum.[45]

The past two decades have seen remarkable changes in New Zealand's youth justice system. Key among these are dramatic decreases in the number of young offenders in custody, and hence the amount of money spent incarcerating youth. Professors Maxwell and Morris described how, in the ten years before 1991, the number of youth custodial residences in New Zealand dropped from twenty-three to four, representing a decrease in bed placements from "400 to 83 of which 71 were for youth justice cases" (a small number in residential care apparently result from child protection placements).[46] Between the mid 1980s and the early 1990s, the total staff employed in these custodial facilities declined "from about 600 to less than 200 and costs, from $24 million to less than $10 million."[47]

Professors Maxwell and Morris observed that broad implementation of family group conferencing—especially for more serious offences—"provides evidence that restorative justice ideas can be incorporated effectively in modern criminal justice systems."[48] They found conferences "that result in remorse and repair of harm can reduce re-offending" and that "[h]igh proportions of those actively participating are satisfied with outcomes."[49] They note, however, that decreases in the budgets of public health, education and welfare services since passage of the *Children, Young Persons and Their Families Act 1989* have lead to limitations on the programs available to help children and youth, and as a result "current policy in New Zealand is not effective in providing sufficient support for the families of young offenders to ameliorate the circumstances that place their children at risk."[50]

The contrast between benefits and challenges of the current system highlights the at times tenuous relationship between how justice is done (i.e., what process is followed and what theory is applied) and long-term resources to help offenders, victims, and families after the court process is complete. In Canada, likewise, a major issue that will likely shape the effectiveness of the *Youth Criminal Justice Act* is whether much needed resources will be made available to support new approaches and types of sentences contained in this Act.

Australia

Adjusted for the relatively small percentage of Aboriginals in the overall population, Aboriginal youth in Australia are incarcerated at a rate of over fifteen times that of non-Aborigine youth. As evidence of this, in the fourth quarter of 2000, 239 Indigenous youth were in custody across Australia, compared to a total of 351 non-Indigenous youth. Prorated to their prevalence in Australia's population, Indigenous youth were imprisoned at a rate of 267.13 per 100,000, while the rate for non-Indigenous youth was 17.18.[51]

Like the Aboriginal people of Canada, the customs and laws of Australia's Indigenous inhabitants are part of an oral culture.[52] Professor James Crawford of Cambridge University and formerly commissioner in charge of the Law Reform Commission's Reference on the Recognition of Aboriginal Customary Laws, described this culture as placing an emphasis on "unity and immutability rather than on plurality and change," but noted that Aboriginal culture is not recorded in "written codes or statements of customary laws such as are found in some other countries."[53] The degree

to which the criminal justice system in Australia has respected and ac-
commodated Aboriginal culture was questioned in a book entitled *Indigenous Legal Issues.*

> From the outset of colonization, an alien system of criminal justice was
> imposed upon the Indigenous population. Initially, Indigenous people
> were punished, sometimes executed, for acts such as traditional spear-
> ing carried out in accordance with their own laws, and for defending
> their land against the British.... Today, despite some reform measures,
> the criminal justice system remains singularly unsuccessful in bridging
> the cultural gap. Differences in language, communications and culture,
> wealth and status still ensure that the criminal justice system remains
> to Indigenous people an alien and oppressive institution, which sys-
> tematically works to their disadvantage.[54]

The death of ninety-nine Aborigines in custody (police lockups, prisons and juvenile detention centres) between 1980 and 1989 led to formation of the Royal Commission into Aboriginal Deaths in Custody. This
commission's final report, in 1991, was very critical of the Australia justice system for allowing this number of deaths in state custody.[55] Among
its findings, the commission "noted that Aboriginal people are incarcerated in police custody at 29 times the rate of the general population, and
in prison custody at 17 times the rate of non-Aborigines."[56] As reported
by author and prison chaplain Jim Consedine, this "commission found
that the underlying issues of Aboriginal disadvantage generally—racism,
poverty, alienation, powerlessness, hopelessness, alcoholism—contributed
more significantly to the imprisonment of Aboriginal people than any
degree of criminality on their part," leading to the obvious conclusion
that "Aborigines were in prison largely because of social and health factors."[57] These same causal factors have contributed to the over-representation of Aboriginal adults and youths in the Canadian justice system and
its penal institutions, especially in the three prairie provinces.

In searching for links between causes of crime and strategies of crime
prevention, professors Ross Homel and Bruce Herd of Griffiths University and Robyn Lincoln of Bond University identified a "culturally specific" set of risk and protective factors for Aboriginal people in Australia.
These academics acknowledged that risk factors for crime in Aboriginal
communities included such standard factors as prenatal brain damage,
substance abuse, family violence, and long-term unemployment, and that
existing standard protective factors in these communities included social
competence, supportive caring parents, and a positive school climate. They
went further, however, in identifying relevant crime and prevention fac-

tors by incorporating "unique aspects of Aboriginal history, culture and social structure."[58]

As a result, the research of Homel, Herd, and Lincoln identified risk factors in Aboriginal communities which included: the effects of forced removal of Aboriginal people from their home communities, the dependant state of Aboriginal people resulting from government actions and policy towards them, institutional racism, the clash between Aboriginal cultural practices and those accepted in the mainstream, and the link between alcohol and violence in Aboriginal communities. Protective factors identified included cultural and personal resilience to the challenges faced by Aboriginals, as well as family controls which included the extended kinship system of child rearing followed in Aborigine communities.[59]

Another issue affecting the relationship of Aboriginal people to the Australian justice system is the level of police intervention they encounter. Author Rob White studied societal responses to the use of public places by Aboriginal youth. He described a New South Wales study which found an over-representation of Aboriginal people charged with offensive behaviour and offensive language offences in public areas. This over-representation was found in areas with both high and low Indigenous populations. In summarizing the marginalized state of Aboriginal youth in Australia, Mr. White concluded that:

> The position of young indigenous people in Australia makes them very vulnerable to over-policing and exclusionary practices. It also makes them angry. For these young people, public space is often experienced as a hostile environment, one in which they are hounded constantly and rarely made to feel welcome. Addressing issues related to young indigenous people and public space will require provision of more community-based resources, and more facilities for the young people. A major shift in public attitudes is needed as well.[60]

This raises the issue of public attitudes towards those marginalized within society. If, as White suggests, this results in increased surveillance and prosecution of those on the margins, this appears to reflect a punitive view of justice—"getting tough" with young people. Professor Arie Freiberg, head of the Department of Criminology at the University of Melbourne, described this punitive focus of Australian government policy:

> Modern Australian governments seem to be ambivalent about imprisonment numbers and rates. They encourage more and longer sentences by increasing maximum penalties, exhorting sentencers and parole boards to be "tough on crime," and introducing measures that limit

judicial discretion. Low imprisonment rates are not causes for self-congratulation.[61]

In attempting to improve the situation of Aboriginal youth while at the same time trying to address what appears to be a punitive focus within the Australian justice system, a number of voices have urged adoption of more restorative and hence less punitive approach to youth justice. Key among these has been Professor John Braithwaite of Australian National University in Canberra. In *Crime, Shame and Reintegration,* Braithwaite argued that the most effective way to deter crime in a community was through an organized form of shaming by the local community, while at the same time reintegrating offenders into that community.[62] Professor Braithwaite has been a continuing advocate of restorative practices that may ultimately be a vehicle for increased community participation and active responsibility on the part of citizens, in contrast to the passive responsibility and dependence on professionals that characterizes the common relationship to criminal justice institutions.[63] Braithwaite has also drawn on Indigenous practices of the Maori of New Zealand and the indigenous inhabitants of North America in suggesting the importance, within restorative processes, of:

- widening the circle by including a "multiplicity of people who are affected in different ways, but particularly people who love and want to support those affected," such as the offender and the victim;

- putting the problem in the centre of the circle, and not the person who committed the act; and

- shifting the emphasis from material to symbolic reparation, including remorse, apologies, love, and even spiritual healing.[64]

An important point in making sense of international developments in youth justice is recognizing the interconnectedness of problems and solutions. The New South Wales Law Reform Commission, in a 2000 report entitled *Sentencing: Aboriginal Offenders,*[65] recognized the commonality between Australia, on the one hand, and Canada and New Zealand, on the other, in considering new approaches to address concerns about Indigenous involvement and treatment in criminal justice systems:

> Within Indigenous communities throughout the world, the place of custom-based resolutions, restorative justice and community healing in the criminal justice system, have been explored in recent years, opening channels for the formal legal system to deal with offenders in ways that show greater understanding of the nature of those communities.

Several countries, notably New Zealand and Canada, have instigated programs to facilitate greater participation of Aboriginal people in the criminal justice system. These examples provide valuable guidance for making the criminal justice system more responsive to the needs of Australian Indigenous people.[66]

Following on the lead of New Zealand, family group conferences were introduced across Australia in the nineties. The first conferencing program began in Wagga Wagga, New South Wales, in 1991. The "Wagga" approach was conducted primarily by police officers.[67] Officer Terry O'Connell of the New South Wales Police Service described how the introduction of conferencing at Wagga Wagga was linked to police cautioning:

> The goal was simple. To find a way to improve the police cautioning process so that those directly affected might feel better satisfied as a result. A police caution traditionally involved a police officer giving a young offender a warning rather than sending the offence to be processed by the courts. When our Police Community Consultative Committee looked at family group conferencing, our focus was largely about improving police processes. Conferencing seemed to offer an uncomplicated way to do that, and it was. We found that by bringing offenders, victims and their respective support people together in a conference, all benefited from this new approach to police cautions.[68]

This level of police involvement in the Wagga conferencing model has drawn criticism. Professor Harry Blagg of the University of Western Australia suggested that the Wagga model had become "the master pattern for schemes in Australia that have explicitly set out to increase the police role."[69] Professor Blagg was critical of the so-called conferencing reforms, and rather described them as a "re-configuration of the juvenile justice system; increasing the scope of police powers in those areas once considered to be the domain of welfare; and giving the police a very direct and overt (as opposed to simply indirect and covert) role in the deployment of punishments."[70] Professor Braithwaite responded to these concerns, observing that police, regardless of their specific role in conferencing, will always remain the "most consequential" gatekeepers in the criminal justice system. He suggested even racist attitudes among police can be transformed, and that society should "give up on stigmatizing the police as essentially and irretrievably committed to the domination of colonized peoples."[71]

Regardless of the perceived advantages or disadvantages of police involvement in conferencing, Kathleen Daly, associate professor of Criminology at Griffith University, in a recent study of conferencing in New

Zealand and Australia, noted that the Wagga model of police-run conferencing is not now the norm in Australia. Among the Australian states (which each have authority to legislate on youth crime and justice), she reported that legislated youth justice approaches, "which incorporated conferencing as one component in a hierarchy of responses to youth crime, emerged first in South Australia in 1993."[72] Since this legislation was introduced, "all other Australian jurisdictions, except the ACT and Victoria, have introduced legislation, with all but one of the six statutory schemes rejecting the Wagga model in favour of the New Zealand model of non-police run conferences."[73]

The South Australian conferencing process was structured similarly to the New Zealand model, featuring a justice co-ordinator who organized conferences upon receiving referrals from judges and the police.[74] Police officers who believed a youth to have committed an offence were given the option of either administering a caution, referring the matter to a conference, or laying charges and proceeding to youth court.[75] The "front end" measures appear to have achieved some prominence in dealing with the overall youth population. Over the first four years after implementation of this legislation, 17 percent of all juvenile matters were referred to conferences, while about one-third resulted in cautions, and only one-half went on to court appearances.[76]

Professor Daly, in a detailed evaluation of conferencing in South Australia called the South Australia Juvenile Justice Research on Conferencing Project, considered the views of offenders and victims who had participated in eighty-nine conferences in 1998.[77] These views were ascertained through an initial interview apparently not long after the conference, and a follow-up interview in 1999. This study found a high level of satisfaction among both victims and offenders regarding issues of procedural justice at the conference, whether they were treated fairly and with respect, and whether they had a say in the agreement. Although finding the conferences had some positive effect in repairing harm between offenders and victims, she questioned whether there may be "limits on offenders' interest in repairing the harm" and "limits on victims' capacity to see offenders in a positive light." In particular, among a "significant minority of victims" (one-third) she found it "was not possible to separate the 'badness' of the act from the person, suggesting little capacity or desire to reintegrate the offender into the community."[78] Other findings were that conferences were generally "calm events" characterized by civility between participants, that conferences brought about a significant decrease in the anger and fear victims had felt towards offenders, and that offenders were "more likely to be satisfied than victims with how their case was handled."[79]

However, regardless of how the new legislative scheme of conferencing may have reduced total numbers of youth in court and assisted victims and offenders, some have suggested that the position of Aboriginal youth within the South Australian justice system remains largely unchanged by the new legal framework; they are still significantly over-represented. Joy Wundersitz, director of the Office of Crime Statistics for the South Australia Attorney-General's Department, analyzed the plight of Aboriginal youth.

> [I]t is clear that Aboriginal young people continue to be over represented in their contact with the criminal justice system. They are more likely to be directed straight to court rather than being given the option of diversion to either cautioning or conferencing, are more likely to be sentenced to detention and are more likely to be placed in custody. This pattern is very similar to that which applied under the old *Children's Protection and Young Offenders Act 1979*, and suggests that the key problems confronting the juvenile justice system in dealing with young Aboriginal people have not yet been resolved.[80]

As mentioned above, the nineties saw much legislative change in youth justice matters across Australia. In 1992, the state of Queensland introduced the *Juvenile Justice Act*[81] which, among other features, formalized the practice of police cautions, introduced new procedural protections for youths suspected of crime, extended the options for sentencing, and "emphasized the importance of diversion from the courts and of imprisonment as a last resort."[82] In 1996, this legislation was amended to allow either police or courts to refer matters to family group conferences. These conferences are conducted by community conference convenors, and usually include the youth and his or her lawyer, family member or other person chosen by the youth, the victim or victim's representative, the police officer directly involved, and the convenor.[83] Three conferencing pilot programs were established in the Queensland communities of Palm Island, Ipswich, and Logan. An initial survey of the conferencing programs showed a high degree of satisfaction—among offenders, their families, and the victims—about both the agreements reached at the conferences and the sense of fairness experienced in the conference.[84] Although this survey did not include reliable data on recidivism rates, "[p]articipant satisfaction levels in many cases were above common international standards of best practice."[85]

The past two decades have seen all Australian states move from a welfare model of youth justice to a justice model. Criticisms expressed about the earlier welfare approach included "the lack of due process rights, the application of coercive penalties for non-criminal matters, net widening, the failure of rehabilitation, indeterminate sentences and administrative discretion and the injustices of needs-based sentencing."[86] The current youth justice policy is illustrated in the states of South Australia and Queensland. Although South Australia "has made a major effort to introduce family conferencing as a response to youth crime," and although both South Australia's *Young Offenders Act 1993* and Queensland's *Juvenile Justice Act 1992*[87] recognize "the developmental needs of children and young people," the primarily legislative focus in each state has been on "protecting the community and holding young people accountable," while child welfare has been a secondary focus.[88]

Connecting International Trends to the Canadian Situation

As Professor David Miers of Cardiff Law School in Wales stated in his recent and wide-ranging study of restorative justice programming, the "substantial international growth in restorative justice provision over the past 20 to 30 years has been remarkable."[89] In addition to the developing initiatives and programs in New Zealand, Australia, and England, Professor Miers detailed developments across many countries of continental Europe. For example, young offender victim-offender mediation is now common in Austria, Belgium, Finland, France, and Germany.[90] Although these civil law jurisdictions have distinct and complex criminal justice systems— a consideration of which is beyond the scope of this book—there does appear to be a clear trend towards seeking new ways of involving victims and offenders in restorative practices. This is happening both as a way of diverting cases from the formal court system and as a way of augmenting the existing practices in youth court.

As an indication of the international prominence being accorded restorative justice, the government of Canada introduced a resolution in April 2002 asking the United Nations to adopt a Declaration of Basic Principles on the Use of Restorative Justice Programmes in Criminal Matters. This action took place at the Eleventh Session of the UN Commission on Crime Prevention and Criminal Justice in Vienna, Austria. This declaration stated, in section six, that "Restorative justice programmes may be used at any stage of the criminal justice system, subject to national law."[91] The parties to be involved in these restorative processes were stated to be "the victim, the offender and any other individuals or community members affected by a crime who may be involved in a restorative process." Restorative processes were defined as "any process in which the victim and the offender, and where appropriate, any other individuals or community members affected by a crime participate together actively in the resolution of matters arising from the crime, generally with the help of a facilitator." These restorative processes "may include mediation, conciliation, conferencing and sentencing circles." Restorative outcomes were said to include "responses and programmes such as reparation, restitution, and community service, aimed at meeting the individual and collective needs and responsibilities of the parties and achieving the reintegration of the victim and the offender."

An international comparison of developments in youth justice practice and programming is one context within which to consider some of the changes being implemented as a result of Canada's *Youth Criminal Justice Act.* One area with an obvious link to the international youth justice developments discussed above are front-end diversionary alternatives. Sections 6 to 9 of the *YCJA* set out options police officers may consider rather than laying charges and beginning judicial proceedings. These are the use and administration of warnings, cautions, and referrals. These front-end options are similar to developments in New Zealand and England, which have sought to decrease the numbers of youth formally charged and brought to court. Taken together with cautioning and referral options, these provisions provide a number of ways that young people who admit responsibility for an offence can be dealt with outside the court system. This option also follows trends in New Zealand, Australia, and England where diversionary schemes have significantly reduced the number of young offenders appearing in court.

Another area where international similarities can be found is restorative conferencing. Conferencing is a key element of the *YCJA*, with section 19(1) stating that "a youth justice court judge, the provincial director, a police officer, a justice of the peace, a prosecutor or a youth worker may convene … a conference for the purpose of making a decision required to be made under this Act." Conferences can consider "conditions for appropriate extra-judicial measures, conditions for judicial interim release, sentences, including the review of sentences, and reintegration plans." This conference process parallels developments in New Zealand and Australia— described by Professor Kathleen Daly as "laboratories of experimentation in one form of restorative justice: conferencing"[92]—where formalized family group conferencing was legislated, albeit in a largely mandatory form as compared the discretionary form now found in the *YCJA*.

As well, youth justice discourse from around the world shows an increasing appreciation of multifaceted and interdisciplinary approaches to addressing the issues of offenders and victims. As seen in the development of Youth Offending Teams in England, an interagency approach through which organizations and employees from a range of services—in such areas as health, education, social services, probation, and police—can be effective in providing a coordinated strategy for specific offenders. This goes at least some distance towards breaking down a long-standing view that suggested that the justice system—as the ultimate symbol of authority and the rule of law in our society—needed to retain an arms-length relationship from these other service providers. An alternate view, however, increasingly being heard on the international stage, suggests that it is exactly this arms-length relationship that has placed barriers in the road of established coordinated and wide-ranging strategies aimed at both crime prevention and at reducing the risk of recidivism by specific offenders.

Any discussion of interdisciplinary approaches to justice underlies the importance of resources in considering alternative programs and approaches within the youth justice system. A move towards more restorative practices has been heralded by many as a way of returning a sense of participation and control to local communities who have experienced a justice system increasingly dominated by the words and actions of professionals. Accepting that there is an important, if not vital, role that restorative practices can play in restoring a sense of participatory democracy, restorative changes have also been viewed as a way of downloading government responsibility and hence cutting costs in the justice system. As Professor Daly explained about restorative developments in New Zealand:

> Conferencing as one kind of restorative justice may be viewed as a less costly method of disposing of cases; it can rely on the labour and good will of citizens, especially with its rhetoric of decentralizing professional authority. In the past decade in New Zealand, it has become apparent that while there is general consensus in the goals and aspirations for juvenile justice (and for child and family welfare) set out in the historic *Children, Young Persons and Their Families Act 1989*, a lack of government provision of the necessary resources has made it difficult to carry out the goals in a meaningful way.[93]

This discussion sounds a note of caution towards any suggestion that restorative practices, in isolation, are a panacea or miracle cure for the myriad of problems facing the youth justice system. Ultimately, it is the level of resources employed within each country that will determine whether policy goals—such as reducing crime and providing safer communities—are achieved. But a factor to any discussion involving youth justice policy and resources is identifying, and questioning, the ultimate philosophy and sense of justice that underlies any criminal justice system. It is to that challenging question we now turn.

"Probation, that's just like being locked up again.

Obviously, not one person in the whole world is

not going to be breach once in a while…"

R.T.

Chapter Six

Crime and Punishment: Getting Tough on Youth Crime

The Punitive Mentality

Few issues in Canada have stirred public debate as has youth crime. Over at least the last decade, cries for a more punitive focus to our statutory young offender law have been frequently and widely heard. The obvious answer to youth crime from this perspective is increasing the level of punishment within the youth system, hence more frequent and longer sentences of custody. Others, however, view this punitive focus as narrow-minded and urge a more balanced and broad-based view of youth crime. Advocates of the latter view focus more on the root causes of youth crime, and often suggest a very different solution to the problems faced.

We believe great caution should be employed when considering the get-tough approach. Punitive arguments on youth crime are often presented in a simplistic manner which focuses solely on the specific crime committed by the young person and not on their background and environment. Yet few people would dispute that a young person's home and upbringing have a major effect on that child's behaviour.

Punishment is one response to crime that clearly forms much of the strategy applied in our justice system. Although most would agree that some form of consequence is required to hold offenders accountable for their actions, there is much disagreement on what form these sanctions should take. Ultimately, our elected governments dictate through legislation what forms of punishment are acceptable. Although much of the collective resources employed within our justice system are directed towards imposing this punishment, there is no universally accepted definition of this word. In reality, the meaning of punishment depends on what each society says it is. Assistant RCMP commissioner Cleve Cooper and Dr. Jharna Chatterjee, in a presentation to the conference "Changing Punishment at the Turn of the Century: Finding a Common Ground" in Saskatoon in September 1999, described how crime and punishment are defined and legitimized in Canadian society in comparison with other countries:

> In the current judicial system, the state represented by the judicial and correctional system and assisted by the police, constitutes the legal machinery of punishment. It is the state that defines through legislation what would be considered a "crime" and establishes the continuum of appropriate negative consequences (i.e., punishment) for a crime. However, we should be cognizant of the fact that it is the society that ultimately legitimizes this definition of crime and appropriate punishment. In some societies, a woman who alleges to have been raped may face the death penalty by stoning because she has committed the crime of adultery. Most other societies would consider this to be a barbaric travesty of justice.[1]

Punishment has long been a central feature of our criminal justice system. Law professor and former defence lawyer and prosecutor David Paciocco argued that being honest about this underlying function is the best way to restrict its destructiveness:

> The criminal justice system isn't just ... a system of negative penalties designed to discourage crime. It is at bottom, a system of values. I think that the people of Canada, as in many other cultures, expect a consequence, expect accountability, when there's been a violation of some basic norm within the society. For the very serious crimes, the ones that cry out for denunciation, the best we've been able to manage so far in demonstrating our disapproval is punishment. We are very, very reluctant as a society and as a legal culture to talk about punishment. Some people become very offended when you even use the word "punishment." It's why we talk about sentencing, as though it can somehow be a more productive euphemistic way of describing the infliction of pain. We're very loathe to admit that we punish.[2]

Professor Paciocco stated that appreciating the damaging aspects of our criminal justice system is important, as it makes society more concerned about such issues as due process and the presumption of innocence and about people receiving heavy sentences. He argued that recognizing the punitive underpinnings of our justice system is crucial, because "if we conceive of the criminal justice system as this great productive social mechanism that does good and forget the harm it does, we're going to become cavalier in how we use it."[3] These comments reflect a view of the justice system held by many—that it should be separate and apart from the systems and agencies aimed at helping people in need. Within this view, the criminal justice system has as its most fundamental underpinning the threat of punishment for those convicted of criminal offences.

For those holding a get-tough philosophy about the justice system, an essential component of punishing criminals is the loss of many rights afforded citizens in the general population. M.P. Jim Gouk, speaking at the "Changing Punishment" conference in Saskatoon epitomized the potential harshness of this view when he stated that "any person who has been convicted in a Canadian court gives up their rights as a Canadian with the sole exceptions of the right to humane and healthful treatment."[4]

This view assumes that harsh punishment will deter crime, as that treatment will remain a bad memory for the offender, preventing further misdeeds. However, the maintenance and use of criminal records by the Crown in criminal prosecutions suggests that the original punishment is actually ongoing, rather than a memory, since that record can form the basis of denying bail or dramatically increasing the level of punishment for a subsequent offence. Moreover, the use of criminal records can negatively influence the rehabilitation and reintegration of those unfortunate enough to have them.

But studies have shown that virtually everyone has committed some criminal offence during their life. This reflects the broad discretion given to police and prosecutors in framing charges. For example, we have lost track of the number of both youth and adults that have ended up charged with mischief, by interfering with the lawful possession of property. This might be thought of as a catch-all section in the *Criminal Code*, and can be applied to incredibly wide range of circumstances. A youth who attends a party by invitation and then becomes unruly can find him or herself charged under this section, without having actually damaged property or committed any form of assault.

If the view represented by Mr. Gouk reflects public sentiment in Canada—which we doubt—then the only hope for Canadians is an extremely inefficient police force because if everyone committing a criminal offence was charged, this theory would see the vast majority of Canadians give "up their rights as a Canadian with the sole exceptions of the right to humane and healthful treatment."[5]

This view is especially troubling, considering other studies which show that once a person has been convicted in criminal court, the likelihood of them committing further criminal acts is greatly increased.[6]

Specifically regarding youth, it is obvious that the way we treat young people within the justice system will greatly influence the way they, in turn, treat others. In the words of a young person who had spent time in custody:

> I got treated pretty much how I treated them. If I was cool, they were too. If I was trouble, they didn't take the time to talk to me. They just put you in your place. I've never had a worker on the "ins" [in custody] or "out" actually sit with me and counsel me. On the "ins" you're just supposed to do your time and get out. On the "outs" they just kind of process you.[7]

If punitive or get-tough views are widespread within the adult criminal system, they appear rampant within youth justice programming across North America. Boot camps have become a common youth justice feature throughout the United States, and to a lesser extent in Canada. These camps function on the philosophy that tough discipline will change the attitude and behaviour of delinquent youth. Boot camps are characterized by "their rigid militaristic style" where youth are "commonly organized into platoons and required to wear uniforms and to participate in daily regimens of drill exercises and physical training."[8] These camps also offer rehabilitative programming, including education and counselling.[9] Research on the boot camp approach—also called "shock incarceration"—has shown that although youth sent to boot camps "tend to develop less antisocial attitudes while at the camp, camps have little or no effect on recidivism after return to the community."[10] Indeed, a study funded by the U.S. Department of Justice found, in general, "no significant differences ... for either adults or juveniles when recidivism rates of boot camp participants have been compared with others receiving more traditional corrections options."[11]

Educational consultant Lon Woodbury of Idaho acknowledged that a tough discipline approach may work with certain mature youth, but warned against this approach for many troubled high-risk youth:

> Boot camps and military schools are based on a punitive structure. When a student makes a bad choice, a staff member determines the punishment. The resulting pain is supposed to teach the child to stop doing what caused the pain. This works for any mature adult who has mastered the concept of cause and effect, and will tend to work with most teens with at least somewhat age-appropriate emotional maturity. For

these children, Military schools and Boot Camps can be very effective and a good growth experience. Punishment, however, is likely to back-fire when a teen is openly rebellious and hasn't learned the relationship between cause and effect. The rebellious teen will not see how his or her actions had anything to do with the resulting punishment. Instead, the lesson learned by a rebellious teen will either be to be more sneaky, so as not to get caught, or to be angry at the staff for picking on him/her. The teen might argue, "I am being punished because that staff member doesn't like me," or the teen might make a manipulative accusation: "That's not fair!" or, the teen might resolve to do something even more objectionable: "I'll show them!" This type of teen truly doesn't get it when it comes to living life effectively, which is why punishment-oriented programs are ineffective for them.[12]

In Canada, Project Turnaround, located near Barrie, Ontario, is a highly publicized example of the military boot camp approach. This camp was opened in July of 1997 as a get-tough response by the provincial government of Premier Mike Harris to the issue of youth crime. Government M.P.P. Allan McLean assured the Ontario legislature in 1998 that "Ontarians called for tougher sanctions against youth crime, and Project Turnaround is answering the call."[13] Given the relatively short life of this program, it is difficult to assess whether Project Turnaround will provide lower recidivism rates for the youths attending this camp as compared to youth in conventional custody facilities. An internal document, obtained by the *National Post* in October, 1999 reported that "nearly 40 per cent of the cadets leaving Turnaround committed new crimes within one year."[14] In March of 2001, however, Rob Sampson, Ontario Minister of Correctional Services, announced that a three-year review of the Project Turnaround pilot project showed that "young offenders who completed the program at Project Turnaround were one-third less likely to re-offend than those who served their sentence in a traditional young offender correctional institution."[15] These results were openly challenged by criminologists at the University of Toronto, who found that "the Minister's own evaluation shows that boot camp 'graduates' are *not* significantly less likely to commit new offences than are youth in standard [custodial] institutions."[16] These criminologists concluded that there "was no evidence of any overall beneficial psychological or academic impact of the boot camp experience over a standard correctional institution" and that the "generalized failure of Ontario's boot camp to show positive effects on youth is consistent with evaluations elsewhere."

Considering the more extensive American experience, it is difficult to find any compelling evidence that boot camps reduce long-term reoffending by delinquent youths. The suggested use of boot camps, however, is compelling for those who believe the current justice system should be tougher on young offenders. In February of 2002, Saskatchewan Minister of Justice Chris Axworthy unveiled a plan to counter the high number of auto thefts by youths in Regina. This included providing more information to judges at sentencing, intensive case management during custodial sentences, and stricter supervision after release. The Saskatchewan government's plan, however, did not include implementing a punitive boot-camp model. "The yelling, the screaming, the pushups, the cold showers, the running in cold weather—that doesn't work, we know that," said Mr. Axworthy. However, opposition justice critic Ben Heppner, a supporter of boot camps for young offenders convicted of car theft, said "the new plan simply wasn't tough enough" and said "it doesn't have the teeth in it, it doesn't have the resources in it, to make it work."[17]

Another example of a program designed to deter youth crime through a tough discipline approach is called Scared Straight. This program has now been in existence for twenty-five years. The original program in New Jersey—subsequently adopted by thirty U.S. states[18]—featured a group of inmates serving life sentences who sought to "scare at risk or delinquent children from a future life of crime." This program featured "an aggressive presentation by inmates" to visiting juveniles which "realistically—even brutally—depicted life in adult prisons" often including "stories of rape and murder."[19] Testing of the New Jersey Scared Straight program showed "no statistically significant effect of the program on its participants"— and actually showed that "participants in the experimental program were more likely to be arrested"[20] than those not taking part in the program. Despite the fact that other research projects "on the effects of crime prevention programs have not found deterrence-oriented programs like Scared Straight effective," belief in the effectiveness of such programs has continued in the United States. This is a result that Dr. Jim Finckenauer of Rutgers University (author of the initial study on the New Jersey program) called "the 'Panacea Phenomenon,' as policymakers, practitioners, and lay person[s] continue to latch onto quick, short-term and inexpensive cures for difficult social problems."[21]

In considering the role of punishment among Aboriginal people, Justice Murray Sinclair stated that punishment is recognized by Aboriginal people, as there are always a small part of any society for which this strategy has to be retained and utilized. He stressed, however, that punishment is utilized carefully within Aboriginal communities, with community protection being the goal of its imposition. He said an orientation towards keeping a community together would naturally lead to a restorative view of justice, but noted punishment is sometimes necessary to protect society and denounce antisocial behaviour. However, he rejected the notion that harsh punishment acts to deter crime.[22]

A recurrent Aboriginal justice theme is replacing the punitive focus of Anglo-Canadian law with an emphasis on restoration of peaceful relations between offender, victim, and community. This view was reflected in the comments of Harry Morin, a Cree man from Sandy Bay, Saskatchewan who was active in the development of circle sentencing within his community:

> Like a lot of times, to me personally, the system is right now just a punishing system, it's punishing. They're not looking at what's causing these problems, they're looking at hey, we have to punish this guy for what he's done, basically, that's all it's at. And a lot of these guys go to jail, and they sit around this ten by twelve cell or whatever size they may be, and they sit there and think. And they get very bitter. They're bitter at the people that put him in there, the victim that reported him. He's mad at the justice system, he's mad at the RCMP. Here in a sentencing circle, we make sure somebody tells the offender that we're here to help, for support, and not only that, if recommendations are made that he takes some kind of programming to better himself back in society, he's not only promising to the magistrate or the probation officer, he's promising it to his own community. And then he knows he's got all that support.[23]

Similarly, Chief Judge Lilles of the Yukon Territorial Court observed from his experience that "concepts of 'punishment' or 'vengeance' are either foreign to Native people or play a much more limited role in their understanding of the meaning of 'justice.'"[24] In studying the various meanings and applications of punishment, it is important to consider the effects of the ultimate punishment in our system: a loss of liberty through imprisonment.

The Effects of Custody

> I remember one young girl, 12 years old. She had spent the weekend in jail for stealing a chocolate bar. They sent her to Kilburn Hall in Saskatoon, now a remand centre for youths. She had been afraid to tell the police officer where she lived. Rather than put her out on the streets, the arresting officer thought she would be better off in custody. As she

asked me for a pen to write down the addresses of the new friends she had met over the weekend, I realized she had her first initiation into the criminal subculture that we have created. Had she been given a warning and sent home, as might have happened a few years ago, she would have gone on her merry way, a little embarrassed but not criminalized.[25]

It is questionable how much in the way of rehabilitation can be expected when a troubled youth is placed into custody alongside other troubled and offending youths. A first-time, naive offender may well be befriended and influenced by other youths more seasoned in a criminal lifestyle. This will likely lead to the opposite of what is hoped, increasing rather than decreasing the chances of recidivism for the first-time offender. Perhaps as a recognition of this danger, the *YCJA* in section 39 now places strict limits on the ability of youth court judge to sentence a young person to custody, making unlikely the chances of a youth with little or no record being incarcerated for a nonviolent offence.

Dr. Martin Brokenleg, a Lakota man and professor of Native American Studies at Augustana College in South Dakota, is recognized as an expert in the area of understanding and helping high-risk youth. During a presentation entitled "Reclaiming Youth at Risk,"[26] while discussing why troubled and high-risk youth often associate with negative peer groups, he stressed the critical human need of belonging. He said that everyone in society has an intense need to belong, and that teenagers, in particular, feel this acutely. He warned that if we cannot find a positive way for our young people to belong within our society, these often troubled youths will find their own way to belong, and these peer connections may be destructive both to the youths involved and to society in general.

Children and youth are in a state of dependency, their development is in a stage of growth, and they rely on their peers. By placing youth into the midst of what is likely a negative peer group environment in custody, the likely result is antisocial, rather than pro-social, changes in behaviour. As Barry Clark, Patricia O'Reilly, and Thomas Fleming explained in *From Care to Punishment*:

> ...Gondreau (1987) succinctly states the problem, the effect created is exactly [the] opposite of that desired. When you do find a correlation between severe punishment and criminal recidivism it is usually in the opposite direction. His assertion finds a sobering resonance in Conrad's (1985) work in Columbus, Ohio. This study reconfirmed the fact that frequent incarcerations actually accelerate recidivism.... More disturbing... was the finding that the younger the person at the first incarceration, the higher the recidivism rate subsequently recorded. One might

assert that while adults adapt to the custodial system, children and young persons are adopted by it....[27]

This discussion raises a fundamental question at the core of our society's criminal and correctional policy: Does punishing offenders reduce crime? The Solicitor General of Canada, the federal government department in charge of corrections including penitentiaries, in a report released in May 2002, has now answered that question. After examining 111 studies, involving 442,000 offenders, who were subjected to a variety of punishments including imprisonment, the conclusion was that not only did harsher punishment of prisoners not reduce future criminal acts, harsher punishments actually increased the chances that offenders would commit future criminal acts. Worse yet, the longer a person was incarcerated, the more likely that they would commit an offence in the future.[28]

And what of the cost of this "incarceration" strategy? In the United States, the Washington State Institute for Public Policy did an extensive cost/benefit analysis of various crime-reduction programs. While they have yet to examine traditional youth custody facilities, they did examine a popular form of custody, boot camps. The Institute found, after examining three federal projects as well as seven boot camps in California and Florida, that boot camps increased recidivism by 10 percent. Naturally this would create a cost to taxpayers and victims. The Institute's bottom line estimate was a loss of $3,578 per youth.[29]

Most people would agree that some form of discipline is a necessary component and tool within our youth justice system. But a difference of opinion would arise over the appropriate form and severity of various disciplinary options. A former young offender, interviewed on CBC Radio, observed that the form of discipline has a major effect on the chances of effecting change:

> The major thing is how the discipline is done. So instead of telling a child that they have to do something, you say, "You know what, I think this would be in your best interest. What do you think is the best way that we are going to accomplish this?" That way they feel they get to keep some of that control, some of that power and they will work with the authorities better that way.[30]

Yet in attempting to devise appropriate and compassionate forms of discipline, care must be taken to consider the backgrounds of troubled youth and their capacity to understand and learn from the "lessons" being taught within the youth justice system. Unfortunately, many of these lessons are being taught to young people behind the walls of custodial facilities, as part of a system caught between public cries for toughness and the obvious need on the part of these youth for healing and understanding.

The words punishment and discipline are often used interchangeably. However, Dr. Brokenleg, while speaking about strategies for reclaiming high-risk and high-need youth, stressed the difference between the two, saying that in many ways they are opposite forces. He equated punishment with revenge, saying that punishment is based on the notion that "hurting you will improve your behavior." He said disciple, however, is an education in responsibility, teaching young people how to make responsible decisions and how to eventually assume independence.[31] In the context of how a child is treated after violating a rule at school, Doctors Richard Curwin and Allen Mendler, in their book *Discipline with Dignity*, contrasted consequences with punishments.[32] They said consequences work best when they are clear and specific, have a range of alternatives, are not punishments, are natural and/or logical, and are related to the rule broken.[33] Although clearly a complex issue, the fine line between meaningful consequences on the one hand, and "getting tough" by inflicting pain through punishment on the other, is one we should be well aware of in designing strategies within the youth justice system.

Indeed, the most telling yardstick for any such strategy is whether it works. In considering the effects of custody, that question becomes: Does placing youth in custody reduce future criminal behaviour by those youth? Elsewhere in this book we have presented ample material to show custody is not an effective deterrent in reducing crime. In fact, we have argued that incarcerating youth likely increases the chances of future criminal activity. However, most studies that have measured the efficacy of custody have compared this strategy to community-based dispositions. We are aware of no study where the recidivism rate of youth in custody has been compared against the general youth population (regardless of involvement with the justice system), or against youths who have committed criminal offences but were not caught and processed through the criminal justice system. This is vital information, as some studies have suggested that, with low-risk youth, the chances of recidivism actually increase with systemic intervention, as compared to diverting and keeping these youth completely out of the system.[34]

Public Perceptions about Youth Crime Versus Reality

Public opinion has become a significant force in shaping justice policy for young offenders. In stressing this point, Professor Bernard Schissel of the

University of Saskatchewan argued that the often-reported concerns about increasing levels of youth crime are misguided. He suggested that such concerns represent "moral panics" which are shaped, to a large extent, by the media and the political elite. He viewed prevalent public attitudes and policy toward young offenders as a form of scapegoating or blaming young people for a multitude of family and society problems that are totally beyond their control.

> [W]e are on the verge of an acute "moral panic" in this country that, if allowed to continue, will result in the indictment of all adolescents, and especially those that are marginalised and disadvantaged. The end result will be the continuing scapegoating of youth for political purposes and, as is the irony of punishment, the alienation of a more uncompromising and disaffiliated youth population. It is not a new insight to say that increasing punishment greatly increases the likelihood of violence and alienation. Despite the political rhetoric to the contrary, we do not collectively consider children our most valuable resource. In fact, we consider them one of our most dangerous threats.[35]

The extent to which court represents the failings of our broader society is, to a great extent, hidden from the public at large. As Professor Schissel argued, the media plays an important part in affecting public perceptions of youth crime. Graphic pictures and descriptions of horrific crimes committed by young persons are frequently reported. These incidents are described to us in great detail. We see innocent people being victimized and feel a sense of shock, violation, and outrage at these crimes. But the public rarely hears the complete story. Media accounts of youth court cases give little information about the background and family history of the young people involved, or about the often poor (or even harmful) social or political decisions involved that contributed to the harm done or, in the alternative, could have prevented it. Although many people comment publicly on issues of youth crime—and are often critical about the system—few people actually attend court or otherwise enquire about the factual basis of specific cases. Information about the background of offenders, and of victims, and about the actual offence—which are largely missing in media accounts—are needed to place into context what occurs in court.

Public reporting about youth crime ignores some obvious realities about marginalized youth. Professor Schissel argued that

> …the primary effect of media and official accounts of youth crime is to decontextualize the act for public consumption, allowing those with direct access to discourse to direct and control public perception. The

portraits of youth criminals that public crime accountants paint are largely portraits of nihilistic, pathological criminals who act alone or as members of gangs, criminals who are devoid of ethical ballast. The decontextualization of youth crime, however, intentionally ignores a fundamental consideration in understanding crime; most repeat young offenders and their families are victims of socioeconomic forces and they are likely to be repeatedly victimized as clients of the systems of law, social welfare, and education. Ultimately, the discourse serves political movements both informally and formally.[36]

While reading media accounts of youth crime, or listening to public debates on the effectiveness of the youth court system, it is easy to be left with the impression of an overwhelming public sentiment towards getting tough on youthful offenders, and hence sending more young offenders to jail for longer periods of time. Criminologist Anthony Doob of the University of Toronto described an apparent public focus on severity as the appropriate measure of our justice system's effectiveness. He said when members of the public are interviewed about sentencing, "they are likely to be asked whether they think it harsh enough and, not surprisingly, most answer that it is not."[37]

As an example, Professor Doob cited a 1993 Statistics Canada poll (the General Social Survey) in which approximately 77 percent of respondents indicated that they thought that sentences were too lenient.[38] But Professor Doob went on to suggest that simple questions about whether the system is too lenient may not accurately measure public sentiment on the variety of public policy issues raised through the sentencing process.[39] His research considered, based on the overcrowding of Ontario penal institutions, whether respondents would rather spend public money on the building of more prisons, or on investing in alternatives to prison. He also queried whether respondents would rather spend public funds on building more prisons, as opposed to crime control programs.[40] In both cases, he found that building more prisons was the least preferred alternative. He concluded that "people may give a simple answer to a simple question (in this case 'Should sentences be harsher?')... [b]ut when pressed to make difficult choices as one almost always does in normal life, different preferences emerge."[41] Later in this article, in considering general support for prison as a criminal sanction, Professor Doob suggested that "[s]upport for the use of prison is soft: it goes down when people are reminded either that offenders are eventually released or that imprisonment is expensive."[42]

There is little doubt that the media plays a large part in how the public gets its information about the justice system. When the Canadian Sentencing Commission (1986) surveyed respondents about where they obtained most of their information about the sentencing of offenders, 95 percent identified the news media as their source.[43] But what effect does reliance on media accounts have on public perceptions of undue leniency in the treatment of young offenders?

A study by criminologists Julian Roberts and Anthony Doob helped answer this question. These academics found that media accounts of sentencing cases did promote a view of undue leniency among respondents.[44] Yet, when part of their study group based their view on the appropriateness of a given sentence after reading a summary of the factual information actually before the court (as opposed to a newspaper account), significantly more of these respondents found the sentence to be appropriate, while feeling less critical towards the judge, and less negative towards the offender.[45]

This research raises the issue of the accuracy and completeness of public reporting about our criminal justice system. Given obvious constraints on space, newspaper accounts rarely include any detailed account of the offence, the offender, or the reasoning and sentencing criteria applied by the sentencing judge. This information, however, is vital to provide context for the complex sentencing decisions in which judges balance competing and often contradictory principles of sentencing (such as rehabilitation, denunciation, deterrence, and compensating victims). The lack of such context can only leave the public confused about how all of these factors are supposed to achieve the goals of reducing crime and protecting our communities. As an example, Judge Barrett Halderman of the Provincial Court of Saskatchewan, while speaking at a public information meeting about court practice, expressed concern over a prominent and complex sentencing he had handled. His decision was produced in written form, and was of considerable length. Yet most newspaper reports about this case were brief, focusing mainly on the offences committed and the resulting sentence. Little, if any, discussion was included on how he had arrived at this result, and hence members of the public were not provided with any context for the ultimate sentence.[46]

Another issue revolving around public perceptions of justice involves to what extent members of the public view crime reduction, and protecting their families, as a responsibility of justice professionals and courts, on the one hand, or the broader community on the other. The Canadian Sentencing Commission conducted a study in which over half of the respondents surveyed felt the responsibility for reducing crime lay with society generally, while only 15 percent identified courts as being responsible.[47] Despite this result, many opinion polls continue to show public scepticism about the effectiveness of those employed within the justice system. For example, on 12 August 2002, Canadian Press reported—based on two surveys conducted by Ipsos-Reid—that "Canadians believe the country's courts are not handing out severe enough sentences to criminals and view judges as the weakest link in the legal process."[48]

Despite the media focus on crime in terms of what happens to offenders in court, families and local community members play a vital in reducing crime. Chief Justice Edward Bayda of Saskatchewan, while speaking at a meeting of judges, lawyers, and members of the Federation of Saskatchewan Indian Nations, expressed his frustration that courts are located at the back end of the criminal justice process. He said that, despite the public focus on what happens in court, and the resulting sentences, we should not forget that a multitude of community and family interactions have affected, and possibly failed, that offender before he or she was ever charged and appeared in the court system.[49] He encouraged all First Nations to consider viable crime prevention strategies in working with their young people. His comments raise the question of whether local communities, as opposed to courts, are best equipped to correct delinquent behaviour.

As seen above, the public expects and demands much from the courts and judges in the sentencing process. Professor Anthony Doob described a study in which a random sample of Ontario residents were asked to rate the importance of five purposes of sentencing: community denunciation, specific and general deterrence, incarceration, rehabilitation of offenders, and compensating the victim or community.[50] For each purpose except incarceration, "the average ratings were very high."[51] As Professor Doob concluded, "[f]or the public, then, nearly 'everything' should be accomplished at sentencing" which is "more than a minor challenge being placed at the feet of judges and the criminal justice system."[52]

In response to these significant public demands, a major frustration for those working in the criminal justice system is the lack of resources available to assist in making changes. While many members of the public may view courts as the ultimate source of power in our society, the reality is that youth court judges can only make limited decisions based on their statutory power, and on the resources available to them within the system. Decisions regarding the allocation of resources are reserved for the legislative and executive branches of government, not the judiciary. As a result, while most if not all of those players involved in a youth court sentencing might agree that an offender requires a specific resource, such as a focused treatment program for FAS/FAE, the court only has jurisdiction to sentence that young offender within the confines of the *Youth Criminal Justice Act* and cannot direct the allocation of public funds towards the creation of a required program.

In *R. v. L.E.K.*,[53] the Saskatchewan Court of Appeal overturned portions of a probation order in which a youth court judge had directed that "a youth court worker with special training and understanding in the organic brain impairment" be "assigned to his file" and had also directed that a "comprehensive case plan be prepared for the day of his release." In ruling that nothing in the *Young Offenders Act* authorized the youth court judge to order the "provincial director or any worker under his supervision to do anything" the appeal court went on to observe "[n]or is there anything that authorizes a judge to order the creation of a new program or expenditure of money for a particular purpose."[54] As can be seen by this example, the reality of sentencing law in Canada, under the *Criminal Code* for adults and under the *YOA* and now the *YCJA* for youths, is that a judge only has power to impose statutorily recognized sentences on an offender. These powers include ordering jail, fines, or probation against the offender. Regardless of the needs of an offender, a judge is restricted to ordering that offender to abide by conditions of a sentence, and has no power to order other people to do anything, or to order the spending of public or other money to assist the offender. This may place judges in a frustrating position.

Chief Justice Edward Bayda of Saskatchewan expressed this frustration through an example of how he would be required to sentence a troubled offender. During an interview with David Cayley of CBC Radio, he questioned what sentence would be appropriate for an Aboriginal offender in his late teens charged with a break and enter. This fellow had "no job, no education, no material goods to speak of and no real sense of his own dignity or worth."[55] Coming from a dysfunctional home life, "his parents are alcoholic, his upbringing has been violent, and his life is without direction and purpose."[56] Recognizing the limits on a sentencing judge, Chief Justice Bayda described the benefit that might be achieved if judges had the power to allocate money that otherwise would be spent on jailing this offender:

> It may be that what this young man needs for the next little while, is an awful lot of guidance from one person, two persons, two elders, who can set him on the straight and narrow. And interestingly, these two elders may well need a young person around their home. After all, they are getting fairly old ... and having a young person around their home may be a very good idea for them. Why don't we put this young man

into the home of these two elders, who are prepared to accept him, and guide him and so on? Why don't we pay these two elders board and room for this young man? After all, we are paying board and room for this young man when we put him in jail. Why don't we use that money to pay these elders? Why don't we put someone in place to monitor this relationship and see if it is actually working? Now, I submit to you that doing something like that will probably be less costly than putting this young man behind bars for the next nine months or the next year. I also submit to you that the dividends we, as society, will collect will be much greater than the dividends that we reap from putting that young man into prison. Now, can I, as a judge, do that today? No.[57]

As these comments suggest, there is a need to consider alternatives to the current processes and practices within our justice system. Yet in doing so, it is important to understand the issue of public support for these changes, as well as the slippery slope of public opinion on matters of criminal justice. Despite their often limited ability to affect or guide the formation of social policy, it is nevertheless the responsibility of professionals working within the justice system to respond to, and correct, public opinion when it leads to inaccurate and misleading conclusions. Defence lawyers and prosecutors, and others working within the justice system, must speak out vigorously in response to public pronouncements that are not based on fact, and in reply to politicians who present short-term fixes rather than long-term strategies for crime control. In responding to the "get tough" view of youth criminal policy, the next chapters of this book consider alternate ways of thinking about and "doing" justice for young people.

"…It's just a sense that I have that if he goes there, he may become like some of the hardened people that are in that system right now. And I don't feel that he is a hardened criminal. I think that this is a first thing for him, and I don't think that prison would benefit."

Calgary store owner

Chapter Seven

A Different Response: Restorative Justice

According to the Ottawa-based Church Council on Justice and Corrections, restorative justice is "the popular name given to a wide range of emerging justice approaches that aim for more healing and satisfying responses to crime. While each approach is different, these processes try to give active participation to those directly involved or affected."[1] Although there a number of definitions commonly suggested for restorative justice, most contain similar themes. Bringing these together, Edmonton-based mediator and facilitator Susan Sharpe described restorative justice, in its many forms, as inviting full participation and consensus, healing what has been broken, seeking full and direct accountability, reuniting what has been divided, and strengthening the community so as to prevent further harm.[2] In whatever way it is defined, restorative justice does provide an alternate approach within a justice system largely dominated by a punitive ideology and methodology, a system that has, until recently, placed strict limits on participation by victims and community members.

The Overreaching Effect of Criminal Law

The evolution of our criminal justice system has shown an increased reliance on criminal law professionals, who have largely assumed the role of trying and punishing those charged within the system. Professor Gordon Brazemore of Florida Atlantic University, in his study of changes to the American youth court system, hearkened back to a day not so long ago when "community members, with the encouragement and support of schools, neighbourhood police, and other institutions, often took care of problems that now end up in juvenile and criminal justice systems."[3] While this historical reflection applies equally to Canada, the situation has clearly changed in both countries.

Bob Gillen, QC, assistant deputy attorney general of British Columbia, speaking at a Restorative Conferencing workshop in Halifax in February 2002, described today's justice system as the vacuum cleaner of society, sucking up all its disputes. He referred to the Ontario Court of Appeal's decision in *R. v. McDougall*[4] as evidence of the overreaching effect of the criminal system. In overturning a conviction of abduction against a father who kept his children one day longer than provided for in a family court access order because a snowstorm made travel difficult on the expected date of return, Justice Doherty commented that "[c]riminal prosecutions cannot become a weapon in the arsenal of parties to acrimonious family disputes."[5] In cautioning against the sometimes over-application of criminal law, Justice Doherty cited with approval the following passage from the Law Reform Commission of Canada's report *Our Criminal Law*:[6]

> Criminal law operates at three different stages. At the law-making stage it denounces and prohibits certain actions. At the trial stage it condemns in solemn ritual those who commit them. And at the punishment stage it penalizes the offenders. This, not mere deterrence and rehabilitation, is what we get from the criminal law—an indirect protection through bolstering our basic values.
>
> But criminal law is not the only means of bolstering values. Nor is it necessarily always the best means. The fact is, criminal law is a blunt and costly instrument—blunt because it cannot have the human sensitivity of institutions like the family, the school, the church or the community, and costly since it imposes suffering, loss of liberty and great expense.
>
> So criminal law must be an instrument of last resort. It must be used as little as possible. The message must not be diluted by overkill—too many laws and offences and charges and trials and prison sentences. Society's ultimate weapon must stay sheathed as long as possible. The watchword is restraint—restraint applying to the scope of criminal law, to the meaning of criminal guilt, to the use of the criminal trial and to the criminal sentence.[7]

In conclusion Justice Doherty, referring to the case before him, said that the "problems underlying these charges involve[d] complex ongoing social relationships and the well-being of two children." He said "other legal avenues" were available to address these concerns which could "more effectively deal with these situations than [could] the blunt broad axe of the criminal law."[8] This decision reflects what many commentators believe to have become an increasing societal focus: turning to the criminal justice system—initially to the police and then to the courts—as an answer to virtually all manner of disputes and transgressions, however trivial. At the same time, it has become increasingly evident that the criminal system is poorly equipped to deal with the myriad of social and economic problems that underlie so many of the situations being processed through it.

In explaining the power held by professionals within the criminal system, Chief Judge Barry Stuart of the Yukon Territorial Court, in an address to a conference entitled Restorative Justice—Working with Youth,[9] described a shift that has occurred across North America over the past twenty years. Communities, he said, have given over much of their power and ability to deal with disputes at a local level, relying instead on the formal institutions of the Canadian criminal system, and on the professionals there employed. Chief Judge Stuart, while recognizing the essential role of an independent judiciary within a democratic state, said a major challenge for professionals within the system is finding ways to give back to local communities this power, responsibility, and control over conflict and crime.

This loss of local control has happened in conjunction with an increasing focus on punishment as a primary means of deterring crime. In the context of youth court in the United States, Professors Gordon Brazemore and Mark Umbreit described a move, in most American states, towards a punitive youth court which they say has "moved further away from its original goal of providing treatment in the 'best interests' of youth."[10] These authors argued that the changes in American juvenile justice have included a heightened emphasis on punishment, and, as a result, have meant "increased incarceration and longer stays in residential and detention facilities" for juvenile offenders in various states.[11]

In both American and Canadian youth courts over the last few decades, an alternate and often coexisting focus to punishment has been treatment. Professors Brazemore and Umbreit, however, criticize both the retributive and treatment approaches in youth court as flawed. They say a punitive focus can lead to "stigmatisation, humiliation and isolation" thereby reducing the chance of an offender regaining self- and community respect. Treatment, on the other hand, failed to recognize any form of sanction on the offender from society, and did not appear to promote any sense of responsibility in the offending youth.[12] This dual focus of retribution and accountability, on the one hand, and treatment and rehabilitation on the other, can be seen in the statement of principles of the Canada's former *Young Offenders Act*. But in considering the very high rates of youth custody in Canada—rates which are higher even than those in the United States[13]—there is little doubt that retribution has become a driving and destructive force in Canada's youth justice system. This has led society to search for new ways of helping youth, while at the same time holding them responsible for their crimes.

A New Means of Victim, Offender, and Community Participation

Although the criminal justice process, from initial complaint onwards, impacts on a broad cross-section of individuals, including victims and local community members, these people have been provided with little opportunity to participate in the process. As an example of this detachment from the system, Judge Barry Stuart (later Chief Judge) of the Yukon Territorial Court, in *R. v. Moses*,[14] described the typical sentencing hearing in a Canadian court:

> The foreboding court-room setting discourages meaningful participation beyond lawyers and judges.
>
> The judge presiding on high, robed to emphasize his authoritative dominance, armed with the power to control the process, is rarely challenged. Lawyers by their deference, and by standing when addressing the judge, reinforce to the community the judge's pivotal importance. All of this combines to encourage the community to believe judges uniquely and exclusively possess the wisdom and resources to develop a just and viable result. They are so grievously wrong.
>
> Counsel, due to the rules, and their prominent place in the court, control the input of information. Their ease with the rules, their facility with the peculiar legal language, exudes a confidence and skill that lay people commonly perceive as a prerequisite to participate.
>
> The community relegated to the back of the room, is separated from counsel and the judge either by an actual bar or by placing their seats at a distinct distance behind counsel tables. The interplay between lawyers and the judge creates the perception of a ritualistic play. The set, as well as the performance, discourages anyone else from participating.[15]

This passage reflects the detachment that has occurred between justice system professionals on the one hand, and victims and local community members on the other. But alternatives that provide a new role for offenders, victims, and community members may be a way of bridging this divide. Sentencing circles, for example, provide a forum in which offenders, victims, and community members can participate in a manner that stands in stark contrast to the conventional system. As then Associate Chief Judge Murray Sinclair of the Provincial Court of Manitoba commented, "the current system is adversarial—we depend on a Crown to prosecute, a defence lawyer to defend, and a judge to decide between the two positions being put forward," but in "circle sentencing the onus is placed on those within the circle."[16]

But changes in process and procedure do not come easily within the conventional justice system. The philosophy guiding justice policy becomes a crucial prerequisite of such change. Professors Brazemore and Umbriet explained the connection between philosophy and alternatives in terms of elements of restorative versus retributive justice:

> Whereas retributive justice is focussed on determining guilt and delivering appropriate punishment ("just deserts") through an adversarial process, restorative justice is concerned with the broader relationship among offender, victim and community [citations omitted]. Restorative justice differs most clearly from retributive justice ... in its view of crime as more than simply lawbreaking—or a violation of government authority. Rather, what is most significant about criminal behaviour is the injury to victims, communities, and offenders that is its result.[17]

Clearly, there is growing interest in restorative approaches to justice, across Canada and around the world. As an example, based on an Ontario survey, Professor Anthony Doob of the University of Toronto concluded that "substantial portions of the population would be interested in becoming involved in structures outside the formal system which, broadly speaking, are reparative in their orientation."[18]

Before considering what form these new approaches might take, it is important to consider, and perhaps rethink, how we define crime and its effects. As an example, Chief Justice Edward Bayda of Saskatchewan stressed the importance of a broad focus when considering how we categorize crime, and focused on the damaging effects of crime on relationships between people:

> We've always treated criminal offences as the "breaking of a law," and the breaking of law has certain consequences. You could end up in jail. But committing a crime is much more than simply breaking a law. Committing a crime is hurting, hurting someone, hurting another person, hurting another group of people, hurting a community, hurting yourself. Should we not be looking at a criminal offence in that light? Somehow I feel that's going to produce a heck of a lot more good than com-

ing down with fire and brimstone and saying, "Okay, now you burn."[19]

A focus on the ways crime hurts people raises issues about how we define and address these hurting effects. Prosecutor and author Rupert Ross of Kenora, Ontario suggested that these damaging effects may be defined differently by victims than by courts and offenders. He said that victims often define a crime as "causing an enduring injury to a central relationship in their lives."[20]

> I recalled the case of a woman walking down the street in her small town when an angry, muttering stranger suddenly veered right at her, grabbed her purse and ran. She was not hurt, but she no longer felt safe on the streets of her own community, worrying constantly if every man coming her way would turn out to be another attacker. Under the relational lens, the real crime was against her relationship with the streets of her neighbourhood. Seen in that way, it was not just a ten-second, once-only event, but something which would continue to infect her way-of-relating to her community long into the future. By contrast, the offender probably believed he "only" stole a purse, and the court probably characterized it as a "momentary threat" and a "minor" property loss. Once again, the relational lens suggested a substantial disconnect, with all the parties coming to very different "definitions" of exactly the same act.[21]

A challenge, but also an opportunity, within the justice system is attempting to heal the many damaged relationships that often result from a criminal act. One way this can be done is considering new ways in which offenders, victims, and community members can participate in the criminal system. Although there is no one method in which such restorative processes may be attempted, some commonalities have emerged from the variety of justice forums which have brought together restorative justice and local community involvement. Professors Gordon Brazemore and Curt Griffiths described four restorative decision-making models: victim-offender mediation, family group conferencing, circle sentencing, and reparative probation. Each model—to varying degrees—involved "citizens and community groups in critical components of justice."[22]

Victim-offender mediation "involves bringing together victims and their offenders along with a mediator or co-ordinator who facilitates the meeting."[23] During the mediation, "victims describe their experiences with the crime and the effect it has had on them and offenders explain what they did and why, answering questions the victim may have."[24] The mediator then attempts to help the victim and the offender to look for ways to make things right between them.[25] Victim-offender mediation programs—also called victim-offender reconciliation programs—have been used in Canada, the United States, and Europe for over half a century.[26] Calgary Community Conferencing, for example, is conducted following a guilty plea and prior to sentencing. (A case study of this organization follows later in this chapter.)

Family group conferencing is discussed at greater length in chapter five. It originated in New Zealand largely as a result of passage of *The Children, Young Persons and their Families Act* in 1989 which, among other provisions, established the use of family group conferences in juvenile delinquency and child protection cases.[27] These conferences were styled after and intended to incorporate elements of Maori culture and restorative practice and were facilitated by a youth justice coordinator. Other participants typically include the young person, any member of the young person's family or community, support persons invited by the young person or his or her family, the young person's lawyer, social workers involved in the case, a police Youth Aid officer, and the victim.[28]

Circle sentencing, or the conducting of sentencing circles, has happened with some frequency over the past decade in Canadian courts sitting in Aboriginal communities. Although the physical setting of circles has varied between judges, communities, and jurisdictions, almost all involve the offender, the judge, a Crown representative, and a number of influential and respected local community members. Other participants have usually been the victim, defence counsel, and family members of the offender and victim. Most of the circles have involved between twenty and thirty participants.[29] A sentencing circle is a sentencing hearing conducted in a circle format. The participants confer in an attempt to agree on a sentence for an offender. The focus is often to find a community-based, rather than a jail-based, sentence for an offender, incorporating whatever lay and professional resources are identified within the circle. Reconciliation and healing between the offender, victim, and community are also a goal, as is reintegration of the offender, and hopefully the victim, into that community.[30]

Community reparative boards are a modern form of the widespread "community sanctioning" response to youth crime which occurred across the United States as early as 1920 in the form of youth panels, neighbourhood boards, or community diversion panels.[31] Reparative boards have existed since the mid 1990s, primarily in Vermont,[32] where they are composed of five local citizens and make dispositional decisions for eligible probation cases referred by the courts.[33] The Vermont reparative boards "are primarily used with adult offenders convicted of non-violent and minor offences; more recently the boards have also been used for with juvenile offenders."[34] Vermont boards meet with offender, and often victims and other affected parties (such as parents of a youthful offender), with the goal of negotiating an agreement, signed by an offender, specifying a set of tasks to be accomplished during a probationary period.[35]

In some cases, restorative processes can provide hope to the parties involved. Despite the obvious limits on what can be accomplished in helping a victim and offender during the limited time available in a restorative meeting, Judge Bria Huculak of the Provincial Court of Saskatchewan stressed the positive effects of restorative justice:

> For me, it is justice as hope. It's the kind of process that gives me hope that something positive can result from a very bad thing. It gives me hope that the victim can go forward and put the criminal event behind them. I know there are horrible things that happen to victims and their families, and it would be silly to suggest that one process alone can resolve that, but it can assist. It gives me hope that offenders can be healed and that they can get the support they need for rehabilitation. But it's only a start, and we can't look at these processes as panaceas.[36]

The advantages of involving victims and community members in a restorative way was seen at the Provincial Court of Saskatchewan in Nipawin in 2000.[37] A young adult Aboriginal man was charged with a serious assault on an elderly man, who was of Mennonite heritage. The assault was random—the two had never met—and occurred while the victim was out for an evening walk. The offender, in a drunken state, had attacked the man, striking him repeatedly.

The assault happened during the course of what was viewed as a local crime wave, involving a large number of break and enters within the town. The assault also occurred in the context of heightened tensions between the town's Aboriginal population and the broader community. After a guilty plea to this charge, Judge Halderman asked the Crown prosecutor and defence lawyer whether there had been any consideration of using restorative methods in dealing with this case, both as way of helping the victim and offender come to terms, but also as a way of trying to heal and help the broader community in coming to terms with issues around crime and its effects. As a result, an initial meeting was conducted with the lawyers, the offender, and the victim (assisted by his daughter). The victim wanted to know why he had been attacked, and what he done to deserve this. The offender, who had no record for violence, and who had suffered many hardships during his upbringing, told the victim repeatedly that the victim was not to blame for what had happened. Although quite emotional, both the offender and victim appeared quite relieved to be able to engage in this dialogue.

From this initial and positive meeting came a subsequent one involving the victim, the offender, and the Nipawin Community Justice Committee. This committee was comprised of a cross section of people from Nipawin, including Aboriginal representation and a representative of the local RCMP. It had been involved largely in administering and conducting alternative measures under the *Young Offenders Act* and, more recently, under the *Criminal Code.* The victim was again accompanied by his daughter, and the offender had his mother and sister present. This discussion was facilitated by a trained mediator, and was conducted in the absence of the judge, although a report on this meeting was forwarded back to him. All participants spoke at the meeting. Most comments from the committee members showed considerable insight into the causes of crime. A number of the committee members stressed that no one group—whether Aboriginal or white or some other group—was responsible for the rash of crimes. The meeting concluded with the tearful victim telling the offender that, if the offender could stop his abuse of alcohol, he would be welcome in the victim's home anytime.

Chief Judge Barry Stuart of the Yukon Territorial Court has argued that the process used in "doing justice" directly affects the outcomes achieved. He said that, in many ways, process is product, as the justice process followed determines who participates, how these participants are involved, the relationships between parties, whether agreements are reached, and, if so, what the content of such agreements are and what commitment the parties bring to carrying out the agreement. In a speech to an Ottawa conference on restorative justice and youth, he urged participants to consider new justice processes, which would empower local communities to take back responsibility for crime. He described this as "creating space to move from a few doing a lot, to a lot doing a little" and as a "move from experts doing it, to little people doing it."[38]

Finding a Place for Restorative Justice in the Current System

One of the challenges of, in Chief Judge Stuart's words, "doing it" is finding ways of discovering commonality between people in conflict, and then using those uniting forces and spirit to produce a solution that respects all the parties to the process. But in Canada, a major obstacle to finding new ways to involve offenders, victims, and lay community members in justice processes is the reality of Canadian criminal law. The vast majority of statutory provisions—which for young offenders include the *Criminal Code* and the *Youth Criminal Justice Act*—deal with clearly defining the processes and procedures followed in determining whether an accused is guilty, and further in protecting the rights of that accused against society's ultimate weapon: deprivation of liberty through incarceration. During an interview on 21 February 2002, Justice Murray Sinclair, formerly co-commissioner of Manitoba's Aboriginal Justice Inquiry, said that most of the sections in the *Criminal Code* deal with procedure and, in effect, are applicable to a relatively small number of accused who go through a trial process. The reality, he said, is that most accused do not have a trial, and many simply wish to admit responsibility for their actions and get on with their lives. Justice Sinclair noted there are few processes in the statutory criminal law to help and heal the majority of offenders who fall into this category.[39]

Our criminal system is set up to handle the most difficult of cases, dragging the simplest cases and least threatening offenders through the same maze. According to author and Crown prosecutor Rupert Ross:

> Everything that we don't like in society gets funnelled into the process that ultimately is set to handle [convicted murderer] Paul Bernardo. We put moose hunters who shoot out of season into that process, drunk drivers, schoolyard fights, all into a process that is ultimately geared to deal with the most dangerous offenders. And when you're dealing with those offenders—people who, for whatever reason, are unable or unwilling to live within society's norms, who are just too dangerous to have on the streets—then we need a process with all of the protections that we presently have in it, because we're saying that the state wants to take away your liberty and for a very long time. And then we need all those processes, those rights, all those protections. And we need the adversariality of it, because it is adversarial. My worry is that, by funnelling absolutely everything into it, we are creating adversarial approaches and antagonisms and angers and alienations in situations where they may be the problem, and we may be adding to the very thing that we're trying to cure.[40]

This raises the issue of whether there is any room in the complex mechanisms of justice for alternative and restorative practices. The reality, however, is that much discretion is left to courts and judges, especially in the area of sentencing. The development of sentencing circles is one example of how this discretion may be applied. Neither the *Criminal Code* nor the *Youth Criminal Justice Act* mention or define sentencing circles. However, both allow broad discretion about who a judge may consult in consider-ing an appropriate sentence. *Criminal Code* section 723(3) allows a judge to "require the production of evidence that would assist in determining the appropriate sentence." *YCJA* section 19 now provides that a judge, pro-vincial youth director, police officer, justice of the peace, prosecutor, or youth worker may convene a conference for the purpose of making a de-cision under the Act, including giving advice on appropriate extrajudicial measures, conditions for judicial interim release, sentences, including the review of sentences, and reintegration plans. These provisions leave much room for courts to consider various forms of restorative practices during the sentencing of both young people and adults. It is interesting, however, that this section in the *YCJA* does not include, or apparently envision, any input from the young person involved, in asking that a conference be con-vened.

Closely tied to the question of what restorative practices might be adopted within the justice system is the question of whether restorative processes are better suited to a setting away from the formal court. Rupert Ross has suggested that the formality of court and the need for judges and prosecutors to address principles of denunciation and deterrence may hinder attempts at restorative justice within open court. He suggested that restorative meetings involving offenders, victims, and community mem-bers might more productively be conducted away from court, in the ab-sence of the judge. Results of these meetings could then be reported back to the formal court.[41] Although such restorative noncourt meetings may be productive, offering some possibility of reconciliation and assistance to the parties, Mr. Ross suggested that these processes may augment, but should not replace, the court process, which he said plays a crucial role in any free and democratic society (including denouncing crime, deterring members of society from committing crimes, rehabilitating offenders, com-pensating victims, and promoting a sense of respect for that society's rule of law).[42]

But within the many objectives pursued by a criminal court, these goals often appear to be at cross purposes. The *YCJA* states the purpose of sen-tencing to be holding "a young person accountable for an offence through the imposition of just sanctions that have meaningful consequences for the young person and that promote his or her rehabilitation and reinte-gration into society, thereby contributing to the long-term protection of the public." Holding a young person accountable through meaningful con-sequences while promoting their rehabilitation and reintegration into so-ciety can often call for measures and strategies that seem contradictory and inconsistent. Indeed, if appropriate remedies are not available, then the resulting sentence may actually increase the future likelihood of criminality. As a result, the task of sentencing young people is made all the more difficult when judges are required to choose between goals whose achievement depends on the availability of often-scarce resources and programming.

The conflicts between the purposes and principles of sentencing make obvious the tensions between differing philosophies of youth justice held in our society. Retribution and punishment, on the one hand, and restoration on the other, would appear to be goals that are diametrically opposed. This raises the question of whether both philosophies can be applied at the same time. As Judge Bria Huculak of the Provincial Court of Saskatchewan explained:

> Our concept of punishment is based on the ideology of individualism. That still remains. The concept of restorative justice, in my view, cannot be an add-on. I don't think you can look at justice with one eye on retribution and punishment and the other on restoration. They're too conflicting.[43]

Supporters of restorative approaches suggest that what may be required is a paradigm shift within the youth court system, from a dominating view of retributive justice to one of restorative justice. District Court Judge McElrea of New Zealand described such a shift in his country:

> The new paradigm does not easily fit within the old parameters—liberal/conservative, justice/welfare, punishment/rehabilitation, justice/mercy. It cannot be described in those terms because it requires a new way of thinking, and of doing justice. My conclusion therefore is that we indeed do have a new paradigm of justice. It is not simply an old model with modifications. A new start has been made, new threads woven together and a new spirit prevails in Youth Justice in New Zealand. It is a spirit which I would characterise as responsible reconciliation. The term "reconciliation" connotes a positive, growing process where strength is derived from the interaction of victim, offender and family in a supportive environment. It is a "responsible" process in that those most directly affected take responsibility for what has happened and for what is to happen. In the process most of the power previously vested in the court is transferred to the local community which now carries this new responsibility. Perhaps when the real strengths of the new model have been understood we will be able to take it beyond the Youth Court, find a mechanism for defining a relevant community group for adult offenders, involve victims and the wider community in find-

ing solutions, and in the process remove from the courts and our prisons much of the burden of unrealistic expectation under which they labour.[44]

The Challenges Facing Restorative Justice

Much has been written about the potential benefits of restorative practices within the youth justice system. The past twenty years have seen an exponential increase in the number of community-based programs that purport to follow a restorative path. But there are also a number of legitimate criticisms and concerns about community justice programming and about the implications of restorative justice theory when applied within the existing youth criminal system.

Despite claims that restorative practices will reduce recidivism among specific offenders, and reduce crime in the overall community, there is little statistical data to confirm whether existing programs are achieving these aims.[45] Clearly, empirical research is required to test the effectiveness of these programs. But, in doing so, it is important to appreciate that many of these programs have multiple aims over and above the question of offender recidivism. As professors Gordon Brazemore and Curt Griffiths explain:

> Many restorative and community justice initiatives have objectives that are far more holistic than traditional crime control responses, which have typically utilized recidivism rates as a primary outcome measure. An evaluative framework for those approaches would, therefore, have to include measurable criteria to assess outcomes of "community empowerment and solidarity," "victim interests," and "crime prevention." The relative importance assigned to such outcomes as community and victim involvement, offender shaming, reparation to victims, dispute resolution, and healing will also determine how one gauges the effectiveness of any model.[46]

Proponents of restorative justice have argued that the existing criminal system offers little support and satisfaction to victims. As mediator and facilitator Susan Sharpe explained, crime "involves much more than breaking rules" as it "involves real actions that hurt real people with real and lasting consequences." She said a justice system "bent on catching and punishing criminals has little to offer victims of crime."[47] But are there also dangers in involving victims in a restorative process? Professor Howard Zehr, a key figure in the U.S. restorative justice movement, sounded a warning that "[o]ften the design and implementation of restorative programs lacks the vital input and direct participation of victims, their advocates, and victim services."[48] This involvement seems an obvious element if these programs are hoped, in part, to help victims deal with the aftermath of a criminal act imposed on them.

An interesting and difficult question regarding the role of victims within restorative processes is whether, like offenders, there might be some expectations or requirements of victims who participate in a restorative process, such as to forgive the offender, or to come up with an agreement for restitution. Author and Crown prosecutor Rupert Ross argued emphatically against any such expectation of a victim:

> I have grown substantially opposed to processes which have as their stated goal any "expectation of forgiveness" by the victim. Placing such a burden on victims, in my view, is wholly unwarranted; they are, after all, the injured and innocent parties, and they owe the offender nothing. Where the harm has been deep and lasting, suggesting in any way that victims carry some civic or other duty to forgive may amount to nothing more than a second victimization. While the parties often do find themselves moving towards some degree of rapprochement when the process is both thorough and faithful to its relational obligations, and such a result should be welcomed, it should not be set out as an expected outcome.[49]

The concern about protection of victims within restorative processes is especially acute when local dynamics dictate that certain victims, such as women assaulted by their spouses, are at a decided disadvantage. Such victims are less likely to have their voices heard and to be assured of ongoing protection within that community. In Canada, Aboriginal women's groups have been critical of the way some community justice initiatives have treated women victims. These concerns are summarized by Professors Gordon Brazemore and Curt Griffiths:

> In Canada, Aboriginal women have voiced concerns about the high rates of sexual and physical abuse in communities and have questioned whether local justice initiatives can provide adequate present and future protection for victims.... Additional concerns as to whether the sanctions imposed on offenders by community justice structures were appropriate also have been voiced. In a study of violence against women in the Canadian Northwest Territories, Peterson[50] found that Aboriginal and Inuit women were concerned about the attitudes toward violence held by community residents and how this would impact the operation of community justice initiatives.... Unfortunately, the failure to address these critical points has led to situations in which commu-

nity justice initiatives undertaken by Aboriginal bands have been first criticized by Aboriginal women and then discredited in their entirety.[51]

These concerns were further articulated by Professor Emma LaRocque of the University of Manitoba. Professor LaRocque challenged commonly accepted theories about Aboriginal justice practices, upon which she said a number of restorative community justice projects operating in Canadian Aboriginal communities apparently had been based:

> In recent times, mediation programs have been promoted by various political interests, church organizations, and an overloaded criminal justice system; they have been adopted, and adapted largely by Aboriginal and other minority groups. It is understandable why these groups would be anxious for alternatives to the racist record of existing justice (and other) systems, and there is nothing inherently wrong with Natives' use of other traditions. The problem is not in borrowing, but in the confusion surrounding cultural and traditional values and their applications, particularly as they relate to the oppression of women and other victims of violence. Mediation programs do present untenable options for the oppressed (i.e., victims of violence) because the pendulum has swung way too far to the advantage of the oppressors (i.e., the offenders) within Native communities. And "culturally appropriate" definitions and applications are paving the way for a pattern of abandoning the oppressed to the oppressed.[52]

Despite concerns about victim participation in restorative processes, there is also wide interest in the ways victims may become more involved in the justice system. Giving crime victims a greater say in the justice system and addressing their needs, while at the same time holding offenders accountable for the harm caused by their actions, are goals shared by many people whose political leanings span a continuum from left to right.[53] But those supporting a heightened role for victims often have come with very different agendas. In an American context, co-authors Sharon Levrant, Francis Cullen, Betsy Fulton, and John Wozniak described the contrasting views, and hence the potentially divergent interests, of conservatives and liberals when viewing restorative justice. Liberals, they say, are more attracted to "restorative justice because of its potentially humanistic and balanced approach to justice."[54] This view sees justice as more than "offender-oriented penal harm," but rather as "community-oriented peacemaking" with a goal of reducing the suffering of offenders, victims and communities and of reducing crime.[55] Conservatives, on the other hand, view restorative justice as a furtherance of the victims' rights movement, promoting victim participation and compensation within the justice system. "In so doing, they often attempt to increase the punishment of offenders at the expense of restoration."[56]

The last decade, across North American and overseas, has seen the influence of victims increase significantly within the criminal justice system. In his book *The Culture of Control: Crime and Social Order in Contemporary Society*, Professor David Garland of New York University described a number of changes within the British and American justice systems in the 1980s and 1990s. Many of these, he said, have involved the role and position of victims vis-à-vis both the overall system and the offender:

> The need to reduce the present or future suffering of victims functions today as an all-purpose justification for measures of penal repression, and the political imperative of being responsive to victims' feelings now serves to reinforce the retributive sentiments that increasingly inform penal legislation.... The sanctification of victims also tends to nullify concern for offenders. The zero sum relationship that is now assumed to hold between the one and the other ensures that any show of compassion for offenders, any invocation of their rights, any effort to humanize their punishments, can easily be represented as insult to victims and their families.[57]

The changing role of victims within the criminal justice system raises the sometimes tricky question of how victims are to become involved in restorative practices, and also a broader initial question of how a victim is to be defined in the first place. Just as most people have committed a criminal offence sometime in their lives (whether they have been charged or not), so too have most people been the victim of one or more criminal acts. The reality we see in court, week after week, is that many of our clients are victims one week, and then offenders the next. While recognizing the restorative processes are not for all victims, and hence no victim should be forced to meet and negotiate with an offender, it equally important that information about the potential benefits of restorative approaches be shared with victims, allowing this to be a viable option if interest is shown.

Restorative Justice and Community Empowerment

Another point of debate about restorative and community justice initiatives is found in the relationship between individual initiatives and the formal structures of the criminal justice system. Rather than representing a sharing or devolution of power, many initiatives quickly become established parts of the criminal justice system, and are controlled by the same decision-makers who regulate the existing formal structures within the justice system. This has led some observers to describe the evolution of community justice projects as representing more a process of co-option than of collaboration.[58] This raises the spectre of whether such community justice programs represent something new and innovative or rather just more of the same within the formalized processes of the justice system.

In considering the question of how, and if, power is being devolved to community justice projects, a study of the sentencing initiatives in six Aboriginal communities of Manitoba and Saskatchewan found much interest among local Aboriginal communities in assuming some of the decision-making authority previously held solely by police, lawyers, and judges within the justice system. Donald McKay, Jr., a Cree man from Cumberland House, Saskatchewan, in discussing the cases being referred to that community's community justice committee by the court, expressed the hope that they would be allowed to consider more serious cases (either for purposes of alternative measures or providing a sentencing recommendation back to the court).

> I guess I questioned the judge a couple of times on what kind of cases we could deal with. I guess the far more serious cases, say assault and stuff like that, are too serious for us, according to the judge or court system, to deal with. But we've been dealing with, say, breaking and enter, mischief, damage of property, and cases like that. Assault charges, maybe, between two young people, stuff like that we've been dealing with. But far more serious assault charges where a weapon was used, those ones we haven't been able to deal with.... [However], I keep saying this—I've probably said it ten times—but we are the ones that live here in this community. We are the ones that have to live with these people that commit crimes. And I think we as a community should be dealing with them.[59]

Closely tied to the question of how much power is devolved from controlling forces in the justice system bureaucracy to the local level is whether so-called community justice initiatives have a primary focus that is restorative in nature, or whether their main focus is to take back control of decision-making from the professionals in the conventional justice system. This is complex question as both restorative and community-empowerment goals may be motivating factors. The sentencing study referred to above raised concerns about imbalances between the amount of attention and support resources being provided to victims within sentencing circles being conducted in northern Saskatchewan and Manitoba.

This is only one example of why caution is required in interpreting and understanding the advantages and disadvantages of allowing local community members a greater involvement in determining sanctions for acts which previously would have been the sole control of a judge at court.

The overall goal of restorative processes is a safer community which would best be achieved by a reconciliation between offender and victim, and a reconciliation of the torn relationship between an offender and his or her community. This raises the obvious need for restorative processes to address how a specific offender might best be reintegrated back into the community. Community interest in reintegration would appear to be more easily achieved in a small closely knit community than in a large diverse one. In the context of family group conferencing, New Zealand Professor Murray Levine contrasted the traditional small Maori community with an urban environment that he suggests detracts from a sense of community responsibility required for reintegration.

> The dense social networks in small face-to-face groups stand in contrast to the many independent social networks and settings in which individuals interact (neighbourhood, leisure, work, church, friendship, community organizations, age, gender, etc.). Dispersion of participation in many single purpose networks may make the restoration of harmony after a breach far less important. Dispersion may undercut the sense of communal responsibility.[60]

But an urban context does not exclude the possibility of a clearly defined community, and a justice process that seeks reintegration within that community as a goal. In *R. v. Morin*,[61] Justice Milliken conducted a sentencing circle for a Métis man living in Saskatoon. His Lordship considered whether there was an identifiable community "interested in helping" this offender "change his life-style." He concluded that the Métis people of Saskatoon were such a community, and proceeded to conduct a sentencing circle involving a cross section of people including the offender, victim, police, and assorted community members.

Although an urban environment is by definition broader and more diverse than a small community, the possibility of achieving a coordinated and supportive community within a city environment is evidenced by the Aboriginal Legal Services of Toronto. This organization provides assistance to Aboriginal people within Canada's largest urban centre, including court advocacy and support, a legal aid clinic, and a community council. The operation of this council shows how community support can be focused in an urban context:

The Community Council is a criminal diversion program for adult Aboriginal offenders who live in Toronto. The project takes Aboriginal offenders out of the criminal justice system and brings them before members of the Aboriginal community. The members of the Council are men and women who represent a cross-section of Toronto's Aboriginal community. The focus of the Community Council is to develop a plan by consensus that will allow the offender to take responsibility for his/her actions, address the root causes of the problem, an reintegrate him/her into the community in a positive way. The concept of the Community Council is not new—it is the way justice was delivered in Aboriginal communities in Central and Eastern Canada for centuries before the arrival of Europeans to North America and also the way that disputes continue to be informally resolved in many reserve communities across the country. This is the first project to apply these principles in an urban setting.[62]

Spirituality and Justice

In considering new philosophies and approaches to justice, a further consideration is whether justice can be said to encompass more than just physical and psychological aspects. Does justice involve a spiritual element as well? This is a complex issue, the consideration of which may lead to more questions than to answers. Indeed, religious freedom is thought to be a deeply personal right in our society. As the primary example, the freedom of conscience and religion is imbedded as a fundamental freedom in section 2(a) of the Canadian *Charter of Rights and Freedoms.*

The links and symbolism between the Judeo-Christian faith and our criminal justice system are obvious, with the Bible present in each Canadian courtroom, and the normal practice being that witnesses are initially asked to swear on the Bible, saying the words: "I swear to tell the truth, the whole truth, and nothing but the truth so help me God." The prominence of Judeo-Christian symbolism in our courts raises an interesting question. One of the underlying tenets of the Christian faith is we should not take "an eye for eye." Yet the converse of this appears to apply within the justice system, as we impose pain and punishment in response to criminal actions. This latter philosophy and practice is perhaps epitomized by the oft-repeated phrase, "if you're old enough to do the crime, you're old enough to the time."

In contrast to the religious acknowledgement followed in conventional Canadian courts, sentencing circles held in Canadian Aboriginal communities have usually begun with a traditional prayer or ceremony representative of that peoples' religious, spiritual, and cultural heritage. This may include a sweet grass ceremony or a prayer offered in an Aboriginal tongue. In discussing the evolution of circle sentencing within Aboriginal communities, Justice Murray Sinclair of the Manitoba Court of Queen's Bench stressed the importance, from the viewpoint of local community members, of any justice process addressing the spiritual beliefs and traditions of that community. He said that while the English common law came to equate the monarchy (or Crown in today's language) with the deity, Aboriginal people more often came to hold a world view that respected the Creator at the centre of their being. Therefore, in acknowledging their spiritual beliefs, ceremonial openings or prayers include a recognition and statement of their responsibility to the Creator to find peace within their community.[63]

A further consideration is the extent to which justice processes encompass a sense of aura and mystique. Justice Sinclair also commented on how rituals are commonly used in conventional Canadian courtrooms (such as the robes worn by judges, or the way court is opened) to create and continue an aura of mystery among those people appearing or attending court. If these rituals were stripped away, he suggested, the court would lose much of its ability to impress these people.[64] Indeed there is a delicate and complex relationship between the processes adopted in court, the religious beliefs of specific communities, and the spiritual or mystical element present in any justice process.

Regardless of the formalities or ceremonial aspects of religion that may form part of the justice system, there is also a question of whether there is a spiritual connection and interaction between people involved in a truly restorative process. This will obviously be a very controversial subject. But we have both, in our involvement within the criminal system, seen and felt what might, to some, be called a sense of intimacy, and to others a sense of spiritual connection, arise between victims and offenders and others in attendance at restorative proceedings.[65] This connection between restorative processes and spirituality was explored by authors Denise Breton and Stephen Lehman in *The Mystic Heart of Justice*. This book argued in favour of rejecting "the paradigm of external control of society found in the retributive model prevalent" in our courts, and the "reward-punishment model for success established in society."[66] The authors, in the alternative, turn to the promising opportunities of the restorative justice paradigm, "exploring justice as a matter of spirit rather than a matter of law."[67]

Perhaps the spiritual elements of justice are best defined through experiences and insights that occur during justice processes. In 2001, a case at Carrot River, Saskatchewan demonstrated this. It involved a prolonged and violent fight at a drinking party on one of the local First Nations. Eighteen people had been charged in this melee. Almost all were both charged with assault and were victims of assault themselves. One man almost died of his injuries after being airlifted to hospital. At the sentencing of all offenders (who were both adults and young offenders), this man told the assembled circle what this incident had meant to his life, which had to that point had been characterized largely by alcohol abuse. By sparing him, this man said he believed God had given him and his family a second chance. Suddenly, it became obvious that this proceeding was more than just the public hearing about a party gone terribly wrong. This man was sharing his story, as a testimonial to the mistakes he had made but also as a statement of the spiritual path he and his family had embarked upon. Perhaps that is how the spirit appears in justice matters, as a reminder that everyone deserves a second chance, no matter what they have done. The spiritual elements of justice will certainly mean different things to different people, but there was a spiritual component to that proceeding at Carrot River.

Many would argue that a spiritual element underlies our entire understanding and practice of justice. Indeed, we see a spiritual presence in many places within the justice system. We see it in the chance of restoring torn relationships between people, and in the hope that offenders and victims will somehow find a healing presence emerging from their anger and grief. We feel it when we question why we are jailing young people and adults rather than looking for alternatives which will address the root causes of their behaviour. And we understand it when we hear a man tell us that God has given him and his family a second chance.

Case Study: Calgary Community Conferencing

In 1998, in a city often thought to be the nucleus of "get tough" opinions about crime and punishment in Canada, Calgary Community Conferencing (CCC) was created, initially as part of a Master of Social Work program before being operated part time by Calgary Youth Probation Services, and then in 1999 expanded through an interagency partnership formed between four sponsoring organizations: City of Calgary Youth Probation Services, the Calgary Board of Education, the Calgary John Howard Society, and the Mennonite Central Committee. Each of these organizations seconded staff to the conferencing project. Probation officer Doug Borch was the initial staff member of CCC, and explained how this organization emerged from an unconventional relationship between government (or system) agencies and nongovernmental (or community) organizations:

> Generally speaking, system driven programs don't have a whole lot of legitimacy in the community because they are seen as another top heavy program from government. At the same time I am not so sure that, generally speaking, community based programs have a whole lot of credibility within the system. The result is that you have these two things that kind of pass in the night with kids, their families, victims and the larger community lost in the middle somewhere. When we started CCC, we really wanted to make an effort to bring representatives from those two generic streams to the same table. So we have a strong organizational structure that is not just a probation program or not just a school board program. It's a true collaboration of these four primary organizations that represent the heavy systems of justice/probation and the school board with their respective bureaucracies but then you've also got these grass roots nonprofit organizations with their own board of directors.[68]

In addition to the sponsoring organizations, the Calgary Police Service, Calgary Family Services, and the University of Calgary Faculty of Social Work are considered partnering organizations providing consultation and resources to the program and its participants. An advisory board of management-level representatives from the sponsoring and partnering organizations assists CCC with the development of funding proposals and with navigating systemic and organizational issues. Financial contributions for this program have been received from the federal Department of Justice, the Alberta Solicitor General, the Calgary Foundation, the United Way of Calgary, and the Alberta Law Foundation.[69]

Staff members of CCC conduct restorative conferences after receiving referrals from two sources. Referrals may come from the youth court following a guilty plea as a pre-sentence measure or from public school administrators to re-establish safety in the school community. The referrals from youth court specifically target high-impact offences where the young person is likely to receive a jail sentence; school referrals target serious incidents where the student is likely to be suspended or expelled.[70] Conferences are usually held at community halls, on weekends, and average three to four hours in length. Two CCC facilitators are involved in each conference. Doug Borch summarized a typical conference:

> People speak one at a time, we put pads of paper and pens in the middle of the circle and encourage folks to keep track of questions or details they want to come back to. The facilitator uses questions to guide the

conference. We've already spent a lot of time with all the participants ahead of time to help them sort through what they hoping the get from the experience. The incident may have happened twelve months ago and they need some real help to figure out what they did and recall the sequencing. After everybody has had a chance to speak there's been made room for discussion then the kid and their supporters which is usually their families and the probation officer or social worker (if they are at child welfare status) or their counsellor or neighbour or whoever they have with them, go into a separate room. The kid comes up with a proposal for the victims so he comes back with five things based on what he has heard them say throughout the afternoon and he presents it back as opposed to sort of a group decision making thing which in my experience gets very adult heavy and very preachy really quickly....[71]

As noted, the process requires an offender, after proceeding through the initial stages of a conference, to come up with a proposal about how they might help and compensate the victim. Doug Borch described the importance of allowing youth time to consider their own response with an example:

A kid was part of a really nasty break and enter where this woman was sound asleep and woke up to see two girls standing over top of her. They didn't realize she was in the bed and suddenly she wakes up, screams, they scream, and out they go. It was a horrific experience and this woman described bluntly how the incident had impacted her. She was having nightmares and she couldn't get to sleep. After hearing her talk about not being able to sleep the young girl had time to consider what she'd heard. She offered to buy the woman a pair of fluffy flannel pajamas as her way of saying, "I now understand that I took your sleep and I hope you can get it back." Now, I don't think a kid is going to come up with that in the original room full of adults who are all going to have their own ideas about what she should do.[72]

The organization of youth court and family services court in Calgary, together with the structure of Crown prosecutor, legal aid defence counsel, and youth probation services, contributed to the development and expansion of CCC. Calgary Family and Youth Court is presided over by eight to ten judges who hear all youth justice and child welfare matters. Calgary also has a single youth legal aid office, with eight to ten lawyers handling up to 80 percent of the cases in youth court. The Crown is represented by the same four or five prosecutors who work exclusively in youth court. Finally, youth probation in Calgary is run by the City of Calgary out of its social services department, as opposed to the provincial justice department. As a result, all youth probation officers are social workers, with a minimum qualification of a bachelor of social work degree. Doug Borch described how all of these factors provided an ideal environment in which to attempt a restorative approach to justice:

> All these factors coming together, a social work approach to probation, consistent judges, lawyers and social workers at youth court lead to strong working relationships. Judges sit in Family Court and so they will deal with a kid when he's ten and he's been apprehended by Child Welfare and they have a pretty good understanding of the dynamics that have led this kid to this [criminal] court room when he is fourteen.[73]

At the start of this conferencing project, Borch approached a number of youth court judges, asking them to consider referrals for a restorative conference before sentencing. He believes his credibility with these judges was an asset, as they already knew and trusted him as a youth probation officer. As a result, the youth court judges began referring cases. From its creation in 1998 to the summer of 2002, CCC has conducted over 140 conferences involving over 1,500 participants, including youth, victims, their respective supporters, relevant professionals, and others from the community.

CCC receives roughly half of its referrals from schools. CCC facilitator Gail Daniels was seconded from the Calgary Board of Education in 1999. During a conference on restorative youth conferencing in Halifax, Nova Scotia in February 2002, she described how school administrators had come to favour the approach used by CCC. In the past, she said, a schoolyard fight had two likely results. One was that police would investigate and lay charges, and another was that at least one child would be suspended. A number of people working within the school system came to see that what was missing in the scenario was a sense of learning from this mistake for the youths involved. Conferencing came to be viewed as a way of letting these youths learn from their mistakes, but also as a way of formalizing a plan about how these often high-risk youths could return to school, while avoiding the criminal process.

The conferences held to date would appear to have had a positive effect on both offenders and victims.[74] Doug Borch said the major impact on offenders is to provide opportunities for them to hear and understand the harm they caused to the victim. Daphne Buffet, a probation officer who has referred a number of youths for CCC, said these conferences made the offence more real for kids as they must meet face to face with their victims. Borch said a conference takes the focus off the offender and places it on the victim and other affected people. It allows the offender to hear first hand the effect of his or her crime, directly from the victim. Offenders also hear from their own family members about how an offence by their son or grandson has affected their life. One conference involved a boy who had robbed two other boys of five dollars, while pointing an imitation pistol at them. Doug Borch described how, during that conference, the young offender sat and listened to his grandmother's reaction to his crime:

> He heard his grandma talk about how disappointed and really disgusted she was with what he did. Now she very clearly separated what he did from who he was. She scolded him: "That you would hold someone up—that happens on TV or in the movies—you held those guys up at gunpoint and you poked a gun in their chest!" She talked about what it was like to stand in court on a very busy Monday morning with all kinds of other people in court while her grandson entered in shackles, and when the charge was read out, people in the courtroom went "ooh." Now he may have heard some of her reaction over the dinner table at home, but there is something different about hearing it in a more public forum.[75]

Regarding victims, youth probation officer Daphne Buffet explained how victims attending a conference want the opportunity to address their fears by asking the offender questions about what happened, and also want the chance to say what they want from the offender as a way of restoration.

> They can have questions answered, like: Why my house? Why did you go in this room in my house? Why did you target my house particularly? Those kinds of questions that they are able to get answers to and for the most part find out that it was generally a pretty random act so I think the main thing for them is to get answers. The other piece that they say is important for them is to make things right with the person who has offended against them. Sometimes in youth court they may be ordered compensation or probation, but that may not be what the victim needs or wants. Being in a conference offers the opportunity to say what is going to make it right for them.[76]

Conferences often lead to a sense of healing between the parties. Daphne Buffet said she had seen relationships repaired where offenders have offended against someone they knew and there has been no communication between the families since the offence. She said she has seen this friendship restored through the conference, and believes this was a powerful experience. Borch described how relationships built between offenders and victims during a conference may result in the victim speaking on behalf of the offender at sentencing. He gave one example of a boy charged in an incident where he threatened a bus driver with an imitation gun on a city bus. It was an emotional conference in which the bus driver told the offender how this offence had affected his life. The driver said he no longer bothered to ask for fares from passengers because it was not worth getting shot over, and also said he had lost most of his pride in his work. But through the restorative process of this conference, the bus driver ended up appearing with this youth during his sentencing, and told the judge, "You know, I've got kids of my own and I see kids every day and I just don't think this is one that needs to go to jail."[77] As a result, this youth did not receive a custodial sentence, despite the severity of the offence.

But reconciliation with the offender may not be the reason a victim chooses to attend a conference. In addition to addressing their fears and having their questions answered by the offender, Doug Borch said many victims simply want acknowledgement of the harm caused by the offender. He explained this point by describing a conference which had brought together three youths who had assaulted an elderly woman on her front walk and stolen her purse, leaving her on the ground:

> This woman was absolutely traumatized. What the boys didn't know was that she had a rare blood disorder and had she cut herself she could have bled out on the doorstep. In her purse was experimental medication for a double blind study she was participating in. It was two days before Christmas and the trial medication could not be bought a pharmacy. Everything has shut down for a week and a half and she's lost all of her medication for a week and a half so aside from the physical impact on her, her doctor was very upset because it impacted this important study.
>
> [For the victim] the immediate thing was these guys lived in her geographic community and knew where she lived. She didn't want anything else from these guys. She didn't want them to cut the grass, she didn't want them to do her walks. She never wanted to see them again. She was very clear about that. In her words, "I'm not doing this because I want to be your buddy, I'm doing this because I need you to know what you did to me and I need to know that you're not coming back at me." She was very clear in asking those questions and these boys just sat and listened—for her it was about acknowledgement and safety.[78]

In most cases where conferences don't proceed, it is because victims are not willing or able to participate. In the few cases where CCC conferences haven't proceeded because of circumstances of the offender, it is usually because a youth is not taking responsibility for the crime, or is simply not able to discuss what happened. Borch said sometimes troubled

youths are so engrossed with their own family issues and personal trou-
bles that they just "shut down," and aren't able to face the victim. He described how invasive a process a conference can be for a troubled youth,
who may be more comfortable appearing in youth court than participating in a conference:

> There have been cases where the kids are just so in deep with their other
> stuff, family stuff, they're just shut down. In those cases I wonder if
> those kids are even capable at that point because they've shielded them-
> selves to such a degree that when we come in and start talking about
> meeting with people face to face which is really an entirely invasive proc-
> ess for the kid, they're used to the court dealing with everything for
> them. The lawyers speak on their behalf and now we're talking about
> sitting in a room on a Sunday morning and you're going to have to walk
> through in minute detail. For some kids, they just say "I can't do it, I'd
> rather go and take my lumps at court." The other significant factor is
> when kids are not supported in the conference process. In our experi-
> ence, this is the greater concern. Being accountable is hard work for any
> of us. But to be the only youth in a room of angry and upset adults is a
> big deal.[79]

Borch said such cases create a real dilemma for CCC facilitators where
they have a victim quite willing to participate and wanting to tell the offender about the pain this offence has caused them. As one victim who
wanted to participate in the conference told Borch:

> I'm not doing this for him to feel better or worse. In fact at this point I
> don't really care about him. I care that my six year old can't sleep in her
> own bed. That's my concern and I need to look this guy in the eye and I
> need to tell him.[80]

But the chance of any form of reconciliation between offender and victim, or at least acknowledgement by the offender, is limited if the youth
refuses to acknowledge responsibility for the offence. Likewise, poor or
inconsistent support for the youth can limit the young person's ability to
follow through on the commitments he or she makes. CCC does not proceed to conference without the involvement of people directly affected by
the incident. This need not be the person named as the victim on the
police report, however there must be some direct impact on the person.

Another issue in restorative conferencing is whether power imbalances
exist between the participants. This concern has been raised by Aboriginal women's groups in the context of sentencing circles being used in cases
of spousal assault.[81] In the context of youth justice conferencing, there are
issues about inherent power imbalances both between youths and adults,

but also between victims and offenders. Doug Borch explained his experience with these imbalances:

> You've got this initial imbalance generally speaking around kid offenders, adult victims, but then you've got this mirror-image thing around kids offending, being in my underwear drawer and my feeling completely vulnerable whether I'm an adult or not. So there's almost a dual imbalance. I guess we are always aware of it and try to be as aware and challenge ourselves and in our team meetings. It's all about picking apart referrals and conferences. What about this, and what about that. What we have tried to do is name it, and be very up front with people if something is feeling uncomfortable. We need to talk about what that is and really try to build in supports for the people in the conference.[82]

Conferences at CCC are not specifically focused on making sentencing recommendations. However, results of what happened at conferences have been referred to and incorporated by judges when sentencing youths who have participated in a conference. An example of the impressive work being done by CCC, and of the effect these conferences can ultimately have on the disposition rendered in court, can be seen in the case *R. v. B.J.K.*[83] As Judge Cook-Stanhope of the Provincial Court of Alberta (Youth Division) recounted, this young person pleaded guilty to a serious robbery at a convenience store, as well as two other related charges. Together with a co-accused, B.J.K., while armed with a knife, accosted two clerks at the store and then stole cash and other merchandise. Before sentencing, the case was referred to CCC for two conferences which involved the offender together with the two youthful clerks, and then subsequently the offender together with the owner of the convenience store.

These conferences produced a proposal for restoration by the young offender, which included direct apologies to the store owner and to the young clerks' parents, payment of $1,700 to the owner, frequent reporting to the store owner by the youth about his progress, help in installing an alley light and security gate at the store, and an invitation for the store owner to attend his disposition hearing. At that hearing, the store owner praised the CCC process, and argued against a custody term for this youth:

> I think that this community conferencing was quite a benefit to me as well as to [the young person]. I think it's a programme, it should be something that should be done on a regular basis. I felt a sincerity from [the young person]. At the same time I feel that you do the crime, you should do whatever needs to be done to pay for what you've done. I don't feel like prison would be a good option for him. ...And that is because it's just a sense that I have that if he goes there, he may become

like some of the hardened people that are in that system right now. And I don't feel that he is a hardened criminal. I think that this is a first thing for him, and I don't think that prison would benefit.[84]

In rejecting the Crown's request for custody, Judge Cook-Stanhope described "a growing sensitivity in our courts to the needs of individuals and communities, who fall victim to criminal offences, to have a voice in the sentencing process."[85] She said this "represents a subtle, but clear shift away from historical approaches to crime and criminality: a move from the mere identification and punishment of offenders by means intended to stop criminal behaviour, to an acknowledgement of not only the causes, but the effects of crime on society and on individuals."[86] She described attempts at encouraging participation within the justice system, with "joint purposes of discouraging criminal behaviour and reconciling the harm done by it."[87]

> A recognition of these dual purposes is an obvious part of the philosophy of the Calgary Community Conferencing Programme, and my examination of the role it has played in a number of cases, before and including the present one, compels me to conclude that a restoration approach within the disposition process for young offenders can and often does have startling results.
>
> It follows that the results of a conference may have a dramatic impact on the eventual disposition imposed. I believe that the imposition of a custodial disposition is only one way to address the traditional aspects of sentencing. Programmes such as the one which was undertaken in the present case, when employed in a proper case, are sufficiently flexible to address most if not all of the expectations of a fit disposition. I am satisfied that the young person's participation in the conferences I have just described justifies a non-custodial disposition.[88]

This is only one example of how a program like CCC, and its restorative approach, can result in a process and disposition that avoids the often damaging effects of custody, but that also holds the young person accountable and provides satisfaction and recompense for the victim.[89] The next chapter considers a number of new and progressive approaches that provide hope towards achieving the goals of reducing youth crime, making our communities safer, and ensuring a fair and supportive youth justice system.

"Instead of looking at you as a criminal, all of them cops, lawyers, judges and youth workers should get to know your good side and get to know what's wrong, and why are you behaving the way you are."

Progressive Approaches to Youth Crime and Justice

Quebec—A Study in Contrast

A number of realities set the Quebec youth justice system apart from the rest of Canada. Most significantly, Quebec has far fewer cases in its youth court system than most other Canadian provinces. Statistics from 2000/2001 show Quebec had a young offender court case rate of 18 cases per thousand youth. This compares a national rate of 41/1,000, and rates as high as 124/1,000 in the Yukon, 94/1,000 in Saskatchewan, 82/1,000 in the Northwest Territories, 71/1,000 in Nunavut, and 68/1,000 in Manitoba.[1] The relatively low rate in Quebec is, in turn, a major contributor to the fact that Quebec sends fewer youths (per capita) to custody than any other Canadian province. In 2000/2001, Quebec had a rate of 4 youths per thousand sentenced to custody, in contrast to the national rate of 8/1,000 and provincial rates including 37/1,000 in the Northwest Territories, 28/1,000 in the Yukon, and 21/1,000 in Saskatchewan.[2]

Despite this lower per capita custody rate, it is interesting, however, that the percentage of Quebec youth sent to custody (out of all those who end up appearing in youth court) is similar to the rest of Canada. In 2000/2001, 22.6 percent of youth court cases resulted in custody, compared to 20.1 percent for the whole of Canada.[3] This reflects a reality that a large percentage of cases are dealt with outside of the Quebec youth court system. With only the more serious cases going to court, the bar is in effect set at a higher level for those appearing in court, but far fewer of the less serious cases see the inside of a courtroom.

The number of cases diverted from the court process, however, is not the only explanation of the lower case-rate in court and a lower per capita custody rate for young offenders. Another major factor underlying these realities is that the overall crime rate is lower in Quebec than most places in Canada. In 2001, Quebec had a crime rate of 5,869 criminal offences per 100,000 population (both youth and adults) compared to a national average of 7,747/100,000. The highest was the Northwest Territories at 30,149/100,000 and the lowest was Newfoundland at 5,635/100,000. By comparison, Saskatchewan's crime rate was 13,458/100,000.[4]

During a House of Commons debate on the proposed *YCJA*, in speaking against the more punitive elements of the proposed Act, Member of Parliament Claude Bachand (Saint-Jean) linked this low provincial crime rate to a Quebec system focused more on rehabilitation than on punishment.

> In other words the youth crime rate in Quebec is lower than in Ontario, Manitoba and British Columbia. The reason is that: Quebeckers consider the youth justice system more as a rehabilitative process. We have to get the young offenders back into society. The bill before the House does just the opposite. It would throw these young people in jail. And as everyone knows, prison is a school for crime.
>
> In prison, 14 year old kids are living among older criminals for whom it is perhaps harder to get back into society because of their age. For a 40 or 50 year old man who has been a killer all his life, rehabilitation is less likely. Of course, Quebec will try to give him a chance, but the most important thing is to give young offenders the opportunity to redeem themselves. Throwing them in jail with hard core criminals would defeat the purpose. Statistics show that Quebec has a higher rehabilitation rate among young offenders because we have come to realize that these young people need support and supervision, not jail time.[5] [translation from French]

The Quebec youth justice system has a number of unique features. One is how cases progress through it, after initial contact between a police officer and a youth. If the incident is not handled by a referral or warning on the street, the officer's report is sent to the Crown. A prosecutor then determines whether there is sufficient evidence to allow a prosecution to proceed. If so, for the majority of offences, the Crown refers the youth's case directly to the youth centre governing that part of Quebec for a decision on whether the case should be diverted for alternative measures, returned to the Crown for prosecution, or simply closed and no further action taken. This process contrasts to that followed in most other Canadian provinces, where decisions on whether offences are to be dealt with by extrajudicial measures are taken either by the police or by Crown prosecutors.

There are seventeen youth centres across Quebec. Each has overall responsibility for both child protection and young offender services, although these are dealt with by separate arms of the youth centre. Upon receiving a file from the Crown, a social worker reviews the file and then meets with the youth and his or her parents or guardians. The social worker also considers a report about the victim prepared by alternate justice organizations called des Organismes de Justice Alternative (OJA), covering the geographical area where the offence happened. After this file review and meeting, the youth centre social worker decides whether to close the file, refer the case back to the Crown for court prosecution, or refer the case to an OJA for extrajudicial measures. In making this decision, the social worker considers whether the youth accepts responsibility for the incident and whether that youth is willing to repair the damage done. The social worker also considers the circumstances and attitude of the youth, and the issue of whether the young person represents a risk to the community.[6] If the social worker decides to refer a youth to alternative measures, the social worker, in determining what type of measures would be appropriate, considers whether such a referral would represent a benefit to the victim (through such means as financial restitution, personal service, an apology or face to face mediation), a benefit to the community (through community service work) or a benefit to the offender (through such means as skills development, other integration programming or counselling).[7]

Charges dealt with outside of the court system are handled largely by OJAs. OJAs are community nongovernmental organizations that receive youth referrals both before and after charges are laid. Serge Charbonneau, head of ROJAQ (an umbrella organization representing OJAs across Quebec), described how community organizations first came to be involved in diversion of charges, after passage of the Quebec *Youth Protection Act* in 1979. In 1984, when the *Young Offenders Act* came into force, there were five OJAs in Quebec. Only a year later, this had mushroomed to thirty-six organizations. Currently, there are thirty-nine of these organizations in Quebec. The number of youth dealt with by the network of OJAs has also increased dramatically. In 1984, a total of eight hundred youth in trouble with the criminal law were referred to the existing OJAs. In 2001, twelve thousand youth were referred to these organizations: 60 percent for purposes of alternative measures from the youth centres, and 40 percent from court for purposes of community service work, offender programming, and in some cases, extrajudicial measures.[8]

The first OJA organized in Quebec was Trajet Jeunesse in Montreal.

This organization grew out of a program begun by two university students in 1980. The original goal of this committee was to provide appropriate interventions for minor youth offences, outside of the court system. The members of this committee carried a reparative focus, looking for types of community service work in which youths could participate. Eventually Trajet Jeunesse grew and took on paid staff. As a sign of its growth, youth worker Michel Côté described how Trajet Jeunesse had dealt with between four hundred and five hundred youth in 1984–85, and how this had grown to fourteen hundred youth per year by 2002.[9]

Trajet Jeunesse follows a philosophy based on the importance of keeping youth out of the court system. Indeed, they appear to be successful, as recent recidivism statistics showed that only 4 percent of youth involved with this organization reoffended.[10] In accomplishing its mandate, Trajet Jeunesse conducts a range of programs into which youth are placed depending, to some extent, on their age and circumstance and the offence they have committed.[11] These programs include a coordination of community service work (performed by youths who are matched with appropriate community agencies and organizations) and also a variety of programs conducted at Trajet Jeunesse called Social Responsibility Awareness Measures. These programs are presented by youth workers, and include sessions in which youths are instructed and challenged on issues around their crime and the effects of their actions. Another option provided by this OJA is having young people make a monetary donation to a charitable organization of their choice. This option requires the youth to meet with a person from that organization who explains the organization's objectives, its nature, and the use that will be made of the youth's donation.[12]

A recent agreement between the parent body for youth centres in Quebec and the ROJAQ shows the increasing role of victims in the Quebec youth justice system. Upon receiving a file from the Crown, the youth centre now immediately sends a copy of the file to the OJA closest to the occurrence. A youth worker from that OJA then contacts the victim, who is asked first whether they would be open to participate in some form of alternative measures with the youth; second, if the matter proceeded to court whether they would like information about the case as it progresses; and finally, whether there is anything they would like to say to the judge hearing this case, should it proceed to court. The OJA youth worker then prepares a report summarizing the victim's response, and sends this back to the youth centre social worker, who considers this report in conjunction with other information on the file, and the meeting with the youth involved.[13]

Similar to the other OJAs across Quebec, programming at Trajet Jeunesse now shows an interesting progression towards a greater recognition of victims. Youth worker Michel Côté indicated that initially the organization's programs focused almost solely on community service work, and programming for youth such as life skills and offender awareness sessions. Beginning around 1997, however, this OJA began to do victim-offender mediations. Mr. Côté said that process absolutely "took off."[14]

In attempting to understand the youth justice system in Quebec, it is important to realize that not any one factor or approach is unique to Quebec. Indeed, many other provinces feature programming that supports views about youth justice advocated in Quebec. As well, in Quebec there is not necessarily a monolithic view about youth justice issues and approaches. As an example of this, Michel Côté described an alternative measures program called Reparado which he said arose out of public cynicism about the effectiveness of community service work for offending youth. This cynicism is comparable to public commentary on youth justice measures we have heard elsewhere in Canada. The Reparado program (modelled after a similar one at the Egadz Youth Centre in Saskatoon) now allows youth to earn money, part of which is sent to the victim as compensation, suggesting a more direct link between accountability by the offender for his or her actions and reparation directed to the victim.[15]

Although there is no single or unanimous view of youth justice in Quebec—reflecting the unavoidable diversity of public opinion existing in any society—the particular emphasis placed on a clinical and rehabilitative approach to youth justice in Quebec distinguishes its youth justice system from others in Canada, especially those west of Quebec.

A number of factors—many of them historic—have contributed to the distinctiveness of the Quebec youth justice system.[16] Key amongst these is that alternative measure programs were up and running in Quebec long before the *Young Offenders Act* came into force in 1984. This made for an easy transition from the *Juvenile Delinquents Act* to the *YOA* as the structures and schemes needed to put into action the alternative measures envisioned in section 4 of that Act were already in place. As a result, Quebec is now able to divert away from the youth court system a greater number of cases than most other provinces. For example, in 2000/2001, 9,836 cases appeared in Quebec youth court, while in 2001 7,200 cases were diverted away from court to alternative measures.[17]

The youth protection system in Quebec appears to be both more active and of wider jurisdiction than most provinces in Canada. Youths up to eighteen years of age can be apprehended by the state if found to be "in need of protection" under the *Youth Protection Act*.[18] This, then, leaves an alternative to the criminal system as a way of dealing with sixteen and seventeen year olds, many of whom would likely find themselves within the criminal system of other provinces had they resided there.[19]

The use of what appears to be a largely institutionalized child protection system might be one explanation of why Quebec's criminal custody numbers are so much lower the rest of Canada. However, it does not appear that the criminal and child protection systems have a great overlap. Professor Trepanier said that, as of 21 September 2002, the Montreal Youth Centre had responsibility for 7,797 youths. Two-thirds of this total (66.67 percent) were there as a result of child protection intervention, 15.04 percent as a result of criminal intervention under the *Young Offenders Act*, and the remaining youth were being dealt with outside both the criminal and child protection systems. It is interesting that only 2.92 percent of the youth—or 228 of the total number of youth of 7,797—had current open files in both the child protection and criminal systems. This suggests that, although there would appear to be a high level of integration between *YOA* (now *YCJA*) and child protection systems within the youth centre structure, there is little overlap between the actual criminal and child protection systems as they deal with specific youth.[20]

Professor Trepanier, however, expressed a concern that the *YCJA*, with its addition of a mandatory supervision order to follow custody (usually one-third of the total sentence), would likely have the effect of increasing the crossover of cases between the child protection and criminal youth systems. He believed that this statutory change would potentially reduce the average custody term, and hence the rehabilitative and clinical focus of services available in custody would be cut short. As a result, youths would be released at a point where there will have to be reliance on child protection services, which otherwise would not have occurred if the entire sentence (as under the *YOA*) had been completed.

Under the *JDA*, provinces were given the option of increasing the upper age limit of youths to be covered by the Act. Most provinces set the upper limit at sixteen years. Quebec set the ceiling at eighteen years.[21] As a result of including sixteen and seventeen year olds under the Quebec *JDA* system, there was little if any negative reaction to including these youth in the *Young Offenders Act* in Quebec, unlike the apparent backlash against this age group in English Canada, where these youths had largely been treated as adults.[22]

The other contrast between the situation in Quebec and that in the rest of Canada was regarding the minimum age of twelve established by the

YOA. Quebec's *Youth Protection Act*, which came into force in 1979, included a few dispositions that applied to juvenile delinquents. This legislation set the minimum age for prosecution under this Act at fourteen years. Professor Trepanier said there had been no constitutional challenge to this provision—although it dealt with some offences that might otherwise have been prosecuted under the *JDA*—and that there "did not appear to be any opposition to this policy, at least in public."[23] As a result, Quebeckers were not as concerned when in 1984 the minimum age was increased from seven years in the *JDA* to twelve in *YOA*. To the contrary, some people saw a problem "more in the sense of lowering the age from fourteen to twelve!"[24]

Clement Laporte, Director of Young Offender Act Services on the island of Montreal, said there is a clear consensus among police, justice officials, lawyers, and professionals employed in the youth centres that the focus of the youth justice system should be rehabilitative—and hence reflect an investment in youth—as opposed to being punitive. This view is obvious in a number of areas of the justice system, even extending to the custodial facilities, which are all named Rehabilitation Centres as opposed to Correctional Centres. As one indication of how prevailing views in Quebec may differ from the areas of Canada to the west, Mr. Laporte described a meeting held several years previous between senior Quebec justice officials and a parliamentary committee looking into youth justice issues. A Reform Party M.P. on the committee openly advocated a punitive view, essentially that if young people "were old enough to do the crime, they were old enough to the time." These comments were challenged by the Quebec officials at this meeting, who asked this M.P. to provide them with any evidentiary basis upon which to base his comments. Mr. Laporte said that this M.P., clearly under attack, fell silent for the remainder of this meeting.

One hypothesis to explain Quebeckers' differing attitudes might be that they are less influenced by the crime and punishment images and focus presented by American television. Professor Trepanier referred to a BBM survey in the spring of 1998, which found that Francophone Quebeckers (the overriding majority in Quebec) spent less than one-fifth as much time watching American television channels as did Anglophone Quebeckers. Whatever the explanation, people working in influential positions within the Quebec youth justice system appear to openly support a rehabilitative model and argue against a punitive one.

Another factor that appears to influence the rehabilitative and clinical philosophy prevalent in the Quebec youth justice system is a strong focus on university training for staff members working with youth. Professor Trepanier said this dated back to the 1950s. The Boscoville Youth Centre—from which a psycho-educational theory of youth rehabilitation emerged—promoted an interdisciplinary view toward young offenders, which resulted in, or from, a large percentage of its staff having a university degree in the social sciences. Mr. Trepanier said that the professionalization which occurred in custodial facilities also occurred in youth probation services. He knew this because he had initially worked as a youth probation officer after graduating from law school in 1966. By the 1980s, Mr. Trepanier said, most youth probation officers were university-trained. Similarly, Clement Laporte indicated that 85 percent of his youth centre's employees working with youth under the *YOA* were university-trained.

Another distinctive feature of the Quebec youth justice system appears to be a widely held and articulated view that specific types of rehabilitation programs are capable of and do in fact have positive effects on youth recidivism. This is an acknowledgement that would be uncommon among senior bureaucrats and politicians in English Canada. An example of empirical research on the efficacy of rehabilitative programming can be found in the writing of Professor Marc Le Blanc of the Université de Montreal. Professor Le Blanc argued against any suggestion that rehabilitative youth programming did not work, or that these programs were "ineffective and a waste of taxpayers' money."[25] After carefully analyzing the research surrounding three rehabilitative approaches to youth (described as psycho-educational, cognitive-behavioural, and cognitive-developmental approaches), he concluded that the psycho-educational approach is the most effective means of achieving young offender rehabilitation, if used in conjunction with techniques from the other two approaches.

The legal arguments against the new *YCJA* heard from Quebec were complex, but, on a practical level, three core criticisms—expressed by senior youth justice system officials and commentators interviewed in Montreal—can be described. First, a concern expressed by the justice system professionals interviewed was that the *YCJA* would reduce the average time of custodial sentences to a point that no effective rehabilitative programming could take place. It was suggested this would happen as a result of mandatory community supervision for the last third of each custodial sentence, and through mandatory credit given for time on remand. Quebec had already experienced a move in this direction, as in 1984/85 11 percent of this province's youth custody sentences were for less than one month. But by 2000/01, this figure had grown to 27 percent.[26] It was feared that the changes being brought by the *YCJA* would exacerbate this situation by handcuffing the ability of custody institutions to provide effective programming and rehabilitation. Hence, the custodial facilities would become detention centres, where youth are warehoused, as opposed to their previous existence as rehabilitation centres. Clement Laporte said he viewed between six and seven months as the minimum time required in custody to effect any meaningful rehabilitation with a youth. He viewed between fifteen and eighteen months as the upper limit, after which programming had little rehabilitative effect.[27]

A second criticism was that the *YCJA*'s focus on violent youth resulted in a type of labelling against youth charged with violent offences. Hence the nature of the charge, rather than the circumstances and prognosis of the youth, becomes the major governing factor in how the youth is dealt with under the Act. Clearly, these provisions in the *YCJA* are viewed as limiting the clinical discretion, which has apparently been used with some success in the Quebec youth justice system.

A final concern about the *YCJA*, which appeared to go hand in hand with increasing similarities between the processes used in the adult justice system, was expressed by Judge Ann-Marie Jones of the Quebec Youth Court. Judge Jones worried about the issue of timely treatment of youths facing the youth court, and noted that youths generally have a far different perception of time than adults. This necessitates that interventions happen sooner than later for the best interests of the child. She viewed *YOA* youth court process in her court as relatively quick. But she was concerned that this might not remain so under the new legislation. In particular, she cited the new process of preliminary hearings for some youth brought before the court. This process is similar, if not identical, to the process used for adults under the *Criminal Code*. She believed that much of the legitimate strategical manoeuvring used by defence lawyers in adult court, largely around the use of preliminary hearings as a means of finding holes in the Crown case, would become a common feature in youth court. Taken together, she thought the changes to the *YCJA* would slow down rather speed up the rate at which youth cases would proceed in court.[28] This is a view that clearly questions the declaration of principle in section 3 of the *Youth Criminal Justice Act* which states, in part, that the youth justice system should emphasize "timely intervention that reinforces the link between the offending behaviour and its consequences" and "the promptness and speed with which persons responsible for enforcing this Act must act, given young persons' perception of time."[29]

Although criticisms of the *YCJA* have been heard across Canada, the government of Quebec, representing the views of many employed with the youth justice system, was opposed to implementation of the *YCJA*. Through a reference to the Quebec Court of Appeal, was the Quebec government sought a declaration that:

1. The federal government exceeded its jurisdiction—and hence encroached on provincial jurisdiction in the area of child protection and the administration of youth justice—in the *YCJA;*

2. The *YCJA* in general, and in particular the provisions regarding sentencing and when names of young persons could be published, violated international law including the *Convention on the Rights of the Child*[30] and the *International Covenant on Civil and Political Rights;*[31] and that

3. Sections of the *Act*—pertaining to when a youth convicted of a presumptive offence should be sentenced as an adult and when the name of a youth convicted of a presumptive offence but given a youth sentence could be published—violated the *Charter of Rights and Freedoms.*

The Court of Appeal in its decision found that the *Act* was within the legislative jurisdiction of the federal government, and that the impugned provisions did not violate international law. The court, however, found certain provisions to violate section 7 of the *Charter of Rights and Freedoms.*[32] In particular, the court held that the sections pertaining to the sentencing of a youth convicted of a presumptive offence[33] violate the *Charter* "insofar as they place on a young person who has committed a presumptive offence the burden of proving the factors that justify imposing a youth sentence instead of an adult sentence."[34] As well, the court held that sections determining whether a youth convicted of a presumptive offence but sentences as a youth should have his or name published[35] violated section 7 of the *Charter,* "insofar as they require the young person to justify maintaining the ban instead of placing the burden on the prosecution to justify lifting the ban."[36]

It is difficult to predict what the long-term effects of this decision will be. The federal government was reported to have decided not to appeal the case, but rather to amend the *YCJA* to address the court's concerns.[37] This federal response, however, drew a critical response from the provinces of Ontario and Alberta. Attorneys General from both provinces attacked the federal government's position, saying the impugned provisions were necessary to hold young offenders accountable and to protect the public, and hence implored the federal government to appeal the decision.[38]

On balance, consideration of the Quebec youth justice system provides an interesting contrast. Not only does this jurisdiction have the lowest youth custody rate in Canada, it also appears to follow a strategy of diverting a large number of cases away from youth court. In a province that enjoys the lowest crime rate of any province in Canada, the emphasis on a rehabilitative and clinical view towards dealing with young people in the youth system may, at the least, suggest an alternative the widely held view, in other areas of Canada, that "getting tough" on young offenders is the preferable answer to youth crime.

Mentoring and Role Modelling

All too often youths on the margins of society find themselves in the centre of our justice system. Most of these young people are disconnected from the positive influences and supports available within the community. Mentoring and role modelling is one way of trying to bring these marginalized youths back into the mainstream of society. As Lynda Fowler of Family and Consumer Sciences at Ohio State University stated in *Adults as Role Models and Mentors for Youth*, the "vitality of our communities and families is linked to the quality of the education, nurturing, and responsible role modelling that adults can provide through mentoring relationships with youth."[39]

The effects of mentoring programs can be impressive. A "controlled experiment with 959 youth in eight cities found that the Big Brothers/Big Sisters program resulted in a 46 percent reduction in drug use, a 32 percent reduction in hitting people, and a 52 percent reduction in truancy.[40] Another example is the Quantum Opportunities Project (QOP) funded by the Ford Foundation. This involved random selection of fourteen-year-old youth from families on welfare living in an impoverished neighbourhood. These youth were provided with

> …caring, competent, compassionate adult mentors who stuck with them for four years no matter what. During that time each youth participated in intensive education, personal development and community service opportunities, strove towards financial incentives and received maximum encouragement to persevere. What did they get in return for their hard work? … [C]ompared to a random sample of their peers who were not enrolled in the program, the Q.O.P youngsters improved their basic skills, graduated from high school and went on to post-secondary school or college. They were also much less likely to have babies or become unemployed.[41]

It should be noted that there seemed to be *no difference* between the QOP youth and the random group after the first year, however by the fourth year the difference was dramatic. Training takes some time. The Washington State Institute for Public Policy found that the QOP reduced crime effectively and calculated a return of $1.87 for every $1 invested.[42]

The effect of the QOP program on future criminal activity was also studied by the Rand Corporation. It conducts research seeking to identify and understand the links between social environment and youth crime. The QOP represented a further subject for inquiry. Researchers at Rand studied the arrest rate of QOP youth in comparison to their peers, and found a remarkable 70 percent fewer arrests for QOP youth as compared with their peers (i.e., brothers, sisters, friends, cousins, next-door neighbours, etc.).[43] When combined with higher rates of high school graduation and college and post-secondary education, along with fewer teenage pregnancies, the QOP becomes even more significant.

Another study reported that mentoring significantly reduced four out of five risky behaviours: carrying a weapon, illegal drug use, smoking more than five cigarettes a day, and having sex with more than one partner in the previous six months. Interestingly, only alcohol use was not reduced by mentorship. The authors were not able to report on the length of time a youth was mentored but noted that longer mentorships may be more effective than shorter. The authors concluded that "the utilization of adult mentorship should be supported as a key strategy in working with adolescents to decrease certain risk behaviors and their consequent morbidity and mortality."[44]

The Washington State Institute for Public Policy also examined mentoring on a cost/benefit basis. The two main studies were Big Brothers/Big Sisters and Cambridge–Somerville Youth Study. The Institute estimated a $5.29 return for every $1 invested in mentoring. Mentoring was found to have strong crime reduction effects. As mentioned previously, the ten boot camps for youth studied had a tendency to increase crime by 10 percent.[45]

The benefits of finding a trusted mentor can be seen in the comments of one Aboriginal youth, interviewed in the presence of his mentor, a trusted Elder within the Saskatoon Aboriginal community:

> [Elder Roland Duquette]… helped me out a lot, keeping me out of jail and getting me into the cultural stuff. Yeah, that really would work, like making a friend rather than a youth worker. A youth worker's just another person telling you what to do. A friend is what you need to help you get through stuff like that. You go through a lot of stuff…. Kids

need friends they can trust, that won't turn their backs, or say if you don't do this to hell with you! You need a friend you can really talk to. It doesn't matter what the age. I talk to Roland a lot, and his wife.[46]

Mentorship need not only occur between adults and youths. Mentorship can and should also happen with young children who may not have the benefit of supportive home environments. The CHUMS program in Tisdale, Saskatchewan is one example of a mentoring program that pairs high school children with elementary school students, and seeks to "promote healthy lifestyles and physical activity," prevent alcohol and drug abuse, and to develop "an awareness of support agencies and recreational and physical activity opportunities" in the Tisdale community.[47]

Case Study: The Manitoba Aboriginal Youth Career Awareness Committee

A Canadian example of using mentoring as a way of helping young people, and by inference keeping them away from the myriad of circumstances and influences that might bring them into contact with the criminal justice system, is the Manitoba Aboriginal Youth Career Awareness Committee (MAYCAC). This committee was originally formed in 1987 among a group of Aboriginal people employed by the Manitoba government, the government of Canada, or private industry.[48] President Clayton Sandy described how these committee members realized that each had attached themselves to and benefited greatly from the support and assistance of a mentor. In discussions among themselves, committee members discovered that each of their mentors was a white person. The committee then began to question how Aboriginal mentors could be recruited to assist Aboriginal youth.[49]

From that beginning the committee developed a plan to help Aboriginal youth in a number of areas. The goals of MAYCAC now include promoting positive Aboriginal role models, providing employment, mentorship and work experience opportunities, encouraging early career planning, and providing career information.[50] Specific activities that MAYCAC is involved in are:

- assisting in the formalizing of an Aboriginal development program;
- assisting in the formalizing of an Aboriginal internship program;
- assisting in organizing career days;
- providing a wide range of Aboriginal role models for career days;
- providing workshops on cross-cultural information;

- providing stories of self-healing and living a healthy lifestyle; and

- providing ideas of how to heal one's self by using community resources.[51]

MAYCAC works towards its objectives through partnerships with a number of government and community organizations. A focus of MAYCAC has been its involvement in internship programs for Aboriginal and black students. The Aboriginal Internship Program began in 1995 through a partnership between MAYCAC, Manitoba Education and Training, the University of Manitoba, and the Manitoba Department of Agriculture. The original goal of the program was to provide students of Aboriginal origin with an opportunity to explore careers in veterinary medicine. The program is now focused on inner-city high school and university students and is expanding to include a wider variety of career options.[52] The current program objectives include providing "inner city high school students of Aboriginal or black origin with the opportunity to explore careers in the financial and business sector," encouraging "Aboriginal and black students to stay in school," and "helping students gain confidence and self-respect."[53] In 2000, the partners in this internship program were wide-ranging and included four inner-city high schools, two credit unions, one bank, the RCMP, a transport company, Xerox Canada, MAYCAC, the University of Manitoba, and Black Youth Helpline Inc.

Much of MAYCAC's work has involved assembling a group of Aboriginal people who are prepared to act as role models and mentors to Aboriginal youth. The numbers of Aboriginal role models now associated with this committee and listed in MAYCAC's role model profile has increased to 650. All role models who agree to appear in this profile are also asked, in addition to being available for career day speaking engagements at schools, to commit to a one-on-one mentoring relationship with an Aboriginal youth. Mr. Sandy noted that, of the many youths mentored through the MAYCAC committee since 1987, 25 percent of these are now active as mentors in this program.

A publication of MAYCAC described the benefit of role modelling and mentoring in the following terms:

> Our young people need to hear about work and education choices from people who have travelled these paths themselves and have faced the same obstacles that the students will face. These men and women demonstrate how hard work and education are instrumental in achieving career goals, just as those virtues are instrumental in achieving any goals

in life. Our role models also recognize that we must acknowledge who we are, be proud of our heritage, and pass that pride on to our youth.[54]

The importance of having faced similar obstacles cannot be overstated as a means of connecting with Aboriginal youth. Clayton Sandy indicated that the original thirty-eight mentors in this program all shared a dysfunctional family background. This, he said, allowed these mentors to connect with the youth to whom they spoke, and their experiences and insights got the attention of and allowed a development of trust with the youth.[55]

Mr. Sandy had personally experienced a family and childhood characterized by "family violence, alcoholism and abuse."[56] This, he said, allowed him make a connection with Aboriginal youth. For example, at a school career day he described to a number of Aboriginal youth how he used to collect beer bottles from his house to get enough money for food. He immediately noticed how this story built a bridge with these young people, a number of whom had experienced this same reality. Mr. Sandy said he doubted another speaker—even of Aboriginal heritage—would have been able to make a connection with these youth without some sense of shared experience.[57]

Mentoring and role modelling can become a positive means of keeping youth away from a criminal lifestyle. During an interview in May 2002, Mr. Sandy described how he was using this strategy in his employment as the manager of Community Relations with the Correctional Service of Canada's Aboriginal Gang Initiative. Among its objectives, this project sought to provide Aboriginal teaching and cultural activities, as taught by respected Elders who characterized "good strong values."[58] Mr. Sandy described how 90 percent of gang members came from single-parent families, the vast majority of which had a single mother as the caregiver. This meant that these male youths grew up without any positive male role model. He was working with gang members, both in jail and on conditional release. With the support of respected Aboriginal Elders, he was using a mentoring approach as one means of allowing individuals to free themselves from their gang lifestyle.[59]

Mentoring and role-modelling is a promising approach. It helps youth to address many of the challenges which they have brought from childhood, but at the same time helps to build lasting relationships which nurture self-esteem and teach the skills needed to become a contributing member of society and the benefits available from doing so. Mentoring programs, as well, evidence the benefits of cooperative and integrative approaches to helping young people, a topic discussed in the next section.

Interdisciplinary and Interagency Approaches to Youth Justice

Looking for answers within the justice system leads to the unavoidable conclusion that many—if not most—solutions to the problems of crime among troubled youth lie outside the control of police, lawyers, and courts. This realization has led many to support a move towards interdisciplinary and interagency approaches to justice. These approaches necessitate co-operation among a broad spectrum of people and organizations, including employees working in various services and agencies inside and outside the justice system together with other groups and individuals within each community. Although many of these people and agencies were not previously considered to be part of the formal criminal justice system, their involvement is now increasingly seen as a key to providing the resources needed to assist offenders and victims. In effect, this approach means putting a new emphasis on a cooperative view of justice. To state the obvious, the role of criminal justice, especially as it applies to youth, is to be one—and only one—of the many tools society uses in improving the lives of its citizens. It is essential that the strategies applied within a society towards the greater good of the community not be at cross purposes.

As a recognition of the need for an interdisciplinary and wide-ranging approach to youth crime, the *YCJA* now contains, in its preamble, a statement that "communities, families, parents and others concerned with the development of young persons should, through multi-disciplinary approaches, take reasonable steps to prevent youth crime by addressing its underlying causes, to respond to the needs of young persons, and to provide guidance and support to those at risk of committing crimes."[60]

At the root of this discussion is questioning how we can expect to change delinquent behaviour if we return youth to the same environment that contributed to their misbehaviour without any change in their personal or home circumstances. In a society where public-sector cutbacks have become a way of life, in the wake of a public clamour for tax cuts, there is an obvious need to pool resources in attempting to address the causes and effects of crime, and as a result to provide safer communities. If our experience as lawyers tells us anything, it is that maintaining the justice system as an island apart from the rest of society's resources is a recipe for further failure. The extent to which the justice system has remained aloof from the rest of society, in contrast to many other institutions, was explained by Chief Judge Barry Stuart of the Yukon Territorial Court in *R. v. M.N.J.*[61]

How can a system remain so robust when no one can make the case it is succeeding and everyone can agree it should be doing much better on almost every front? When the evidence for changing to a holistic, coordinated, value-based approach is so overwhelming, how can the justice system remain a jungle of complex, disjointed interactions that preserve numerous self-serving fiefdoms, all with different values, different objectives? When the public has not merely challenged, but penetrated and participated directly in the shaping of other public processes (Education, Health, Environment, Labour Relations, etc.), how has the justice system managed to keep the public at its outer gates, misinformed and ineffective in changing our arcane processes? We have achieved, often despite our best intentions to be otherwise, a level of excellence in maintaining the status quo, despite constant external pressures to change.[62]

As a signal that those employed within the justice system must be open to new partnerships with other agencies and community members, the general principles of the *Youth Criminal Justice Act* state that measures taken against young persons who commit offences should, "where appropriate, involve the parents, the extended family, the community and social or other agencies in the young person's rehabilitation and reintegration."[63] This section is also a recognition of the complexity of today's society, and hence the need to pool and focus the effort of people and organizations in providing service and supports to young people, and an increased sense of safety at the local level.

Unfortunately, the most common changes we see being implemented within the justice system across Canada are attempts at simply shoring up the established enforcement system with more police, more Crown prosecutors, and more emphasis on offender accountability through the ultimate weapon: custody. Obviously, this strategy can have little positive effect and may actually have a negative impact without at least a coexisting strategy of addressing the underlying causes of crime, and of effecting positive changes in behaviour for the young person involved.

As a particularly discouraging measure of how lax Canadian society has become in dealing with a primary, if not *the* primary, cause of youth crime, statistics on child poverty are not encouraging. In a report entitled *Child Poverty in Canada: Report Card 2000,* the group Campaign 2000 recalled and restated a resolution of the House of Commons in 1989 to "seek to achieve the goal of eliminating poverty among Canadian children by the year 2000." This report found that goal to be elusive, observing in the year 2000 that "one in five children in Canada still lives in poverty—an increase of 402,000 since 1989."[64] The extent to which "the rich are becoming richer and the poor are becoming poorer in our society" was shown in a report on poverty released by the Canadian Council on Social Development in November 2002, which found that between 1984 and 1999, "the average net wealth of the top 20 per cent of couples with children increased by 43 per cent" while for "families at the bottom of the income scale, net wealth fell by more than 51 per cent."[65]

The need for justice professionals to step outside their conventional boxes in considering new partnerships and new approaches to youth crime and in helping young offenders has never been more pressing. In considering how this transformation can happen, and in addressing the cycles of crime and suffering and repeat offending, Chief Judge Stuart suggested a holistic approach, involving agencies and family and community members:

> The justice system alone cannot stop this cycle. The state, even if it finally turned from its turf-conscious, truncated approach to an integrated systemic approach, could not stop this cycle. The cycle can be stopped—but only if we turn to address the causes and not the symptoms; only if we recognize that professionals and state agencies cannot do the work that communities and families must do, only if we accept that legal solutions have never, and can never, solve social issues, and especially only if we acknowledge that simple solutions, like punishment, exacerbate rather than solve complex social problems.
>
> There is hope, but it does not lie with more justice resources—it lies with less. It lies with a different approach, with different objectives, different resources, different people. It lies with giving a greater voice to communities and to those skilled in rehabilitating individuals, families and communities. Let us embrace crime as an opportunity to understand what is wrong, not just with an individual like M.N.J., but with our system that would enable M.N.J. to become so estranged from us that he could commit such a crime. Let us use crime as an opportunity to discover what is wrong with our institutions, with our communities that hindered our ability to intervene long before this crime.[66]

Similarly, Shay Bilchik, administrator of the Office of Juvenile Justice and Delinquency Protection of the United States Department of Justice, in an article entitled "A juvenile justice system for the 21st century," stressed the need for an integrated and coordinated approach to youth justice, by implication requiring policy decisions to be taken both with the help of, and considering the best interests of, the broader community.

> An effective juvenile justice system must meet three objectives: (1) hold the juvenile offender accountable; (2) enable the juvenile to become a capable, productive, and responsible citizen; and (3) ensure the safety

of the community.... These objectives are best met when a community's key leaders—including representatives from the juvenile justice, health and mental health, schools, law enforcement, social services, and other systems—are jointly engaged in the planning, development, and operation of the juvenile justice system. Juvenile justice system reform must be part of a broad, comprehensive, community-wide effort to eliminate factors that place juveniles at risk of delinquency and victimization, enhance factors that protect them from engaging in delinquent behaviour, and use the full range of resources and programs within the community to meet the varying needs of juveniles.... It is essential that, in engaging the community in this undertaking, the juvenile justice system also include greater public access to both the court and the system. This access will ensure a proper role for victims, a greater understanding of how the system operates, and a higher level of system accountability to the public.[67]

Although there is much to be said about how interagency and interdisciplinary approaches to justice can help youths caught up in the justice system, another very significant aspect of this form of cooperation lies in the area of crime prevention. This is an overarching goal that most politicians at all levels of government will claim to support. Yet the movement of resources away from enforcement and punitive arms of the justice system towards services, which will in the short run address the root causes of crime and in the long run reduce crime levels, can be a tough sell. We suspect that this has much to do with issues surrounding the reporting of youth crime and how public perceptions are shaped by the sensational accounts of individual cases.

The notoriety and public attention garnered by one serious youth crime often overrides any publicity about a multitude of success stories involving youths who received help and then stayed out of trouble. One way of trying to reverse this trend toward sensationalism is continued and increased emphasis on crime prevention. As an example of this, the English use of Youth Offending Teams (YOTs)—integrated teams made up of social workers, education and health staff, prison staff, magistrates, and probation officers—has brought a new emphasis on dealing with the underlying causes of youth crime, and hence on crime prevention. An article evaluating these interdisciplinary YOTs stated that the "teams not only work with 10 to 17 years olds within the criminal justice remit, such as supporting a young person through their community punishment orders, but also provide preventative work for young people who have yet to get involved in the criminal justice system."[68]

As a further recognition of the importance of crime prevention, the

Youth Criminal Justice Act now provides, as a key principle of interpretation, that the youth criminal justice system is meant to "prevent crime by addressing the circumstances underlying a young person's offending behaviour."[69] As an example of the importance of crime prevention as a social priority, the Manitoba Aboriginal Justice Implementation Commission devoted an entire section of its report to the important connection, and causal link, between community development and crime prevention. The commission observed that the roots of over-representation of Aboriginals in the justice system are not "found only in the justice system, but in the broader social setting, and will require concerted action from all three levels of government in Canada."[70] The commission suggested a co-ordinated crime prevention approach, addressing the many problems faced by Aboriginal people.

> The justice system is reactive. The changes proposed in this section are preventative. They build on people's strengths and encourage community building. And, at the same time, they recognize that Aboriginal people who are at risk of becoming involved in crime often face multiple problems: racism, domestic violence, community violence, poor access to health care and education, inadequate housing and limited employment options. These problems generate hostility, stress, and demoralization, and can lead to criminal behaviour. A successful crime prevention approach will address all these issues in a coordinated fashion.[71]

One of the challenges in preventing youth from getting caught up in the justice system is keeping them out of it in the first place. Regarding young people, the commission recognized the interconnectedness of young people, their families, and their communities, and stated "there is clear evidence that money spent on early years' education decreases the likelihood of a young person's coming into conflict with the law."[72]

We suggest that each youth is a potential ally in future crime prevention. For example, one youth with extensive experience in a custodial institution advised:

> If I was to change the way the youth system worked, I'd have way more community involvement. And I'd use new concepts, new programs because kids want to be a part of new things. I'd use that to make sure I hooked them up with something good, and use that to show them how their whole life could be better. I'd start as soon as someone was put in custody, I'd ask them what they'd really like to do, hear all their ideas. Leave them with pens and paper to keep thinking about it when they're alone.[73]

Prevention strategies can begin at, and be focused on, an early age, even including prenatal concerns. An example of this is the *Kids First* program, currently operating in a number of Saskatchewan communities. *Kids First* is a "voluntary program that helps families build on their strengths and have the healthiest children possible."[74] The *Kids First* program is focused on providing for the unique needs of each family, and is designed to enhance existing programs already in the community. The range of services provided under the *Kids First* umbrella include prenatal outreach, home visiting, childcare and early learning, and family support services. This program benefits youth and families in a number of ways. Prenatal women benefit from being offered the support they need to have the healthiest babies possible. Postnatal women and their families benefit by being assessed and offered services based on identified needs. Families benefit through programs built around parenting, literacy, nutrition, and other needs. Children benefit through early learning opportunities. The long-term benefit of such a program for all of society is obvious: fewer high-risk youths coming into the justice system.

Programs such as *Kids First* show a response to the obvious need for preventative services, and for early diagnosis of behavioural problems. For too long, the justice system has been the site where such problems, and hence troubled youth, are identified. In many cases this is grossly after the fact. As a result, other locations within our communities need to be used to identify trouble signs long before a youth finds him or herself in a prisoner's box, looking across at the prosecutor and judge. Where, then, are these focal points at which problems can be identified and addressed long before a young person can develop into a young offender? In *R. v. J.K.E.*,[75] Judge Lilles of the Yukon Territorial Court suggested that schools are one such location.

> In many cases, schools are in a position to identify problems at an early stage. Currently youth who, without obvious reason, begin missing school or are habitually late or whose classroom performance and participation deteriorates noticeably are disciplined and may eventually be suspended or expelled. The underlying problems are neither identified nor addressed. A community circle at this point will greatly increase the likelihood of identifying the issues, which are often complex, and the solutions, which are beyond the capability of any one agency.[76]

Few would dispute the correlation between regular and active school attendance by youth and a reduction in criminal risk for such young people. But the importance of our educational institutions goes far beyond this. They are a place where potential problems can be identified and corrected as an alternative to involving the criminal justice system, a place that can serve as a hub of social activity, and a central point from which service delivery can occur.

The *School PLUS* strategy of the government of Saskatchewan envisions schools as an integral and central part of the interagency network serving and supporting at-risk youth. To meet the diverse and holistic needs of children, "schools need access to array of social services and supports."[77] In February 2002, the Saskatchewan government stressed the importance of continued service integration and interagency collaboration in addressing the needs of high-risk youth.

> Volunteer efforts at interagency collaboration and service integration have achieved important advances. Heightened effort and more systemic actions are needed, however, for these initiatives to realise their potential in supporting the developmental and educational needs of children and youth. The Task Force [on the Role of the School] identified that up to 25% of children and young people are at risk of not completing high school and thus of experiencing limited life chances, and that this number could rapidly climb to 40% unless significant action is taken. Moreover, because schooling is compulsory and because schools are located close to families at the community level, they are a logical place from which to deliver needed support services. The need to access other human services in support of learning has reached a critical state.[78]

Similar to what is happening in schools and the educational system, the idea of involving a broad cross section of people and organizations in assisting young people within the youth justice system is an approach now promoted within the *YCJA*. Under the community conferencing provisions of this Act (in section 19) a "youth justice court judge, the provincial director, a police officer, a justice of the peace, a prosecutor or a youth worker may convene or cause to be convened a conference for the purpose of making a decision required to be made under this Act."[79] These conferences, presumably, will involve the participation of a variety of people who previously would not have had their voices heard in youth court or elsewhere in the youth justice system.

Youth justice committees are another organization that will play a part in promoting community-wide consultation and cooperation on youth justice matters. The *YCJA* provides that the functions of youth justice committees include "ensuring that community support is available to the young person by arranging for the use of services from within the community, and enlisting members of the community to provide short-term mentoring and supervision" and "when the young person is also being dealt with by a child protection agency or a community group, helping to coordinate the interaction of the agency or group with the youth criminal justice system."[80]

One example of an integrated and coordinated process for working with high-risk youth and their families comes in the so-called Wraparound process. Based in large part on the work of Dr. John VanDenBerg, this process is used to "help communities to develop individualized plans of care."[81] This process has been implemented broadly across North America, and focuses on an individualized plan for each youth and his or her family. This plan is developed by a Wraparound team—usually four to ten people who know the youth and family well—which must be no more than half professionals.[82] Dr. VanDenBerg describes the nature and prerequisites of an individualized Wraparound plan:

> The plan is needs-driven rather than service-driven, although a plan may incorporate existing categorical services if appropriate to the needs of the consumer. The initial plan should be a combination of existing or modified services, newly created services, informal supports, and community resources, and should include a plan for a step-down of formal services. This plan is family centred rather than child centred. The parent(s) and child are integral parts of the team and must have ownership of the plan. No planning sessions occur without the presence of the child and family. The plan is based on the unique strengths, values, norms, and preferences of the child, family, and community. No interventions are allowed in the plan that do not have matching child, family, and community strengths.[83]

The Wraparound process, which focuses primarily on youth and family strengths (rather than deficits), is an encouraging example of how individual plans can be prepared for high-risk youths. Although this approach looks more at helping individual children rather than setting policy direction for the entire community—the trees rather than the forest—its application toward an increasing network of high-risk youth and families would clearly pave the way towards preventing youth crime and bringing more and more marginalized youth into the mainstream of society.

One problem marginalized families and youth face is the number of agencies and workers they deal with. In their report *Helping At Risk Youth, Lessons From Community Based Initiatives*, Morley and Rossman stated "[c]ommon sense and years of research suggest that at risk youth and their families have multiple needs and interrelated problem behaviors that are not likely to be successfully addressed by single response stand alone initiatives." Yet chaos can result if these services are not coordinated. Morley and Rossman suggested that services integration and case management was one of the "critical components of community based options for youth at-risk, yet local programs often experience difficulty implementing them."[84]

This can be seen in Saskatoon, for example, where between 1993 and 1995 an attempt was made to make sense of the specialization that seemed to be preventing people and agencies from seeing the big picture. The Saskatoon Children's Services Integration Project discovered that one family, in a two-year period, had 40 different agencies working with them, and had 120 different people acting as service providers. When they documented this, the Children's Service Integration Project entitled the table that listed agencies and providers, "How Can One Mother Make Sense Of This?" If placed in the same position, none of us could take advice from 120 different people in such a short time.

In the same city, Judge Mary Ellen Turpel-Lafond of the Saskatchewan Provincial Court had before her a young person with Fetal Alcohol diagnosis. She discovered that no one knew what could be done to address the problem despite the number of years that have elapsed since it has been recognized. She ordered that Social Services, Saskatoon District Health, and the youth worker meet to devise an appropriate plan. These agencies appealed to the Court of Appeal for Saskatchewan, who, it would appear, reluctantly ruled that these agencies could not be forced by the courts to meet and prepare a treatment plan.[85]

Despite the Children's Integration Project and Judge Turpel-Lafond's attempts to force discussion, the response of the Saskatoon community is still not unified. Clearly, a lack of coordination of agencies and services, including those within the criminal justice system, does not help promote positive change for offenders, victims, and their families. Yet a call to change the way agencies function and interact is often met with resistance, as it represents a threat to those who wish to protect their turf, or a challenge for already overworked employees. Yet the need for change is obvious, and if the means of achieving this can be made less threatening to those working within the system, the results can be positive.

As an example, the Washington State Institute for Public Policy's study of community integration revealed some astonishing results. By spending a small amount—$603 per person advocating for a youth's right to already existing services, effecting a "wraparound" of services—a bottom-line benefit of $25.29 resulted for every $1 spent. The coordinated services in this study were found to reduce crime by 14 percent. In comparison, an extensive study of juvenile boot camps showed that spending $15,424 per participant would result in a 10 percent *increase* in crime.[86]

Another example can be seen in the Seattle Social Development Project. This was a successful project that involved many agencies in an integrated, multilevel or multicomponent intervention. An editorial of *Archives of Pediatric and Adolescent Medicine* stated that "the result of this program's broad focus on youth development provides evidence that strengthening social and psychological skills, rather than targeting specific risk behaviors, can protect against an array of health risks." The editorial later states that earlier reports on the program "demonstrated its measurable beneficial effects on violent and nonviolent crime, substance abuse, sexual activity, pregnancy, school achievement, grade repetition, dropping out of school, suspension and expulsion and delinquency." Previous studies generally dealt with one risk factor at a time, but "[b]ecause adolescent behavior is influenced by factors at different levels, intervening at more than one level could produce an additive or synergistic effect greater than any single intervention in isolation.… This approach can remedy the fragmentation of prevention and clinical services that adolescents so often face." While the editors stated that pediatricians and adolescent and family medicine specialists were not part of the Seattle Social Development Project, they suggested that it would be beneficial for them to consider joining so "adolescents communicate effectively with their health care providers and make healthier decisions."[87]

Contrary to the positive results in Seattle, the factual scenario in *R. v. M.N.J.* provides a vivid example of a lack of community and interagency coordination and programming over this offender's life. By any standard, it is a shocking history of neglect and abuse, from four years of age onwards. For five years of his childhood, M.N.J. lived for the most part with his grandparents, and during this time was "repeatedly taken into, or voluntarily placed in, the care of the department" of Social Services. This home environment "was not just chaotic due to the number of children, but in this home he was severely victimized by his family." Court records showed "M.N.J. was sexually and physically abused by uncles living in the home." As an often neglected child, "emotionally and physically, when he became too difficult, or simply too much to look after, he was given to, or taken by, the department," often for months at a time. Chief Judge Stuart summarized M.N.J.'s situation by saying nothing "in the evidence suggests this home provided, or could provide, a nurturing home for any child, but especially for a child abandoned and brutalized by his natural parents," and that since 1981, "doctors, public health nurses, teachers, foster parents and people in the community have reported to the department various concerns about the abuse and neglect M.N.J. suffered."[88]

Despite the many people who tried to help this offender during his developmental years, there was an obvious lack of coordination. Chief Judge Stuart described a breakdown in community and professional services in this case.

> Without the necessary support systems of family, community, friends or professional services desperately needed to diffuse his well-documented capacity for sexually inappropriate and aggressive expression, Mr. M.N.J., living alone in the community, was a ticking bomb. He had been through more than a dozen placements before he was 18. Numerous professionals had worked with him or assessed him. Everyone knew his propensity for violence and for sexually inappropriate behaviour. No effective intervention occurred to help him change or to prevent further anti-social behaviour.[89]

But as sad as these circumstances are, they also form a blueprint for how the various players within the justice system, and the larger community, might better organize and coordinate their services, to avoid a repeat, or escalation, of M.N.J.'s story. Chief Judge Stuart used the analogy of moving a rock when he described the need for integrated community planning that was capable of making a difference:

> The M.N.J.s within our system are victims of the lack of an integrated plan. Imagine for a moment that the cumulative effect of all the abuse youth such as M.N.J. endure creates a festering mass of anger, pain, frustration, and an irrepressible yearning to strike out at authority. Think of this mass as a large rock—so large that no family, no community, no professional, no agency can alone lift this rock to a better place. Everyone tries. Repeated efforts leave them exhausted, burned out, despairing and resigned to failure. Yet if all took on the challenge in a coordinated effort, the rock can be moved. M.N.J. was too much for his family to manage. He was too much for social workers, probation officers, judges, psychologists—too much for any one person or agency to manage alone. So many times in dealing with young people like M.N.J. everyone struggles essentially alone, without an integrated effort that reaches far beyond the specific resources they possess. They all do their jobs, but the job needed to make the difference does not get done. As long as we fail to work together, we will fail to make a difference.[90]

There are no easy answers about how professional agencies, community leaders and volunteers, families and youth can work together in a more integrated and productive manner, and ultimately keep more troubled youth out of our courts and custodial facilities. There are, however, some positive signs, if we only take the time to see them.

For example, in northeast Saskatchewan, the Nipawin Integrated Services Committee has been functioning since 1997. This committee has broad representation from this town, including Métis Local 134, the RCMP, the Nipawin School Division, the Kelsey Trail Health Region, Cumberland Community College, the town of Nipawin administration, and the Department of Social Services. It works to facilitate integrated planning and service delivery that meets the needs of at-risk populations in Nipawin, specifically: early childhood (0–4 years), children (5–11 years), youth (12–19 years), young adult (20–30 years), and citizens generally in vulnerable situations.[91]

This committee's goals are to: co-ordinate local needs assessments, work towards integrated service delivery, co-ordinate funding allocations, research and access funding to support integrated services, and establish project and program accountability at the local level. In its short existence, this committee has coordinated a variety of programs to the Nipawin community, including a youth counsellor, a youth group, an outreach program, a student support centre, a preschool program for at-risk children, a nutrition program, and a pre- and post-natal program for at-risk mothers and children.[92]

Resiliency and Marginalized Youth: Bottling the Magic

If asked what the goal of criminal justice should be, most of the youth we represent would talk about reducing the number of harmful acts against others in the community. Most of these young people take no pride in hurting others. Many of their crimes are committed spontaneously, often in response to extreme pressure of circumstance.

The consequences of these circumstances are dire. Most of our clients believe that if sent to custody, they must be prepared to vigorously defend themselves from aggressors. As a result, even for nonviolent youths, the effects of this "learning" experience are difficult to overcome.

An example of the sort of learning experience that custody can bring was seen recently in the case of *R.* v. *E.T.F.*[93] E.T.F. was a seventeen-year-old youth charged with three counts of mischief and three counts of theft. He had one previous conviction for assault, committed while in the care of Children's Aid (after being sexually assaulted by his biological father). Apparently as a result of being homeless, this youth remained on remand for ten days at the Toronto Youth Assessment Centre. He was beaten repeatedly by other youth being held in the centre—both in the centre and while being transported to court. Justice Brian Weagant found this youth had been held for ten days "in a hellish system reminiscent of Dickens and Lord of the Flies." He found, among other things, "manifestly unaccept-able" physical conditions for this youth at the centre for at least the first four days, that lack of supervision made it possible for another youth to steal E.T.F.'s food, and that E.T.F. suffered a series of assaults at the hands of another resident. Justice Weagant said his injuries "would have been evident to any correctional worker as they were in court," and found the staff placed the onus on E.T.F. to lay charges, and acted in a callous man-ner in response to this youth's request for medical help with his asthma condition. In shocking terms, Justice Weagant described the transporta-tion used to take accused youth to court:

> The transportation system epitomizes the consequences when detained young persons are not adequately supervised. Unobserved and unsu-pervised, these teens are free to torment and physically abuse each other. The vulnerable victim has no adult to come to his protection, nor can the young person escape the situation. Removing the most violent young persons from the others and locking them in separate cages at the front of the van (and presumably in view of the escort in the front seat of the van), does not prevent violence. As E.T.F.'s testimony demonstrated, other boys are under a compulsion to act on behalf of the isolated boys. They act as soldiers and carry out orders.[94]

It is understandable that a youth subjected to such conditions might learn to react with anger and aggression. But despite any aggressive be-haviours they have adopted while within the institutions of the criminal justice system, our clients still believe, at some level, that hurting is wrong. In looking for strategies that build on and support this basic belief, two realities must be considered. Most of these youth come from backgrounds that predict a high likelihood of involvement in crime, characterized by such factors as unemployment, low education rates, high suicide rates, prenatal maternal consumption of alcohol, and poor health. But most also share a desire to move out of the margins of society into the mainstream. This desire, if encouraged, is a powerful force militating against further harmful acts.

In our practice as lawyers, we see youth who return time and again to youth court, often in police custody. We also see youth who, for whatever reason, offend for a period of time, and then are not seen again in court, having become contributing members of society. And finally we see, or hear about, young people—perhaps siblings of those young offenders we represent—who experience the same terrible circumstances as those caught up in our criminal justice system, yet do not get into trouble with the law.

What allows some youth to rise above enormous misery and beat such substantial odds? What helps a youth to change his or her life, away from criminal activity? Perhaps part of the answer lies in the concept of resiliency.

The initial studies of children who go through life circumstances that seem to encourage crime come not from the crime control industry, but rather primarily from the fields of health, education, and community development. For example, a 1979 study on the Isle of Wight and in a poor neighbourhood in London found that six family-based problems were linked to a greater likelihood of psychotic disorder in children.[95] Another researcher, Dr. Norman Garmezy, found that all six of these stressors accounted for a 33 percent increase in psychiatric disorder. Similarly, Sameroff and his colleagues used a list of ten stressors in families and found that the accumulated stresses "had a pronounced negative effect on the child's cognitive and social development." Sameroff suggested that "the presence of each adverse factor ... cost the child 4 IQ points."[96] These studies of children born and raised in highly stressed environments used the phrase "risk" to describe those stressful factors.

As various studies from different disciplines were examined, one point became obvious. Some children did relatively well, even though they lived in difficult environments. In 1993, Dr. Garmezy observed there was a knowledge gap in the accumulated research focus, as "only in recent years have investigators begun to explore the lives of similarly disadvantaged children for whom positive outcomes have been reported."[97]

Who were these children who excelled out of chaos? What unique features did they share? Some called them "invulnerable" children, although the more risk factors and the longer children were left in abusive situations the less invulnerable they seemed. Now they are commonly called resilient. The question for us, in looking to make our communities safer, is what can we learn from the resilient behaviours of children, and what can we do to encourage and assist others to respond with resilience?

Studies of resiliency show that learning to handle traumatic events, as resilient youth do, depends on an interconnection of personal and social factors. It is one thing to face trauma, but the most traumatic situations are those that also threaten our concept of self, and our view of the world. People can easier face trauma, even death, if the trauma and death do not threaten their view of self and especially their understanding of what it means to be a member of their community.[98]

Every crisis is a threat. The ultimate examples are starvation and brutality. But a sense of crisis can be felt differently depending on its source. If a crisis emanates from dealings with those thought to be friends, or in response to good acts and intentions, the crisis is all the deeper.

This raises the subtle but vital relationship between factors such as positive self-image and social support in dealing with crisis. Clearly, resilient children cannot stand alone. Resiliency is largely facilitated by one individual learning from and being supported by others. This learning involves acquiring needed skills in understanding what disruption means, in accessing assistance (both material and interpersonal) within the community to help face this disruption, and finally in developing the personal skills and social supports needed to cope with these anxieties.

Many, if not all, of these skills can be taught. Studies have shown that some aspects of resiliency are aided by genetic biological factors, but as author Jennifer White points out, "traits develop and are re-enforced through a child's lived experience." White says this "is through the *process* of being in relationships and through interacting with key socializing environments."[99] But what are the specific factors and strategies that facilitate resiliency, and can these be used to diminish future criminal acts by marginalized youth who are already involved in the criminal justice system?

Dr. Susan Fine, senior lecturer in psychiatry at Cornell Medical College, conducted a study of persons in many fields who often prevailed over extraordinary hardships. Dr. Fine's study concluded that resiliency was facilitated by social support, by teaching youth new problem-solving techniques, and by encouraging youth to find hope, meaning, and purpose in life while at the same time rejecting negative and limiting labels.[100]

Hope, in our experience, especially realistic hope, is in short supply among the high-risk youth we often represent. It is evident in their disconnection from school, and in their expectation of employment. We hear comments ranging from "I'd really like a job, any job, I don't care what," to "I'm going to be a judge," even though the speaker cannot read or write and refuses to go to school. Hope, however, helps these children to be resilient, and can be seen in a determination not to give up, or a desire to one day to expose the injustice some have been subjected to. Clearly, realistic hope is dependant on societal and community supports that surround these youth.

Affiliation to a social group can be a powerful way to help face extreme situations, and to ensure a sense of belonging. This, in turn, can promote a moderation in behaviour. In a study of the attitudes of homeless males in Edmonton, it was found that the men who believed others who cared for them would be disappointed by further criminality on their part felt that this disappointment was a deterrent. In fact, these young men were more fearful of criminal sanctions.[101]

Dr. Fine identified the process of stepping back to be able to describe one's experience in a new way and engaging in a search for the meaning of it all as an important technique used by the resilient. Being able to transform some part of oneself into something that adds to the lives of others is a powerful remedy to "risk," and a characteristic of the resilient. For example, Buster Keaton could not laugh spontaneously and so he made others laugh. Charles Dickens, Pablo Picasso, Anton Chekhov, and Buster Keaton were all highly stressed and traumatized children. They gave to others, to make their own lives more bearable.

Resiliency in children, while it seems to appear spontaneously in unexpected places, relies largely on positive social interactions that assist children in developing appropriate skills. For example, Dr. Steinhauer, speaking in relation to early childhood development, stated:

> Many children experience high levels of chronic stress and adversity in regard to their health or their environment as they develop. But risks experienced within one aspect of their life, for example chronic illness, maltreatment, or growing up in poverty, may be counteracted by protections provided by other aspects in what is called the protective triad (i.e., individual opportunities, close family ties and external support systems, including the school and the community: Garmezy 1991) Given such supports, some children become resilient despite chronic exposure to disadvantage and some are even strengthened by their struggle against adversity (Sinnema, 1991: Ciccetti et al., 1993).[102]

Dr. Fine refers to this process as learning to help "transform the dross of their adversity into the gold of their accomplishments."[103]

Although resiliency is a topic of much study in health and education circles, the same cannot be said of the criminal law system. That is surprising because this concept represents a successful response to traumatic backgrounds, a common denominator for most young people appearing in youth court. Yet in Canada, the techniques and understandings that explain and facilitate resiliency are not mentioned in either the *YOA* or the *YCJA*, leaving a vacuum in attempts at understanding the often complex relationship between youth crime and resiliency. The *YCJA* does, however, state that measures taken against young offenders should "be meaningful for the individual young person given his or her needs and level of development and, where appropriate, involve the parents, the extended family, the community and social or other agencies in the young person's rehabilitation and reintegration."[104] This appears to be a recognition of the difficult circumstances that may have brought the child into the justice system, and further of the need to respond to each child's unique situation by providing family and community supports. It is also a recognition of the absolute necessity of reintegrating youth into the mainstream of our society.

The causes of youth crime, and the factors that have a direct correlation with criminal activity, were discussed in chapter three. Successfully addressing these factors may go a great distance towards increasing the number of children who respond to adversity in a resilient fashion. In the United States, the Rand Corporation, in a report entitled *Diverting Children from a Life of Crime*, while not specifically mentioning the word resiliency, clearly identified many factors that, acting together, affect the chances of criminality:

> Delinquency is not a problem that appears alone. Delinquent youths are also at higher-than-average risk for drug use, problems in school, dropping out of school and teenage pregnancy (Elliot, Hulzinga and Menard 1989, Greenwood 1993). Research attempting to explain the likely sequence or relationship among these various behaviors now supports an international model in which all are interconnected, with causality flowing both ways between any two (Thornberry, 1987). Given this perspective, any intervention that reduces the incidence of one of these problem behaviors is likely to reduce the others as well. Thus, beneficial secondary effects on crime might be anticipated from interventions that have been shown to reduce drug use or teen pregnancy or to increase educational achievement.[105]

While our society is supposedly built on a philosophy of equality before the law, to ensure personal power does not sway justice, many decisions made formally and informally within a community create conditions affecting the chances of youth entering the criminal justice system. For some youth, these conditions are so pervasive as to actually be prenatal. In many ways, the chances of success for these youths are the opposite of equal. As Bob Dylan said in *Like a Rolling Stone*, "when you ain't got nothing, you got nothing to lose."

Following this theme, academic writing and studies about resiliency show how difficult success is to come by when socially stressed people are not considered in their social context. As a result, helping these people overcome their stressed backgrounds requires a focus on social and personal success. One place such a focus can be seen is in restorative justice practices, which promote a positive focus, building on the strengths of offenders and victims, as well as the community. This positive focus goes hand in hand with questioning the negative effects of punishment on self-esteem and self-worth, and hence on the prospects of positive change.

Like refocusing on the successes of marginalized youths, the broader challenge becomes finding different approaches to changing behaviour. Jennifer White described such a change in the context of preventing suicide:

> We need to place a deliberate emphasis on building the strengths and competence of children and youth and work to increase protective factors across a range of socializing contexts. Ideally then, when confronted with change, loss and other conditions that could potentially put them at risk for suicide, young people can bring more competence or "hardiness" to the experience or challenge at hand. The key environmental contexts should support and reinforce children's adaptive behavior and healthy choices, which will ultimately heighten the likelihood of a resilient outcome.[106]

This analysis applies equally to the risk of criminality. Stressful environments create a variety of responses: sometimes suicide, sometimes criminal acts—attempted suicide was itself a crime in the 1970s. As a general statement of principles Ms. White's words are just as relevant to dealing with marginalized children before and after they have been charged with an offence. Restorative justice practices directly or indirectly encourage an exploration of resiliency.

The choice of appropriate treatment for those in need is also highly significant in facilitating resiliency. Dr. James Bonta of the Policy Branch, Solicitor General of Canada, in an address to the Association of Parole Authorities International, pointed out that where treatment of sentenced persons was appropriate then a 50 percent reduction in recidivism could be expected. Contrast this to another study from the Solicitor General referred to earlier in this book, which showed that incarceration caused an increase of up to 6 percent in recidivism. In his paper, Dr. Bonta explained the characteristics of an appropriate program. Just as significant as the positive effects of appropriate treatment of high-risk offenders, he showed that using intensive programs (for example counselling or monitoring) for those who were not at a high risk to reoffend (perhaps those who had developed resilient techniques already) actually increased recidivism.[107]

We suggest that this is because such programming interferes with unique strategies that the person has already developed. In considering what offences should be dealt with by extrajudicial measures outside of our youth court system, we must be cognizant of the reality that bringing low-risk and often first-time offenders into the mechanisms of the criminal justice system may well increase their chances of further criminal activity. This makes essential the task of accurately assessing the risk level of offenders, and employing strategies that reduce the chances of youth returning—in a revolving-door fashion—to crime and the structures of the criminal justice system.

For persons at a higher risk to offend, counselling and monitoring may be effective because the high-risk person has fewer skills to deal with crisis. Dr. Bonta found that counselling and cognitive-behaviour programs showed the best results. High-risk persons tended "to be concrete oriented in their thinking, not very verbal and inadept with certain pro-social skills (e.g., work, interpersonal)."[108] According to Dr. Bonta, an effective cognitive-behaviour treatment program required a focus on training behaviour skills and needed clear structure, and required a therapist who was openly warm yet firm and consistent, and who modelled the appropriate behaviour and provided feedback. He said this therapist should reinforce pro-social behaviour and discourage antisocial behaviour.[109]

Our youth custody facilities are filled with those marginalized by race, disability, mental illness, poor education, and traumatic childhoods. These are the unresilient. Understanding the concept of resiliency, and what factors influence and promote resilient behaviour amongst young people, is new and dynamic area. According to Dr. Susan Fine, the good news about this inquiry is "that those who rise above adversity do not belong to an exclusive club."

> It is not a closed system. However some people are their own best facilitators while others need help. Neither group should face its ordeals at the hands of care givers and environments that induce more stress by diminishing humanistic contacts and links with reality, by neglecting the person's need to predict or anticipate outcomes, or by ignoring the inner elements of coping and competency behaviors. It is troubling to note how well many of our treatment centers fulfill the criteria for extremely stressful negative life events.
>
> The variability of resilience may come as bad news for some, because it does not permit a simple recipe for treatment. Instead, we must commit ourselves to understanding the complexities of personality, coping capacities and environmental influences and use them to identify goals, interventions and environments that are meaningful to a given person under a given set of circumstances.[110]

Perhaps the above statement describes why marginalized youth from traumatic backgrounds so often do not become more resilient or crime-free after being incarcerated. It is however possible that, while incarceration in general raises crime rates, if our youth justice system drastically reduced custody for marginalized children, incarceration may be an effective response to crimes by middle-class, nondisabled children.

Jumping out of the Box: Effecting Change within the Youth Justice System

As we have shown in the preceding sections and chapters of this book, there are techniques and approaches that are capable of reducing crime and making our communities safer. Yet many of the approaches currently used in the youth justice system appear to hinder rather than help us in achieving this goal. To effect constructive change within the system is a goal shared by most justice professionals, from police officer to judge, from youth worker to prosecutor, from defence lawyer to therapist. Making this change is difficult, but not impossible.

People working within the youth justice system, however, often face a dilemma. They are usually drawn to this employment, at least in part, through a desire to help and improve the lives of those youth caught up in the system. Yet, at the same time, they experience and see structural inflexibilities and inequities within the system that seem to choke off the prospects of positive intervention and change. That leaves many workers with a lasting frustration, concluding that change is outside their grasp, and that they are powerless in the face of unbending bureaucracy. Others, however, reject this view, and spend their working days striving for change both on an individual level—working with youth—and at an organizational level—striving to make their organization more efficient, effective, and proactive.

At a conference in November 2001 entitled "Restorative Justice: Working with Youth,"[111] Chief Judge Barry Stuart of the Yukon Territorial Court stressed the need for those within the criminal justice system to get outside of the box of conventional practice and to consider new processes, rather than the existing ones that created the problems in the first place. A few months later, in *R. v. M.N.J.*, he further articulated this view in simple terms, saying it "is time—past time—to step outside of our cocoons."[112] There are many examples of people and organizations who have been able to achieve change, often against tall odds. The following discussion offers three examples of how people and organizations can effectively become agents of change.

Youth justice systems of Massachusetts and Pennsylvania

Dr. Jerome Miller was appointed commissioner of Youth Services for Massachusetts in 1969, and was subsequently appointed to a variety of influential positions within the American youth justice system. His story provides an excellent example of how an individual can promote change in responding to the needs of youth. It also shows how it is possible to respond to, and disprove, public perceptions about the necessity of punishing and incarcerating children.[113]

Dr. Miller came to see that developing individualized plans for young people that respected their desire to be a part of an effective community achieved less crime in society. In pursuing new options for young offenders, Dr. Miller suggested that, rather than the two existing options of jail and probation, there should be thirty to forty times that number. Rather than legislators determining the options by referring to the crime (i.e., legislating incarceration for numerous breaches of probation, adult sentences for certain numbers of certain offences) skilled diagnosticians would suggest appropriate plans. They would be expected to take the time with the youth to see what was necessary to go beyond criminal behaviours, and then match the youth's needs to the available programs. In practice, the debate in criminal justice circles became how to fund such a diverse approach.

Jerome Miller showed that he could think far ahead of common practice. He looked carefully at how many children really needed to be in custody. He considered how well community safety would be served by each child being in custody rather than being in one of the seventy to eighty programs outside of the custodial facilities. The answer was it was better for the youth, and better for the community, that money for such programming be found even if that meant less money for custody. In Massachusetts, for example, after being unsuccessful at convincing institutions to be more humane, he closed down the custody facilities for youth in the state.

That was clearly a dramatic step. Of course he met fierce resistance. During the years of his reforms, youth crime was going up all across North America (basically because at that time youth were a greater percentage of the population), but researchers at Harvard University[114] found that in regions where Miller's reforms were accepted and implemented, youth crime dropped significantly. However, in regions where his reforms were resisted, youth crime increased. This study found that resistance to the reforms essentially attempted to recreate custodial institutions.[115] Jerome Miller's experiment in Massachusetts showed that youth crime can be reduced by appropriately situating and supporting young persons in the community, rather than in custodial facilities.

Some time after the controversy of his Massachusetts's reforms lead to his removal, Dr. Miller went to work in the Pennsylvania youth justice system. As commissioner there, he convinced Governor Shapp to implement a proposal similar to that tried in Massachusetts. Dr. Miller's ability to try again was probably due to public outrage over a specific case. A sixteen-year-old boy had hung himself while serving time at an adult prison. This case began when the youth's mother found a marijuana roach in his jacket pocket. This woman called the local police chief, who suggested incarceration to scare the boy. However, whether because he was scared or for other reasons (if he was like our clients he was both scared and believed that his new friends in custody were his only friends) he escaped with an older boy.

Because of his escape, this youth went to adult prison, where he hung himself. At that time there were four hundred youths in adult prison in Pennsylvania. Jerome Miller described the reforms of this system he undertook, largely focused on his strategy of devising individual plans for young people.

> We moved those kids out of there, and, in doing so, we developed individualized plans for each of them. It might involve a group home, it might involve a return home but with other kinds of supervision or it might involve community service. It might involve a treatment centre, it might involve outpatient drug treatment, depending on the kid and why he was there. And it worked really very well. We individualized the plans.[116]

In order to follow his strategy of keeping youth out of custody and preparing plans of them, each child had to be assessed by a team of diagnosticians. But that raised the question of what constituted an effective diagnosis, and placed an emphasis on the range of viable options and alternatives available for high-need youth. Jerome Miller described the process of diagnosis he had applied in Massachusetts:

> It was a good experiment, incidentally, in diagnosis, because the same 400 kids had been diagnosed a year or so before I came to the state by a group of diagnosticians that the Probation Department and the Department of Corrections had hired. And they came to the conclusion that of the 400, 380 needed to be in secure settings, because they were truly dangerous. When we diagnosed the same group our diagnosticians said only 40 needed to be in such a facility.
> And you say, Well what's the difference? Did you pay the diagnosti-

cians to give you a fixed diagnosis? No, we didn't. We had some marvellous, independent, well-credentialed psychiatrists, psychologists, social workers. But what we did with them is we paid for their time to come to a day-long training session, in which we discussed what we would like to do with these kids, and we said that if the diagnosticians spent a lot of time with a kid and could come up with any kind of alternative plan— supervision, hiring someone to be on his arm 24 hours a day—you name it, anything they could come up with, we would pay for that kind of plan. So that freed the diagnosticians.[117]

Our discussion in the previous section of this book began with a question about why some children from terrible backgrounds still succeed. The answer, in social science circles, came to be known as resiliency, a behaviour that could be encouraged and facilitated. In order to promote resilient behaviour among its youth, a community must carefully consider the strategies being employed in dealing with children from terrible backgrounds. Jerome Miller explained:

> Diagnosis in the area of criminal justice is primarily determined by the risk at which diagnosticians think they are putting themselves, so they tend to be very, very conservative, unless it's their own kids or their neighbours kids. Then they can get pretty open and decent. When we have a system as we have now in this country (U.S.A.) which relies so much on imprisonment, it stultifies that whole field that deals with people. Everybody gets very narrow in their conceptions of what offenders are all about. If we had a system of a wide range of options, then our view of everybody in those options would change dramatically.[118]

Dr. Miller found that one needed flexibility and adaptability in dealing with problems encountered in making plans for young people. He made it clear that when dealing with these youth the plan may have to be renegotiated. He also saw clearly, decades before resiliency research, how thoroughly those concepts could increase the efficiency of the criminal justice system. For example, the QOP program discussed earlier achieved a 70 percent decrease in crime. The advantages of QOP were largely invisible one year into the program, but were astounding after four years. Jerome Miller explained:

> You need continuity. And you need a person who can arbitrate and negotiate that system and be around for an extended period of time. Because even learning self-discipline is still a matter of relationship. It's not a matter of imposed discipline, which is what prisons give. They impose it but when the person walks out the door, there's no one going to be standing there, threatening them. So, it comes from a relation-

ship. The Latin *disciplina*, comes from *discipulus*, the word for a disciple of a revered person, who you so revere that you want to be like them, and, therefore, you learn to internalize control, you learn to internalize discipline. Reliance on prisons does precisely the opposite. It prepares people to function in totalitarian societies or dependant societies, where everything is preordained and set out and on schedule and you'd just better adhere to everything you're told to adhere to. Now, that is not a preparation for a citizen in a democracy. The other is far better. So, you try to build that into the alternative plans.

And now there's no reason that can't be done. I mean, we're paying in this country an average of $25,000 a year now for the average inmate. For juveniles, we're paying an average $60,000–70,000 a year for them to be in reform schools that do nothing but make people worse. Well, my gosh, if I were given $60,000 for a delinquent youngster in my family, I could do very, very well.[119]

The Harvard University study of Jerome Miller's reforms in Massachusetts concluded that for "the state as a whole, … the reforms did not go nearly far enough…."[120] Dr. Miller's reforms in 1969 still had measurable effects in 1985. In 1969, before the reforms, 35 percent of adult inmates in Massachusetts were graduates of juvenile corrections. In 1985, about fifteen years after his reforms, only 18 percent were graduates of juvenile corrections.[121] It appears that paying careful attention to underlying problems and needs of children can have positive results.

Operation Help

If the story of Jerome Miller teaches us anything, it is that one determined and insightful person can make a difference. This is so even in the face of significant odds. Yet as much as Dr. Miller's story stands out, there are many similar ones within our own communities. In Saskatoon, for example, consider the impressive work being done in *Operation Help*.

Any lawyer appearing in Saskatoon youth court before Operation Help came into existence can testify to the tremendous agony that resulted from sex trade charges being laid against children and youth. There appeared to be nothing, other than custody, for these young people. Although there were strong people outside the youth justice system who tried to and did help some of them, other forces in the justice system suggested custody was the way to deter these children from being sexually exploited by johns on the streets. Many of these young people came to realize that most of their time at court was spent in a long debate over whether or not they should remain in custody, and if so for how long. The alternative was to have a youth worker, and often these young people saw this as a recipe for disaster; expecting them to become middle-class overnight. This meant keeping a strict curfew, ignoring their friends, keeping away from booze and drugs, going to school every day no matter what, and keeping a strict schedule of appointments with them. They feared an inevitable breach and a return to custody. It was not unusual for these youth to wail loudly the entire time they were in custody.

Naturally, none of this reduced the number of children living on the street. Below the surface, we suspect the situation made police, custody workers, prosecutors, judges, youth workers—everyone—heart sick. But what were the options? As Abraham Maslow pointed out, if the only tool you have is a hammer, you tend to see every problem as a nail.

Then, along came a strange alliance. The advocate for the youth on the sex-trade stroll at the time was the Egadz van. The chief person in this van was an Aboriginal man named Don Meikle. For years, his relationship with the police had been somewhat stormy because he kept information about children and youth confidential. He had a friend, social services worker Mike Dumphy, who supervised youth released on bail from custody. They approached Randy Hiusman, a city police officer they trusted. They also enlisted a local lawyer, Katherine Grier. Together, they looked at an idea from Edmonton that hadn't gained the support of police and bureaucrats there. Eventually the challenges they encountered in getting this program underway were overcome, and their team was expanded to include three police officers, a lawyer, a social worker, a street outreach worker, an Elder, a survivor of the sex trade, an Aboriginal court worker, and a worker to do follow-up.

Now, when the police decide to do their stings (pretend to be johns in order to arrest persons involved in the sex trade in public spaces), the Operation Help team waits in the library at the police station. There they have coffee, cookies, etc. Kathy Grier explained: "We all come from different backgrounds, actually we all used to fight each other, but now, I don't know if it's because we all see the tragedy or because we are all still up at 3:00 a.m., we've become close."[122]

When the arrested women are placed in the cells, the Operation Help team go down and invite them to join them. Social Worker Mike Dunphy described this situation:

> They're shocked... they're shocked that they aren't going to be charged... they can't believe they're going home with [their] plan... and we're there to support them... some of the toughest are shocked because they are used to being looked down upon... you see the Elder stroking their hair while they're crying... the way they describe it... there's love and

caring... because we don't judge, they have to be out there for one reason or another.[123]

Department of Justice (Canada) described this program as "an innovative, non-traditional, inter-agency outreach" which "seeks to make a difference in the lives and behaviour of these young people."[124] Operation Help "uses a focussed, co-ordinated approach to provide support from various community agencies," has allowed officers "to break down barriers and stereotypes held by these young, mostly aboriginal, women and work in partnership with them."[125]

This program is modelled after traditional Native healing circles.[126] A support circle comprised of a representative from each of the involved community agencies attempts to provide an environment of support and encouragement for the young person.[127] This circle, convened the same night a youth is apprehended by police, provides timely support and encouragement to the youth. According to the Justice Canada, "*Operation Help* seeks to reduce the re-arrest cycle; promote confidence and self-worth; emphasize rehabilitation not criminalization; deal with root social problems; and promote positive lifestyle changes."[128]

Constable Grant Obst, one of the police officers involved in this program, described Operation Help as a new approach, "a lot different than the old way of doing things" when we "were out there arresting people, attempting to suppress the sex trade."[129] This program, he said, focuses on underlying causes.

> We work to get to the underlying reasons why she's on the street... Is there somebody at home compelling you to work the street or reaping the revenue from you working the street? Are you an intravenous drug user? Or some other type of substance user?[130]

The Operation Help team has chosen not to charge those youth apprehended from the street with breach of probation or with communicating for the purposes of prostitution. As a result, there have been no charges under section 213 against sex-trade workers (either youth or women) for two years in Saskatoon court. Operation Help members now have the loyalty and respect of the youth and women they deal with, along with a range of police, social workers, lawyers, elders, outreach workers, survivors of the sex trade, and Aboriginal court workers.

We asked several of those involved with Operation Help—the police, the outreach worker, the lawyer, the social worker—how putting themselves on the line, working overtime, getting more involved in the lives of people in pain, committing yourself to them, how it affected them, their jobs and their stress level? "This is so much better than regular police work. I like it," said one police officer. "Best job I ever did," said one lawyer. "Best piece of social work I've ever done," said a social worker.

Indeed, the social worker told a story about how an Operation Help client was having difficulty with her social worker. He volunteered to go with her, to speak with her worker. "This worker didn't know me. I was shocked. She talked to this woman like she was dirt, just plain dirt." He then identified himself as a colleague, and as the chief steward for their union, and the other's attitude quickly changed. "So why would I reach out for help if I was in her circumstances? We do get burnt out, you hear these tales, but there's no way that someone should be treated with that much animosity and that much 'no time of day for you.' That's horrid." Yet, sadly, that was often the case before Operation Help looked at an old problem in a new way.

In Boston in October 2002, Operation Help won an award and international recognition from municipal governments for being a brilliant new way of dealing with the problem of the abysmal lives of those working in the sex trade.

The Alternate School (Tisdale School Division)

Another example of how individuals and organizations can make a difference for marginalized youth comes from Tisdale, Saskatchewan. One of the realities of community development is that although in one sense any initiative must "come from" and be supported by community members, one or several individuals almost always act as a spark plug. Starting and persevering through the period of change and development, these movers and shakers are absolutely essential. As a result, progressive initiatives happen because some people are prepared to take risks and question the status quo. In Tisdale, one such person is Tim Tarala, director of the Tisdale School Division.

Mr. Tarala, upon assuming his post in 1998, quickly came to see, as others had before him, that the established high school was not meeting the needs of all teenagers. Indeed, many were falling through the cracks, and either quitting school or becoming seriously truant. He set out to construct an alternate school for these youths. More than anything, this represented a philosophy of education and training for marginalized youth rather than any physical building or structure. The alternate school idea was an attempt to meet a whole series of needs held by these youths, including academics, economic training and career, life skills, addictions and family counselling, and a whole range of other needs.[131]

Mr. Tarala described how the children who fall through the cracks often come from families where there are serious parenting issues. These may be include alcohol and drug abuse by the parents, abusive behaviour towards the children, or simply a lack of appropriate supervision, often meaning that older children have been forced to assume the role of parent for their younger siblings. The youths themselves may have adopted many of their parents' behaviours, including addictions problems and inappropriate interpersonal behaviour.

He was adamant that the education system has to be flexible and capable of reacting to and compensating the unfulfilled needs of its subjects. If the problem is that children are coming to school hungry, feed the children. If they are lacking life skills, this is one of the things they should be taught. If young people have no job skills or knowledge about the work world, nothing stops this from becoming part of the curriculum under the education system umbrella.[132]

Mr. Tarala described how marginalized youth, because of their background and upbringing, often do not realize the educational and employment opportunities that are open to them. He said such youth simply do not have a connection to the community, and do not believe what the community has to offer is accessible to them. As a result they often react with anger, despair, and apathy towards the community. Mr. Tarala said the challenge is to reconnect these youth with the broader community, and to convince them that they can become a contributing member of it and, at the same time, receive those benefits they previously believed were off limits to them.[133]

Mr. Tarala also described how many of these youth often ended up in the justice system. Children without any hope of a future act out in inappropriate ways and fall into destructive patterns of behaviour, both for themselves and for the community at large.[134]

The Alternate School initiative is based around a philosophy of adapting to the individual needs of youth. The plans formed for each youth and the services and networks that are put in place to help meet each child's individual needs are dynamic and constantly subject to change. That said, the Student Support Centre forms a major part of the Alternate School Program. Located on Tisdale's main street, this centre provides a place where students can work towards a grade twelve education, at their own pace, and at the same time have many of their previously unaddressed needs met.

One such need is in the area of job skills and training. The Student Support Centre building is attached to a bicycle repair shop, which the students operate as a business. The *Tisdale Recorder,* reporting on the grand opening of the centre on 28 November 2002, said "the turn of the millennium ushered in a new approach to meeting the needs of at-risk students within the education system, but outside the box of traditional thinking."[135] Similarly, an online news service reported about the centre in the following terms:

> There is no question that this project offers young people who for all sorts of individual reasons have been unable to work through conventional high school the intense focus on skill development, mastery of content (this programme is a very academic oriented alternative programme) and the benefit of achievement that allows success to build upon success has and will continue to provide for more and more young people who might otherwise [have] found themselves at a dead end even before their adult life has begun.[136]
>
> The project provides the students enrolled in an entrepreneurial high school credit so that part of each day is spent working on bike repair and learning how a business works. Adam explained that part of each day is spent on this part of their project and the rest of the day is spent on course material. From the way he and Lindsay talked they are really enthusiastic about the practical nature of what they are learning and there are plans to see the shop continue operating as a summer project.[137]

Development of the Student Support Centre showed the vital role of community partnerships. These partners included the Tisdale School Division, the Rural Municipality of Tisdale, the Tisdale Credit Union, and the Métis Nation of Saskatchewan (Eastern Region). The first three partners were instrumental in facilitating the opening of the centre building on Main Street, while the Métis Nation "will provide the extensive *Pathfinder* hardware and software package that permits individualised self paced learning experience."[138]

The challenges of such a project should not be underestimated. Mr. Tarala described how, despite the broad and influential community support that this centre has come to enjoy in Tisdale, there clearly were other voices. There was local opposition to locating the Student Support Centre in the heart of downtown Tisdale. Some people suggested these high-risk students should be located in an out-of-the-way location. However, Mr. Tarala was adamant that, if these youth were to be brought back from the margins of society, they should be located in the centre of the business community. He will be conveying to the students at the Support Centre the importance of building relationships with the businesses next to them, through such outreach activities as visiting the neighbouring business owners, and goodwill gestures such as buying doughnuts for them.[139]

The Alternate School Program acts as a form of interagency network, through which students can access a myriad of services and agencies. As

Mr. Tarala told the Student Centre opening:

> Now that other agencies have seen the success of the integrated services agenda and that, with the infrastructure in place, the funding goes right to helping the kids, this only the beginning. Each time, addressing needs of students leads to more questions about what we can do. It's exciting to have flexibility that way.[140]

Mr. Tarala was quick to note that not all youth will finish grade twelve. As a recognition of this, the school division is involved in having youths placed into job opportunities through an Opportunities Project. This approach further emphasizes the importance of organizational flexibility and resiliency in reacting to the challenges faced.[141]

The Alternate School Program, including the Student Support Centre, is still in its infancy. As Mr. Tarala explained at the opening of this project, the Student Support Centre was designed to "provide an alternative to students who do not want to end their education but find it difficult fitting into the conventional structure of regular high school."[142] The extent to which this has happened can be seen in the comments of students, made at the Centre's grand opening. Support Centre student Gordon Deforest said: "It helped me to realize how important school is and also how important it is to respect those who have the desire to help us achieve our goals."[143] Student Randi Smith "told the audience that the Student Support Centre is a great place to learn because it provides more one-on-one help, an aspect which has helped her to greatly improve her grades."[144]

Sergeant Ken Homeniuk of the Tisdale RCMP confirmed that, over the short three years that the Alternate School Program has been functioning, youth crime in Tisdale has dropped substantially.[145] He said that although other factors such as increased public education by police may have affected this as well, the school has been a major contributor to decreased crime. This result is encouraging, and has lead Mr. Tarala to propose an overall crime-prevention strategy for Tisdale and area. This is based on the holistic and integrative model of the Alternate School, and seeks to engage the Tisdale area proactively in crime prevention, rather than what Mr. Tarala described as the reactive approach through the justice system.[146]

This section has provided only three examples of how individuals and organizations can think outside of the conventional box and provide progressive services, approaches, and responses for high-risk youth. Many more examples of such innovative individuals and programs exist. These people and organizations contribute both by helping to meet previously unaddressed needs of troubled youth, but also, and ultimately, by providing for safer and more compassionate communities.

"Quit putting them in jail, if that's possible in a dreamland world. Get them help with the issues they are facing, not only to heal themselves or to tell them what they should do."

S.N.

Chapter Nine

Future Directions for the Youth Justice System

Charting directions and strategies for the youth justice system is a complex challenge. So many factors come into play, and so many people—both adult and youth—are involved. But although the issues and debates are often interwoven and confusing, we suggest that there should be one guiding light: Underlying all thoughts about how the system should and can be made better is the reality that we have a responsibility to our youth to provide them support, training, guidance, protection, and assistance.

The *YCJA* seems to further stress these societal obligations, as its preamble states that "members of society share a responsibility to address the developmental challenges and the needs of young persons and to guide them into adulthood." The preamble further says that "communities, families, parents and others concerned with the development of young persons should, through multi-disciplinary approaches, take reasonable steps to prevent youth crime by addressing its underlying causes, to respond to the needs of young persons, and to provide guidance and support to those at risk of committing crimes."

These provisions are significant, yet not all of our societal obligations within the youth justice system are statutory. Our communal responsibilities to young people also arise under constitutional provisions and international covenants. The *YCJA* preamble recognizes this, providing that "Canada is a party to the United Nations Convention on the Rights of the Child and recognizes that young persons have rights and freedoms, including those stated in the *Canadian Charter of Rights and Freedoms* and the *Canadian Bill of Rights,* and have special guarantees of their rights and freedoms."

In *E.T.F.*, Justice Weagant referred both to this constitutional protection and to Canada's international obligations. Regarding protections under the *Charter of Rights,* he cited the case of *R.* v. *T.M.*,[1] which considered the right of young people to be free from cruel and unusual punishment. In the *T.M.* decision, Provincial Judge Lynn King found that "substandard conditions in a holding cell" contravened the *Charter,*[2] and directed a judicial stay of proceedings. Regarding Canada's international obligations, Judge Weagant said:

> I also note that Canada is a signatory nation to the 1989 United Nations Convention on the Rights of the Child, [1992] Can. Tr. Ser. No. 3, wherein Canada undertook to ensure such protection and care as is necessary for the well-being of children and to take all appropriate legislative and administrative measures (article 3). Further, Canada agreed to recognize the right of every child in the juvenile justice system to be treated in a manner consistent with the promotion of the child's sense of dignity and worth (article 40). E.T.F. fits the definition of "child" for the purpose of the Convention and Canada's obligations thereunder.
>
> Correctional workers and court security personnel knew that this young person was being injured and knew that he faced further potential victimization in the unsupervised atmosphere of the back of a transportation cube van. The system made no changes to itself to prevent peer-on-peer violence. The system then, or its commanders, was arguably complicit in the resulting peer-on-peer violence; the lack of supervision in known high-risk situations amounts to a reckless disregard for the well-being of the young person in provincial care.[3]

Clearly then, we as a society are obligated to support and care for young people found within the institutions and processes of the youth justice system. Our societal obligations, however, are broader. We have discussed in several places within this book how the youth found in our custodial facilities in no way represent a random sample of the young people across our communities. Indeed, among these youths there is an undeniable over-representation of disabled, Aboriginal, poorly educated, and poverty-ridden young people. In short, most of the youths in custody are marginalized in one way or another. As a result, a further, and perhaps the most critical, challenge for our society is how these youth can be brought into the mainstream.

As we discussed in our consideration of the concept of resiliency, study and dialogue about how to bring marginalized youth back into mainstream society come largely from outside the strict confines of the justice systems. Parenting experts such as Barbara Coloroso tell us that the most important focus in making better lives for our children should be on giving education and training, and hence in creating skills in our children.[4] Such education and training requires often expensive resources. But to put this into perspective, the Crime Prevention Council of Canada, in 1997, estimated costs of up to $100,000 per year for each youth in custody.[5]

Considering the *E.T.F.* case and other stories we have heard from the young people we represent, we wonder what lessons are being taught to children in custody, and how the dollars currently being spent in the youth correctional system might better be redirected. Directing at least some of these funds towards resources that would provide youth with the necessary skills to make them contributing members of their community and keep them out of the criminal justice system seems to be a much more promising strategy than that currently being followed.

When asked where the money currently being spent on custodial facilities could be redirected, a young Aboriginal woman with broad experience in the youth justice system suggested it could be better spent on programming for the youth and their families.

> Maybe they could spend it on programs that help youth. For example, it could be a program to help kids wanting to exit the sex trade. We know for a fact that no one will help us do this, and we can't wait forty years for it to happen, so it has to be ourselves who change it; for youth to change it and to exit the street trade. And we don't want to focus on the youths alone. We also want to focus on their families, or people they have in their lives. When we do something positive, like going out to eat, or a movie, or doing a workshop or a conference or a meeting, it has a positive effect not only on the youth but also on their family.[6]

In considering the challenging question of how to provide education and training for our youth, we must never forget that penal institutions are themselves a form of education. This point was stressed by Dr. Nils Christie:

> Instead of looking at prison as an answer to crime, one might turn it upside down and look at social phenomena as an answer to prison conditions. Children are sent to business school to learn. From teachers, from fellow students. And they will gain friends, and colleagues—for life. Prisons are no different, and they have their own curriculum.[7]

Vice-Chief Lawrence Joseph of the Federation of Saskatchewan Indian Nations stressed this point during an address to an Aboriginal justice conference in Regina. Vice-Chief Joseph described the impact of prison on young people, and the lessons learned there. His concerns were evidenced through the words of an Aboriginal youth recently released from custody, who described which youth became his peers while he was incarcerated.

> If you're shoplifting, and you are on probation, you are going to jail. More rules. Every time I go to jail, I see the same people in there. They may have just got picked up. The same old people. Obviously, they'll end up in jail. Some that's all they know how to do. They don't want to go to school. They think it's a waste of their time. Ten years to learn stuff, and then go to college. All I learned how to do was B&E's and stealing cars. Friends and relatives taught me, a fast way to get cash. That's all I knew how to do.[8]

Vice-Chief Joseph referred to jails as "universities of crime," and reminded conference delegates that sending an offender to prison has the effect of locking up the family as well. Indeed, discussion at this conference on so-called youth gangs confirmed that recruitment by these gangs has now become focused in correctional facilities.[9] This brings us back, once again, to the question posed by Justice Weagant in Toronto: to what degree are young people being endangered and put at further risk, as opposed to being protected and then rehabilitated, within our custodial facilities?[10]

We must always remember that there is no one way to "do" justice. If our discussion of restorative and other practices shows anything, we hope that it is that the future of the youth justice system is not set in stone. Indeed, it is dynamic and fluid, and we do have the power to change our practices in a way that will both reduce crime and ultimately make better citizens of our troubled youth. For those who suggest that getting tough on young offenders by putting more into custody for longer periods is the way to make our society safer, we have a simple answer. There is no empirical evidence to support this view, and as we have argued throughout, much to support the contrary.

In Canada, we have just embarked on a new statutory regime with the recent proclamation of the *Youth Criminal Justice Act*. As we have shown, this Act draws in large part on international experience in the area of youth justice. The sections dealing with extrajudicial measures (otherwise called diversion or alternative measures), conferencing, and interdisciplinary and interagency approaches to justice are clear examples of this. Yet making sense of the *YCJA* requires some consideration of the diverse and at times diametrically opposing views facing the federal government in drafting this legislation. Many provincial voices and federal politicians (largely from the right wing) urged a tougher and more punitive response to youth crime.

Other voices objected to the phenomenally high levels of youth custody in Canada and questioned whether there was any evidence that locking up our youth was having a positive effect on our society.

As a result of these often contradictory voices and factors, in many ways the *YCJA* represents a schizophrenic piece of legislation. On the one hand, it contains provisions that lower the age for which youth can be sentenced as adults for more serious crimes of violence and reduces the court's discretion to deal with these youths. On the other hand, the Act loudly asserts that every reasonable alternative to custody should be pursued, and states that the criminal justice system should not "use custody as a substitute for appropriate child protection, mental health or other social measures."[11]

Despite its mixed message, this Act clearly forms a framework underpinning the youth justice system. It sets out the principles and policies underlying the system, and provides the process and options open to police and to courts. But as important as the *YCJA* is to the justice system, it paints only part of the youth justice picture. Just as significant are the resources available to support offenders and victims within a community. Ultimately it is this range of agencies and services, and their collective ability to adapt to the challenge presented in helping and educating at risk youth, that will make a difference.

In chapter eight we described how some individuals and organizations have jumped out of the metaphorical box of established practice and applied new philosophies and approaches. To do so requires both initiative and courage, and illustrates the importance of applying knowledge gained in one sector of society to another area.

As an example of how effectively such an interchange of knowledge can be applied, consider how established rules for success in business might help devise strategies for the youth justice system. *Fortune* magazine recently contained an article entitled "10 Rules for Making Billion Dollar Business Ideas Bubble Up From Below."[12] These rules can easily be applied to youth justice policy.

Rule #1 was *set unreasonable expectations.* This reflects the idea that the higher goals are set, the more workers and managers will re-examine their assumptions and then strive to be more successful. If the vision for our justice system is a more peaceful community, with liberty and the right to pursue happiness, and if our mission statement is to reduce harm to others, then the hard business question is why do we spend eighty to ninety cents out of every available dollar on incarceration? Doesn't this appear to work against our goals?

Rule #2 was *stretch your business definition*. This means stop defining your business by what you do; define yourself by what you know and what resources you have. For example, General Electric "tells its business leaders that only companies with expansive business boundaries will outgrow its competitors." In many parts of this book, we cite justice commentators who argue this very point in relation to criminal law. "It's just a punishing system" is a common complaint. Unfortunately, so often those working within the youth justice system do not show the breadth of vision evident in the work of Dr. Jerome Miller, Tim Tarala, and those involved in Operation Help.

Rule #3 was *create a cause not a business*. If the mission is a peaceful society for all in a democracy, need we say more?

Rule #4 was *listen to new voices*. To follow up on these billion-dollar business ideas, we suggest listening to the youth involved, our clients. As well, listen to those outside the conventional justice system who have been successful in working with our clients. To do so would increase dramatically the chances of societal productivity.

Rule #5 was *design an open market for ideas*. The youth justice system is resistant to new ideas. We need to listen to people who approach the same old problems in a new and inspirational way, rather than rejecting any vision that does not fit with the status quo.

Rule #6 was *offer an open market for capital*. What is wrong with taking small amounts of capital from unproductive sectors (such as incarceration) and transferring it to support new ideas and approaches?

Rule #7 was *open up the market for talent*. *Fortune* magazine says workers "jump for the chance to work on the next great thing," and that companies "pursuing killer opportunities attract the best talent." When, we wonder, was the last time Dr. Jerome Miller, Dr. Nils Christie, Dr. John Braithwaite, or Sir Charles Pollard were invited to improve your community's youth justice system? Are the intelligent and creative people in your community—and you do have them—being invited to work on youth justice improvement? Or are the established youth justice players left to do what they will with the system?

Rule #8 was *lower the risks of experimentation*. See the comments above on rule #7. This is still true.

Rule #9 was *make like a cell—divide and divide*. *Fortune* magazine explains: "Cellular division drives innovation in many ways," largely by freeing up "human and financial capital from tyrannical orthodoxy of any single business model." Moreover, they say, it allows the nurturing of entrepreneurial talent, and keeps managers close to customers. The youth justice field is littered with successful experiments that have not replaced the unproductive practices largely because of the forces that resist changing our established models of youth justice.

Rule #10 was *pay your innovationors well.* We're sure you see this point on your own.

The unorthodox yet relevant linkages made above between business and justice strategies illustrate the many ways in which we can look at and rethink policies and approaches within the youth justice system.

A key focus for us in this book has been how our system currently handles charges of breaching a court order. The numbers of youth sent to custody for such "system-generated" offences is staggering, and a terrible waste. We wonder why many if not most breach charges could not be dealt with in a different way, either by diverting breach charges from the court system, or simply by an administrative act without the necessity of laying a charge.

The number of youth in custody for property offences is equally surprising. We wonder why more property offences could not be dealt with by way of a restitution order and an apology. Some of the money spent on custody for such offences could be used to find jobs for youth so that they could pay restitution to their victims.

Finally, in searching for new frontiers within the justice system, we encourage further and wider application of restorative processes involving young people, their families, community members, and youth system workers in a new and more constructive fashion.

To managers of young offender programs, to prosecutors, and to judges, our message is simple. We know you sense the futility of our present youth custody process. We know, from watching and talking to many of you, that you often feel powerless to do anything positive in the face of such challenges. In a strange way, you are like our clients: isolated, even marginalized, and frequently blamed for the system's failures, with little power to change the underlying problems. The challenges of an intransigent system are significant. Perhaps Machiavelli, in *The Prince,* said it best:

> It must be remembered that there is nothing more difficult to plan, more doubtful of success, no more dangerous to manage than the creation of a new system. For the initiation has the enmity of all who would profit by the preservation of the old institution and merely lukewarm defenders in those who would gain by the new ones.[13]

But change can happen. In pursuing new ideas and approaches, we urge those employed within the youth justice system to seek alliances with those who will support change. However, in doing so, we caution against applying programs that are intensive and designed for high-risk youth to low-risk youth. We now know that intensive programming provided to low-risk youth increases recidivism. Although many workers within the system would prefer to use intensive programming on low- rather than high-risk youth, to do so would only increase recidivism rates of the "treated," while further denying high-risk youth the intensive services they need to address their problems and reduce their chances of further crime.

A number of years ago Nike ran a commercial with the slogan "Just Do It!" For those employed within the youth justice system, we urge you to act on your inclinations towards change. We recognize it may be difficult for you to do so, and that there will likely be many obstacles in your path. But the risk will be worth the result, especially for many youth now looking out from the confines of our youth justice system. As Colin Wilson suggested: "Freedom lies in finding a course of action that gives expression to the part of him [that searches for meaning]."[14]

In attempting to figure out what approaches and policies work within the youth justice system to reduce crime and make our society safer, we return to a point made early in this book. Locking up young people has not been shown to reduce future criminality. In considering the effects of incarceration, a young Aboriginal woman with many past connections to the justice system was asked what she would change, if she could, in the youth justice system:

> Quit putting them in jail, if that's possible in a dreamland world. Get them help with the issues they are facing, not only to heal themselves or to tell them what they should do. It's really with their whole family, that's the problem. Help the whole family because the whole family could be suffering from abuse. My parents suffer from tremendous abuse in their childhood and their lives. And they think maybe this generation, their children, will be better and a lot more healed, but we are suffering the effects of it.[15]

The Washington State Institute for Public Policy found that boot camps increased recidivism by 10 percent. In Canada, a Solicitor General study found incarceration increased recidivism by as much as 6 percent. Yet, many children and youth still go into custody in Canada. We wonder what odds we are promoting by this strategy. As an interesting comparison, the vice president of Casino Regina was interviewed and explained the existing odds in favour of the casino.[16] He said the odds in favour of the house on blackjack (if the player is highly skilled) were 0.62 percent, for Chemin de Fer (James Bond's game) 1.25 percent, and for roulette 2.7 percent.

Putting this into perspective, it appears that the odds of promoting further criminality by incarcerating youth are significantly higher than the odds enjoyed by a casino.

That of course leads to the question of what works in reducing crime if it is not custody. We have no certain answers to this question, but from decades of standing beside youth, families, victims, youth workers, prosecutors, and police we have a number of suggestions.

First, the youth who are either in custody or in danger of custody agree that harming others is wrong. They say they act in hurtful ways largely because of their circumstances. These include social factors—such as poor family relationships, poverty, racism, poor role models, disabilities, a past history of abuse, living in disorganized neighbourhoods, and being unable to fit into education and other systems—as well as poorly developed life-skills about how to deal with problems and conflict. Programs that address and help to overcome social and life-skills deficits are likely to reduce the number of harmful acts by these youths, and hence reduce the number of them appearing within the youth justice system.

Second, young people agree that a strong relationship with one mentor, one person who cares, one person who can teach them pro-social skills, one person who likes them, is the key. One youth interviewed in Saskatoon in the presence of a respected Aboriginal Elder described him as a friend and guide. This young man had a very large, well muscled body, and his peers expected him to act like he looked. His mentor challenged this youth to live in peace.

Another youth, a young woman, described her life on the street. She was sexually abused by johns and pimps at eleven and twelve years of age. Then she went to Vancouver to attend a conference including other youth from around the world who had been similarly abused. When she returned to Saskatoon, she had changed. She started an organization called Sexually Exploited Youth Speak Out (SEYSO). At the same time, she came to intuitively realize that she needed a mentor.

Two other youth we spoke to had artistic talent. They were fortunate enough to find SCYAP (Saskatchewan Community Youth Arts Project). The program involved a school day–type schedule with a warm, energetic, compassionate professional artist whom these two youth clearly admired and wished to emulate. The young person we interviewed who had been successfully matched with a mentor and become active in the artistic program said:

> Now people trust me, now I'm responsible. For me, doing what I want is big. Everyone told me I could be a great artist, and I wanted to be one

bad. But I had no chance. Now I do. It's exposure to the good stuff. My teacher [an artist] is going to get me work on a 20x60-foot mural.[17]

One of these youths described the strong relationship he had enjoyed with one youth worker, in contrast to others:

> Once I had a worker who really tried. She made me feel like trying. She really badly wanted me to do alcohol treatment, so I did. I tried real hard cause I really respected her. I really didn't pay much attention to youth workers who didn't respect me.[18]

Third, youth we talked to said that it's important for them to be involved in something that improves their community. Earlier we referred to the judge from St. Kitts who became disillusioned with her country's state-sanctioned beating of young offenders. The idea she took back to St. Kitts with her from Canada was the importance of youth working in partnership with other people committed to making the community better. This reflects the importance of connecting marginalized youth with those movers and shakers within a community who can make a difference for them. These youth need to be befriended. They expect rejection, but if welcomed, they will return this gesture in an enthusiastic way, committed to the cause of community betterment.

Finally, in seeking to involve these youth constructively within the community, find something that these young people really enjoy. If at all possible, link these youth with someone who is very good in that pursuit, and encourage them to learn self-discipline and learning with pleasure. The process of changing oneself is hard, and it's important to know that joy and not more pain is the goal. The young woman speaking out publicly against sexual exploitation of youth, the two young men learning art, the young man partnered with an Elder, all speak of the power of linking enthusiasm to growth. One of the young artists referred to above said that for years now he's had a problem with alcohol—it was a factor in all his crimes—but that art was far more fun than drinking.

We end then, as we began, not claiming to have all the answers about the challenges facing the youth justice system, but rather raising concerns, based on our experience, and suggesting alternatives. We do so largely in response to, and perhaps on behalf of, the children we represent. Webb Hubbell, once Arkansas chief justice and associate attorney-general of the United States, and subsequently a serving prisoner, once said, in referring to the those imprisoned:

> In addition to punishment we should also offer compassion, forgiveness and a chance for true freedom. If we begin to steer a new course we

will reduce the chance of creating a permanent caste of untouchables who are bitter, resentful and vengeful....[19]

Perhaps the most important factor underlying changes to our youth justice system is effecting a shift in societal attitudes towards young people and their often desperate circumstances. If our work has done anything, we hope that it has begun the debate that will result is such a shift. In the long run, only strategies designed to include youth, and especially marginalized youth, in our broader societal plans will bear fruit. This was recognized by the business development branch of the government of Canada, whose Innovation Strategy for 2002 centred on the importance of inclusion.

> In the new global knowledge economy of the 21st century property depends on innovation, which, in turn, depends on the investments we make in the creativity and talents of our people. We must invest not only in technology and innovation but also in the Canadian way, to create an environment of inclusion, in which all Canadians can take the advantage of their talents, their skills and their ideas.[20]

Notes

Introduction

[1]Although the slightly lower youth incarceration in the U.S. may be influenced significantly by the high rates of young people transferred to adult court and sentenced there as adults (hence reducing the number of youth in juvenile detention), the fact is that Canada has an unacceptably high rate of youth incarceration.

[2]*R. v. J.K.E.* [1999] Y.J. No. 119 (Yukon Ter. Ct.—Youth Ct.) at paragraph 61.

Chapter 1

[1]The figures in this comparison are taken from M. Oulmet, "Explaining the American and Canadian Crime 'Drop' in the 1990's" (January 2002) Can. J. Crim. 33–50.

[2]D. Cayley, "Prison and Its Alternatives" *Ideas* (CBC Radio transcript, 1996).

[3]D. Cayley, *The Expanding Prison: The Crisis in Crime and Punishment and the Search for Alternatives* (Toronto: House of Anansi Press, 1998) at 67.

[4]*Ibid.* at 90. Cayley cites Mathiesen, *Prison on Trial* at 54 as the source of these quotes.

[5]N. Christie, *Crime Control as Industry: Towards Gulags Western Style,* 3d ed. (London: Routledge, 2000) at 200. Also see the discussion about Europe and the United States in chapter 3.

[6]Canadian Centre for Justice Statistics, *Youth Custody and Community Services Canada, 1999/00* Statistics Canada Cat. No. 85-002-XPE, 21:12 at 4 (Figure 1). Saskatchewan's Aboriginal youth are said to make up 75 percent of secured custody admissions, while comprising only 15 percent of the youth population. Other interesting comparisons are seen in Manitoba (79 percent of secured admissions compared to 16 percent of the overall youth population) and Alberta (35 percent of secured admissions to 5 percent of the overall youth population).

[7]Y. Henteleff, *Position Paper on the Proposed Amendments to the YOA* (Ottawa: Learning Disabilities Association of Canada: 10 October 1996) at 52 (Appendix III). In Virginia, the Department of Criminal Justice Services, in a published report in 2000, stated that: "In Virginia, data on juveniles with special education needs in the juvenile justice correctional system ... between 1993–1998, approximately 39% to 42% of juveniles committed to the Department of Juvenile Justice were identified as being eligible for special educational services at the time of commitment. One of the most frequently identified special educational needs was services for learning disabilities." As well, "Keilitz and Dunivant (1987) indicate that adolescents with learning disabilities were 220% more likely to be adjudicated than other adolescents." *Crime Times* 8:1 (2002) at 5.

[8][2001] Y.J. No. 45, 2001 YKTC 501.

[9]*Ibid.* at paragraph 39.

[10]D. Cayley, "Prison and Its Alternatives" *Ideas* (CBC Radio transcript, 1996) at 1. This same research by Dr. Christie was discussed in D. Cayley, "Crime Control as Industry" *Ideas* (transcript, Canadian Broadcasting Corporation,1993) at 2.

[11]J. Marquat, S. Ekland-Olson & J. Sorenson, *The Rope, the Chair, and the Needle: Capital Punishment in Texas, 1923–1990* (Austin: University of Texas Press, 1998).

[12]This point was discussed during an interview with Professor Tony Doob, University of Toronto (9 October 2002) Toronto, Ontario.

[13]Rodger Doyle, "Reducing Crime: Rehabilitation is Making a Comeback," *Scientific American* (May 2003) 33A.

[14]Alan D. Gold's Netletter, Issue 213 (ADGN/2000-1552) at 11, citing "Research Shows That Punishment Does Not Lessen Crime" Iceland Review (30 October 2000).

[15]"Research Summary: The Effects of Punishment on Recidivism," from P. Smith, C. Goggin & P. Gendreau, *The Effects of Prison Sentences and Intermediate Sanctions on Recidivism: General Effects and Individual Differences* (Ottawa: Solicitor General Canada, 2002), User Report 2002–01, online: Solicitor General of Canada <http://www.sgc.gc.ca/corrections/publications_e.asp>.

[16]R. Corrads & A. Markwart, "The need to Reform the YOA in Response to Violent Young Offenders: Confusion, Reality or Myth?" (1994) 36 Can. J. Crim. 343 at 366.

[17]*Ibid.*

[18]B. Clark & T. O'Reilly-Fleming, "From Care to Punishment: Rehabilitating Young Offender Programming in Ontario" in B. Clark & T. O'Reilly-Fleming, eds., *Youth Injustice: Canadian Perspectives* (Toronto: Canadian Scholars Press Inc, 1993) 189 at 194.

[19]See J. Miller, *Last One Over the Wall* (Columbus, Ohio: Ohio State University Press, 1991).

[20]Associated Press report (14 December 1999).

[21]*Baltimore Sun* (15 December 1999).

[22]As a further caution in applying the adult correctional model to young offenders, Professor Nicholas Bala of Queen's University observed that the evidence is clear that increasing the number of youth transferred to the adult system does not reduce their future crimes and does not improve community protection. "The 1995 YOA Amendments: Compromise or Confusion?" (1994) 26 Ottawa L. Rev. 643.

[23]"Coming to a Neighbourhood Near You" *The Economist* (5 May 2001) 23.

[24]Poor school performance (or poor attachment to school) has been found to be the best and most stable predictor of criminal offending. See M. LeBlanc, É. Vallièères & P. McDuff (1993). "The prediction of males' adolescent and adult offending experience" (1993) 35 Can. J. Crim. 459–78 at 459. The same is true of education levels of youth when they "graduate" to the federal penitentiary. Approximately 65 percent of offenders test at lower than a grade eight graduate. Further, 82 percent are less than grade ten. This was referred to in a publication of the Correctional Service of Canada, Correctional Education Programs, September 1992.

[25]D. Cayley, "Prison and Its Alternatives" *Ideas* (CBC Radio transcript, 1996) at 49.

[26]B. Clark & T. O'Reilly-Fleming, *supra* note 18 at 195.

[27]Jerome Miller, "Prison and Its Alternatives" *Ideas* (CBC Radio transcript, 1996).

[28][2002] O.J. No. 4497. Toronto Registry No. YW000914 (Ontario Court of Justice).

[29]Interview with B.W. (19 December 2002) White Buffalo Youth Lodge, Saskatchewan.

[30]12 June 1999.

[31]Interview with R.T. (19 December 2002) Saskatoon, Saskatchewan.

[32]P. Monture-Okanee, "Thinking about Aboriginal Justice: Myths and Revolution" in R. Gosse, J. Youngblood Henderson & R. Carter, eds., *Continuing Poundmaker's & Riel's Quest* (Saskatoon: Purich, 1994) 222 at 227.

[33]Cayley, *supra* note 25 at 25.

[34]Trevor Sanders, "Sentencing of Young Offenders in Canada, 1998/99" 20:7 Juristat at 7. The total youth custody count for Canada in 1996/97 of 25,278 represents 105 per 10,000 youth in the Canadian population, secure custody 49/10,000, and open custody 56/10,000.

[35]M. Shaw, book review of *Detention in Greenland* by H. Brochman (2002) Can. J. Crim. at 97. (Meffelester on Greenland. Man and Society 25. Copenhogem: Danish Polar Centre 2001.) According to this book review, in Greenland jails, "[l]ength of sentence or the seriousness of the offence are of limited significance." After a few weeks everyone, including those convicted of murder, are allowed weekend passes and evening passes. The staff takes prisoners hunting and

for the mentally unstable fishing. Family visits are held outside the institution, not in. But the prisoners feel the deprivations weigh heavily on them and they want better educational help, better community understanding, and "what the inmates find lacking in the staff is kindness, encouragement—in general more positive attitude—and the ability to deal with conflicts." The staff would like more training and more treatment programs.

[36]Interview with R.T. (19 December 2002) Saskatoon, Saskatchewan.

Chapter 2

[1]K. Lane, *The Philosophy of the Young Offenders Act and Its Impact on the Formal Legal Education and Practice of Advocates for Youth.* (LL.M. Thesis, Univeristy of Alberta, 1995) at 6.

[2]*Ibid.*

[3]*Ibid.* at 27.

[4]J. Hak, "The Young Offenders Act" in J. Winterdyk, ed., *Issues and Perspectives on Young Offenders in Canada* (Toronto: Harcourt Brace Canada, 1996) 45 at 48.

[5]J. Braithwaite, *Crime, Shame and Reintegration* (Cambridge: University Press, 1989) at 111–18.

[6]This wording is taken from section 3(1)(f) of the YOA.

[7]K. Roach, *Due Process and Victims' Rights: The New Law and Politics of Criminal Justice* (Toronto: University of Toronto Press, 1999) at 207–8.

[8]T. Milner. "Juvenile Legislation" in J. Creechan & R. Silverman, eds., *Canadian Delinquency* (Toronto: Prentice Hall, 1995) 65 at 69.

[9]Section 12 *Juvenile Delinquents Act* R.S.C 1970 CJ-3.

[10]R. Smandych & B. Hogeveen, "Origins of the Newly Proposed Canadian Youth Criminal Justice Act: Political Discourse and the Perceived Crisis in Youth Crime in the 1990s" in R. Smandych, ed., *Youth Justice: History, Legislation and Reform* (Toronto: Harcourt Canada, 2001) 144.

[11]*House of Commons Debates* (20 February 1995).

[12]*Ibid.* (21 October 1999).

[13]C. Schmitz, "Youth Court Cases Down 7.4 Percent Since '92–3" (9 June 2000) 20:6 *The Lawyers Weekly* at 1.

[14]T. Quigley, "Some Issues in Sentencing Aboriginal Offenders," in R. Gosse, J. Youngblood Henderson & R. Carter, eds., *Continuing Poundmaker's & Riel's Quest* (Saskatoon: Purich, 1994) 269 at 278–79.

[15]*House of Commons Debates* (22 March 1999).

[16]Smandych and Hogeveen, *supra* note 10 at 145.

[17]*Ibid.*

[18]S.C. 2002, c. 1 (37th Parliament, 2d Session).

[19]Subsections 3(1)(b)(iv) and (v) of the *YCJA*.

[20]Subsection 3(1)(c)(iv) of the *YCJA*.

[21]In subsection 3(1)(c)(ii).

[22]In "The Good, the Bad, and the Unaltered: An Analysis of the Youth Criminal Justice Act" 4 Can. Crim. L.R. 249 at 253–54, Professor Sanjeev Anand of the University of Alberta, a former prosecutor, expressed concern over the potentially onerous weight these provisions may place on prosecutors. While acknowledging the importance of treating victims with courtesy and compassion and answering their questions and responding to their concerns, Professor Anand stated that prosecutors—already under heavy caseloads in many provinces—will face even more responsibility if required to notify "victims of crime about the sometimes numerous court appearances of a young offender." This, he said, would lead to "the necessity of hiring more prosecutors," and redirecting funding from "much needed youth crime prevention and diversion programs."

[23]*Ibid.* at 251.

[24]Interview with S.N. (18 December 2002) Saskatoon, Saskatchewan.

[25]Interview with R.T. (19 December 2002) Saskatoon, Saskatchewan.

[26]In subsection 3(1)(d)(i).

[27]Justice Canada PowerPoint presentation, "The Youth Criminal Justice Act: Overview" PARCA Youth Conference (12–13 March 2002).

[28]L. Tolstoy, *Anna Karenina.* (Toronto, London, etc.: Penguin Classics, 2001), 1.

[29]A prohibition under section 161 of the *Criminal Code*—which prevents an offender convicted of a sexually-related offence from attending at public areas frequented by children or from being employed by or volunteering for an organization where that offender would be in a position of trust over children—cannot be made against a young person charged under the *YCJA*. Further, section 51 of the *YCJA* sets out a mandatory firearms and weapons prohibition for a young person found guilty of an offence referred to in subsections 109(1)(a) to (d) of the *Criminal Code* (encompassing certain offences involving violence, firearms, and/or weapons or involving trafficking, importing, or producing drugs).

[30]Interview with Professor Sanjeev Anand (21 August 2002) via e-mail.

[31][1999] Y.J. No. 119 (Yukon Ter. Ct.—Youth Ct.).

[32]*Ibid.* at paragraph 60.

[33]Statistics Canada, "Youth Court Statistics 1998–9" (Ottawa: Canadian Centre for Justice Statistics, 2000).

[34]Interview with R.T. (19 December 2002) Saskatoon, Saskatchewan.

[35]P. Greenwood & S. Turner, *Selective Incapacitation Revisited: Why High Risk Offenders Are Hard to Predict* (Washington: National Institute of Justice, 1987).

[36]J. Miller, *Last One Over the Wall* (Columbus, Ohio: Ohio State University Press, 1991) 182.

[37]R.S.O. 1980, c. 400, s. 70(3).

[38]T. Quigley, "Some Issues in Sentencing Aboriginal Offenders," in R. Gosse, J. Youngblood Henderson & R. Carter, eds., *Continuing Poundmaker's & Riel's Quest* (Saskatoon: Purich, 1994) 269 at 283.

[39]Anand, *supra* note 22 at 265.

[40]N. Bala, "The 1995 Young Offenders Act Amendments: Compromise or Confusion?" (1994) 26 Ottawa L. Rev. 643 at 662, quoted in *ibid.* at 265.

[41]Anand, *supra* note 22 at 266.

[42]In section 71.

[43]*House of Commons Debates* (30 January 2002) 135.

[44]Interview with R.T. (19 December 2002) Saskatoon, Saskatchewan.

[45][1999] 1 S.C.R. 688, (1999) 133 C.C.C. (3d) 385, 23 C.R. (5th) 197.

[46]*Ibid.,* paragraph 33.

[47]1992, 71 C.C.C. (3d) 347 (Yuk. Ter. Ct.) at 355–56.

[48]N. Poetschke, Community Group Conferencing Statistics (Calgary Police Service, Research and Development Section, June 2000).

[49]Interview with Cst. Leah Barber (11 December 2000) Calgary, Alberta.

[50]In section 38(2)(e)(i)-(ii).

[51][1990] 2 S.C.R. 755, 79 C.R. (3d) 219, 59 C.C.C (3d) 1.

Chapter 3

[1]M. Geigen-Miller, *Policy Implications and Implementation Strategies for Section 35 of the Youth Criminal Justice Act* (Ottawa: National Youth in Care Network, 2002) at 15–16.

[2][2001] Y.J. No. 45, 2001 YKTC 501.

[3]At paragraph 39. "Recent studies of federal inmates have shown that they have a far higher rate of major disorder (e.g., schizophrenia, major depression, bi-polar disorder) than that of general Canadian population." Of federal inmates with mental disorders, 55.0 percent had anxiety disorders, 29.8 percent had depressive disorders. Unfortunately, less than half had reported their symptoms to a physician or mental health professional. *Offender Profiles* (Canada: National Crime Prevention Council, September 1995) at 2.

[4]N. Bala, *Young Offenders Law* (Toronto: Irwin Law, 1997) at 18.

[5]J. Winterdyk, *Issues and Perspectives on Young Offenders in Canada* (Toronto: Harcourt Brace Canada, 1996) at 24.

⁶*Ibid.*

⁷*Ibid.* at 29.

⁸*Ibid.* at 30.

⁹*Ibid.* at 30–36.

¹⁰I. Gomme, "Theories of Delinquency" in J. Cheechan & R. Silverman, eds., *Canadian Delinquency* (Toronto: Prentice Hall, 1995) 155 at 157.

¹¹*Ibid.*

¹²Winterdyk, *supra* note 5 at 26.

¹³*Ibid.* at 27.

¹⁴*Ibid.* at 27.

¹⁵Merton discussed in Gomme, *supra* note 10 at 158.

¹⁶*Ibid.*

¹⁷Winterdyk, *supra* note 5 at 25.

¹⁸Gomme, *supra* note 10 at 158 & 159.

¹⁹*Ibid.*

²⁰Winterdyk, *supra* note 5 at 26.

²¹American Psychological Association, Commission on Youth Violence, *Violence and Youth, Psychology's Response* (Washington: American Psychological Association, 1993) at 17, as cited in Bala, *supra* note 4 at 19.

²²D. O'Mahony & R. Deazley, *Juvenile Crime and Justice* (Belfast: Northern Ireland Statistics and Research Branch, Criminal Justice Police Division, 2000) at 13.

²³*Ibid.*

²⁴These factors were summarized in *ibid.* at 13 and were taken from D.P. Farrington, *Understanding and Preventing Youth Crime* (York: Joseph Rowntree Foundation, 1996) and D.P. Farrington, "Human Development and Criminal Careers" in *The Oxford Handbook of Criminology*, 2ᵈ ed. (Oxford: University Press, 1997).

²⁵O'Mahony & Deazley, *supra* note 22 at 15. Citations were omitted from the end of this quotation.

²⁶Bala, *supra* note 4 at 20.

²⁷CBC Radio "This Morning" (26 May 1998).

²⁸*Ibid.*

²⁹Interview with S.N. (18 December 2002) Saskatoon, Saskatchewan.

³⁰J. Conry & D. Fast, *Fetal Alcohol Syndrome and the Justice System* (Vancouver: Law Foundation of B.C., 2000) at 1.

³¹F. Boland, R. Burrill, M. Duwyn & J. Karp, *Fetal Alcohol Syndrome: Implications for Correctional Service* (July 1998) [unpublished] at 14.

³²Conry & Fast, *supra* note 30 at 1.

³³[2001] S.J. No. 70 (QL) (Sask. Yth. Ct.).

³⁴*Ibid.* at paragraph 25.

³⁵Boland, Burrill, Duwyn & Karp, *supra* note 31 at 2.

³⁶*Ibid.* at 22.

³⁷D. Bray & P. Anderson, "Appraisal of the Epidemiology of Fetal Alcohol Syndrome among Canadian Native Peoples" (1989) 80 Can. J. Public Health 42–45.

³⁸Boland, Burrill, Duwyn & Karp, *supra* note 31 at 24.

³⁹*Ibid.*

⁴⁰*R. v. R.C.P.* [2000] S.J. No. 373 (QL) (Sask. Youth Ct.)

⁴¹Conry and Fast, *supra* note 30 at 2.

⁴²*R. v. Abou* [1995] B.C.J. No. 1096 (QL) at paragraph 11.

⁴³*W.D., supra* note 33.

⁴⁴*Ibid.* at paragraph 35.

⁴⁵*Elias, supra* note 2.

⁴⁶ *Ibid.* at paragraph 39.

⁴⁷[1994] B.C.J. No. 3160, November 24, 1994, B.C.S.C.

[48][1998] B.C.J. No. 3135, June 10, 1998 (Prov. Ct.).

[49][1999] A.J, No 1357, October 26, 1999 (Prov. Ct.);

[50][1998] B.C.J. No. 1505, June 23, 1999 (B.C.C.A.).

[51][1999] Y.J. No. 57, July 2, 1999, (Yukon Terr. Ct).

[52]Conry & Fast, *supra* note 30 at 69.

[53]*Ibid.* at 72.

[54]*Ibid.* at 73.

[55]*R. v. M.L.* [2000] S.J. No. 17 (QL) at paragraph 58 & 59.

[56]*R.C.P.*, *supra* note 40 at 17 & 18.

[57]Although not dealing with a victim of FAS, Judge Sheila Whelan of the Youth Court of Saskatchewan, in *R. v. J.A.P,* provided a thorough consideration of the issue of legal capacity regarding a mentally handicapped youth said to be functioning intellectually at lower than the first percentile of the general population. This decision provides an interesting discussion of the problem faced by a court in deciding between conflicting expert opinions on the fitness of a youth to stand trial. Judge Whelan accepted the opinion of two psychologists, which contradicted that of a psychiatrist, in finding that the defence had proved the mentally handicapped boy was unfit to stand trial. [2000] S.J. No. 260 (QL) (Sask.Yth.Ct.)

[58]*W.D., supra* note 33, at paragraph 20.

[59]M. Vandenbrink, "Counsellor Challenge: The Addictions Client with Fetal Alcohol Damage" (October–November 1998) 18:5 *Developments: FAS/ARBD.*

[60]Conry and Fast, *supra* note 30 at 104.

[61]*M.L., supra* note 55 at paragraph 60.

[62]Conry and Fast, *supra* note 30 at 105.

[63]*Regina Leader Post* (21 December 2000).

[64]National Institute of Justice, Looking at Crime from the Street Level conference, USA (November 1999) abstract online: <http://www.ilj.org>.

[65]K. Makin, "Judges Live in Torment, Study Finds" *Globe and Mail* (14 August 2002). As well, the *Guardian Weekly* (17 March 1996) quoted Lord Taylor (Lord Chief Justice and Senior Judge of England and Wales) as saying that any evidence that harsher sentences "will achieve anything beyond a bonanza for prison architects simply does not exist." The article went on to quote from many who favoured harsh punishments. One of these critics, rather than presenting any evidence to contradict Lord Taylor, replied that judges were "only lawyers in extremely dodgy clothing."

[66]Lawyers Concerned for Lawyers (an independent association of lawyers and judges), undated pamphlet.

[67]Interview with Mike Dunphy (25 November 2002) Saskatoon, Saskatchewan.

[68]"Round Up the Usual Suspects" *Globe and Mail* (10 April 2000) A13.

[69]Interview with B.S. (21 May 2002) Saskatoon, Saskatchewan.

[70]In section 39(5).

[71]Dr. Szasz's theory was taken from "School Shootings and the Death of Common Sense," PSYCHNEWS International 6:1 (May 2001), at 1.

[72]Saskatchewan, *Report of the Indian Justice Review Committee* (1992) 13.

[73]*Ibid.*

[74]*Explaining Aboriginal Corrections,* Research Summary 1:4 (November 1996) at 2.

[75]M. Males & D. Macallair, "An Analysis of Curfew Enforcement and Juvenile Crime" Western Criminology Review (1999) at 2.

[76]*Ibid.*

[77]*About Youth Crime and Youth Court* (Department of Social Services, Government of Saskatchewan, 1997) YOP-2 03/09.

[78][2002] BCJ No. 1877 (QL), 2002 BCSC 1198.

[79]At paragraph 18.

[80]T. Gabor, *Everybody Does It! Crime by the Public* (Toronto: University of Toronto Press, 1994).

[81]*Ibid.* at 52.

[82]*Ibid.* at 54.

[83]*Ibid.* at 56.

[84]*Ibid.* at 54.

[85]Interview with R.T. (19 December 2002) Saskatoon, Saskatchewan.

[86]If one considers that most people have committed crimes, then those calling for more and harsher punishments have probably themselves committed a crime. Certainly, several people close to them—their parents, aunts and uncles, siblings, their own children, their siblings' children, their best friends at work and in the neighbourhood—have committed a crime. If everyone who has committed a crime should be caught and punished harshly as they advocate, the question must be asked who amongst their close family and friends would they turn in? If, however, the purpose of all actions in this field is to reduce the harmful acts to each other, why are they asking to increase spending on our most expensive option (incarceration) which increase recidivism?

[87]*Ibid.* at 16.

[88][2002] B.C.J. No. 1877 (QL) (B.C.S.C.).

Chapter 4

[1]Interview with R.T. (19 December 2002) Saskatoon, Saskatchewan.

[2]Our work is shaped by the words, insights, and struggles of the many Aboriginal youth who have been our clients and who have confided in us. The description of the historical record comes from those conversations, and will vary considerably in form and content from most historical versions found in academic literature.

[3]In 1805, Indian leader Red Jacket (or Sagayewatha) described dealings between his people and the newcomers:

> If we had any dispute about hunting grounds, they were generally settled without the shedding of much blood: but an evil day came upon us; your fore fathers crossed the great waters and landed on this island. Their number were small; they found friends, not enemies; they told us they had fled from their own country for fear of wicked men and came here to enjoy their religion. They asked for a small seat; we took pity on them, granted their request, and they sat down among us; we gave them corn and meat; they gave us poison in return. The white people had now found our country, tidings were carried back and more came among us; yet we did not fear them, we took them to be friends; they called us brothers; we believed them and gave them a larger seat. At length, their number had greatly increased; they wanted more land, they wanted our country. Our eyes were opened and our minds became uneasy. Wars took place; Indians were lured to fight against Indians and many of our people were destroyed. They also brought strong liquors among us; it was strong and powerful and has slain thousands."

In K. Goodenham, *I Am An Indian* (Toronto: J.M. Dent and Sons, 1969), online: Solicitor General of Canada, Conquest by Law <http://www.sgc.gc.ca/publications/abor_policing/Conquest_by_Law_e.asp>.

[4]"And the Indians had said 'Keep your wine and your brandy in prison. It is your drinks which do all the ill and not we Indians.'" A.G. Bayley, ed., *The Conflict of European and Eastern Algonquian Cultures, 1507 to 1700* (Toronto: University of Toronto Press, 1969) at 66, online: Solicitor General of Canada, Conquest by Law <http://www.sgc.gc.ca/publications/abor_policing/Conquest_by_Law_e.asp>.

[5]For example, the enormously important fur trade was largely made possible by Indian women. Sylvia Van Kirk writing in *The Beaver* (Winter 1972), a Hudson's Bay Company publication, stated at 4:

> By the time of the union of two companies (Hudson Bay Company and the North-West Company) in 1821, taking a native woman for a wife was a widespread social prac-

tice.... The first missionaries who arrived relatively late in Rupert's Land were horrified by the Europeans' uncivilized treatment of their Indian wives.

⁶For example, Professors Russell Smandych and Anne McGillivray of the University of Manitoba examined the writings of Jesuit Father Lafitau, 1712 to 1717. They quote Lafitau:

> They let them (their children) do everything that they like when they are very young, under the pretext that they are not yet at the age of reason and that, when they reach those years, they will follow the light (of reason) and correct themselves... no one moreover would dare strike or punish them... which indicates that in methods of bringing up children, gentleness is more efficacious then punishment, especially violent ones.

R. Smandych & A. McGillivray, "Images of Aboriginal Childhood" in M. Daunton & R. Halpern, eds., *Empire and Others: British Encounters with Indigenous Peoples, 1600–1850* (University of Pennsylvania Press, 1999) 238 at 242. Also, Smandych and McGillivray (at 246) quote explorer David Thompson, in 1812, referring to child-rearing practices of the Cree:

> The children are brought up with great care and tenderness ... the constant company and admonition of the old people is their only education ... impressing on their minds, that the man truly miserable is he, who is dependent on another for his subsistence.

Smandych and McGillivray (at 251–52) contrast these practices with those of Reverend William Cockran, an active missionary at Red River from 1825 until he died in 1865. He started a mission school to which, it seems, Indian people did not want to send their children. Using pleas and at least once threatening physical coercion he was able to get some to agree.

> Cockran's punitive pedagogical style and his frequent recommendation that "children must be systematically broken, normally by corporal punishment," would have been a profound shock to aboriginal and perhaps country born children. This pedagogy, premised on European images of appropriate child-rearing was experienced by subsequent generations of aboriginal children whose parents were convinced or forced to send them to government funded mission and residential schools. [citations omitted]

⁷"...[T]here were occasions (especially during the drunken days of the trade wars [between H.B.C. and North-West Company]) when Indian women were abused by the traders..." Sylvia Van Kirk, *supra* note 5 at 4.

⁸See D. Brown, *Bury My Heart at Wounded Knee* (Bantam Books, 1970). The author refers to the Sand Creek massacre (at 85), and describes the Wounded Knee massacre (at 416), both in the United States. Many of the surviving Dakota-Sioux and Cheyenne fled to Canada, most to what is now Saskatchewan. The movie *Little Big Man*, starring Dustin Hoffman, depicts these events.

⁹For example, the *Indian Act* provided:

> Every Indian or other person who engaged in, or assists in celebrating, or encourages either directly or indirectly another to celebrate any Indian festival, dance or other ceremony, in which goods or articles of any sort forms a part or is a feature (the Potlatch) ... and every Indian or other person who engages or assists in any celebration or dance in which the wounding or mutilation of the dead or living body of any human being or animal forms a part or is a feature (the Sundance) is guilty of an indictable offence and is liable to imprisonment for a term not exceeding six months and not less than two months.

E. Ahenakew, *Voices of the Plains Cree* (Toronto: McClelland & Stewart, 1973) at 182, online: Solicitor General of Canada, Conquest by Law <http://www.sgc.gc.ca/publications/abor_policing/Conquest_by_Law_e.asp> at 88.

¹⁰For a detailed history of the effect of Indian residential school on the students and their families, see: J. Milloy. *A National Disgrace: The Canadian Government and the Residential School System—1879 to 1986* (Winnipeg: The University of Manitoba Press, 1999); C. Deiter, *From*

Our Mothers' Arms: The Intergenerational Impact of Residential Schools in Saskatchewan (Toronto: United Church Publishing House, 1999); B. Johnston, *Indian School Days* (Toronto: Key Porter Books, 1988); and J. Miller, *Shingwauk's Vision: A History of Native Residential Schools* (Toronto: University of Toronto Press, 1997).

[11] [1999] 1 S.C.R. 688, (1999) 133 C.C.C. (3d) 385, 23 C.R. (5th) 197.

[12] *Ibid.* at 67.

[13] Canadian Centre for Justice Statistics, *Youth Custody and Community Services Canada, 1999/00*, Statistics Canada 21:12 (Cat. No. 85-002-XPE) at 4 (Figure 1). Saskatchewan's Aboriginal youth are said to make up 75 percent of secured custody admissions, while comprising only 15 percent of the youth population. Other interesting comparisons are seen in Manitoba (79 percent of secured admissions compared to 16 percent of the overall youth population) and Alberta (35 percent of secured admissions to 5 percent of the overall youth population).

[14] T. Quigley, "Some Issues in Sentencing Aboriginal Offenders," in R. Gosse, J. Youngblood Henderson & R. Carter, eds., *Continuing Poundmaker's & Riel's Quest* (Saskatoon: Purich, 1994) 269 at 272–77.

[15] Interview with S.N. (18 December 2002) Saskatoon, Saskatchewan.

[16] Interview with R.T. (19 December 2002) Saskatoon, Saskatchewan.

[17] L. Fisher & H. Janetti, "Aboriginal Youth in the Criminal Justice System" in J. Winterdyk, *Issues and Perspectives on Young Offenders in Canada* (Toronto: Harcourt Brace Canada, 1996) 237 at 242.

[18] Interview with M. Sinclair (17 January 1995) Winnipeg, Manitoba.

[19] *Globe and Mail* (November 2001) at F2.

[20] A. Schkilnyk quoted in Fisher & Janetti, *supra* note 17 at 243.

[21] (London: Vintage, 1990).

[22] *Ibid.* at 141 & 142.

[23] C. LaPrairie "Aboriginal Over-representation in the Criminal Justice System: A Tale of Nine Cities" (April 2002) Can. J. Crim. at 201.

[24] T. Clear & D. Rose, "When Neighbors Go to Jail: Impact on Attitudes About Formal and Informal Social Control" (summary of a presentation to National Institute of Justice Research in Progress seminar series, July 1999), online: National Institute of Justice <http://www.ncjrs.org/pdffiles1/fs000243.pdf> 27 at 42. See also J.P. Lynch, W.J. Sabol, M. Plant & M. Shelly, "Crime, Coercion and Community: The Effects of Arrest and Incarceration Policies on Informal Social Control in Neighborhoods," National Criminal Justice Reference Series, online: National Institute of Justice <http://www.ncjrs.org/pdffiles1/nij/grants/195170.pdf> 27 and 30.

[25] The substantial growth of the U.S. crime control industry is a major focus of Dr. Nils Christie in *Crime Control as Industry: Towards Gulags Western Style*, 3d ed. (London: Routledge, 2000). The extent to which this growth in the youth correctional system has happened through privatization can be seen in a report titled *At Risk Youth... A Growth Industry* (Sun Trust Equitable Securities, 1997, one of the leading investment firms in the United States). Jennifer Walhfun, in the December 2002 edition of the *Atlantic* magazine described this report in the following terms:

> The Sun Trust report ... [included] a diagram titled the "Privatization Spectrum" which showed how companies could profit as children cycled "from schoolhouse to the jailhouse" passing through one publicly funded, privately run facility after another. Arrows marked the flow of kids to companies offering programs in special education, child welfare and juvenile justice. No arrows indicated how these children might one day exit the system and lead ordinary lives.

[26] T. Clear, "Ten Unintended Consequences of Incarceration" (Spring 1997) 1:2 Management Quarterly at 25.

[27] A. Doob & J. Sprott, "Interprovincial Variation in the Use of Youth Custody" (1996) Can. J. Crim. at 401.

[28] Interview with Jim Richards (15 August 2002) Melfort, Saskatchewan.

²⁹*Custody Snapshot Analysis: Executive Summary* (Regina: Department of Social Services). This analysis did not include data for open custody youth in community homes, nor for the open custody youth in Dales House in Regina.

³⁰Saskatchewan's population in 1950 was 833,000. By January 1, 1999, this had increased to 1,026,156. Online: Sakatchewan Bureau of Statistics <http://www.gov.sk.ca/bureau.stats/pea/rbpop1.pdf> and <www.gov.sk.ca/bureau.stats/pop/pop2.pdf>.

³¹M. Jackson, "Locking Up Natives in Canada (1988–89)", 23:2 U.B.C. L. Rev. at 215.

³²*Ibid.*

³³*Supra* note 11 at paragraph 68.

³⁴*Supra* note 31 at 216.

³⁵Interview with E. Gamble (19 April 2000) Saskatoon, Saskatchewan.

³⁶[1999] Y.J. No. 119 (Yukon Ter. Ct. - Youth Ct.).

³⁷[2000] S.J. No. 17 (Sask. Yth. Ct.).

³⁸Interview with S.N. (18 December 2002) Saskatoon, Saskatchewan.

³⁹Address to CAIJ, Social Context for Aboriginal Peoples of Canada (1999). See Jeremy Webber, "Relations of Force and Relations of Justice: The Emergence of Normative Community Between Colonists and Aboriginal Peoples" (1995) 33 Osgoode Hall L.J. 623; M. Jackson, "Locking Up Natives in Canada" (1988-89), 23 U.B.C. L. Rev. 215 (article originally prepared as a report of the Canadian Bar Association Committee on Imprisonment and Release in June 1988), at 215–16.

⁴⁰Interview with S.N. (18 December 2002) Saskatoon, Saskatchewan.

⁴¹P. Monture-OKanee, "Thinking about Aboriginal Justice: Myths and Revolution" in R. Gosse, J. Youngblood Henderson & R. Carter, eds., *Continuing Poundmaker's & Riel's Quest* (Saskatoon: Purich, 1994) 194, 222 at 227.

⁴²*Ibid.*

⁴³*Ibid.* at 229.

⁴⁴Isaiah 10:1–4, *New English Bible* (Oxford University Press, Cambridge University Press, 1970).

⁴⁵Matthew 25:44–46, *New English Bible* (Oxford University Press, Cambridge University Press, 1970).

⁴⁶These examples are cited from D. Van Ness, *Crime and Its Victims* (InterVarsity Press, 1986) at 64. Mr. Van Ness examined many of the same problems as we have in this book from a predominantly Biblical and Christian perspective; it is interesting how similar his conclusions are to those reached here.

⁴⁷E. Adamson Hoebel, *The Law of Primitive Man: A Study in Comparative Legal Dynamics* (New York: Atheneum, 1973) at 279, referred to in Van Ness, *supra* note 46 at 223. Arguably the reason that Japan today has such low crime rates is for the same reason: the need to restore community harmony by restoring the relationship between victim, offender, and the community.

⁴⁸Harold Berman, *Law and Revolution, The Formation of Western Legal Traditions* (Cambridge: Harvard University Press, 1983) 314.

⁴⁹D. Van Ness, *supra* note 46 at 67.

⁵⁰*Ibid.* at 67.

⁵¹In "Prisons and Executions—The U.S. Model: A Historical Introduction" (July/August 2001) 53:3 Monthly Review at 3.

⁵²Joseph H. Kinsey, *Strange Empire: The Story of Louis Riel* (Toronto: Swan Publishing Co., 1965) 414.

⁵³W.J. Chambliss, *Crime and the Legal Process* (Toronto: McGraw-Hill, 1969) at 422.

⁵⁴Albert Einstein, *Why Socialism?*, online: <http://www.monthlyreview.org/598einst.htm>.

⁵⁵D. Mathews, "The Southern Rite Of Human Sacrifice," online: Journal of Southern Religion <http://jsr.as.wvu.edu/mathews.htm>.

⁵⁶*Ibid.*

⁵⁷*Ibid.*

[58]Brock quoted in B. Coloroso, *Kids Are Worth It: Giving Your Child the Gift of Inner Discipline* (Middlesex: Penguin Books, 2001) at 40.

[59]*Money* magazine quoted in *ibid.* at 5.

Chapter 5

[1]1998, c. 37.

[2]Youth Justice Board, "The Aim of the New Youth Justice System Is to Prevent Offending" (London: undated pamphlet).

[3]*Ibid.*

[4]*Ibid.*

[5]Youth Justice Board, *The Preliminary Report on the Operation of the New Youth Justice System* (London: November 2001) at 6.

[6]*Ibid.*

[7]Nacro Youth Crime, youth crime briefing, (London: December 2001) at 1.

[8]*Ibid.*

[9]Youth Justice Board, *Delivering Change: Youth Justice Board Review 2000/2001* (London: 2001) at 8.

[10]Oxfordshire Youth Offending Team, "What is a YOT?" (Oxford, undated).

[11]Youth Justice Board Preliminary Report, *supra* note 2 at 10.

[12]D. Farrington, "The Nature and Extent of Youth Crime" in R. Smandych, ed., *Youth Crime: Varieties, Theories and Prevention* (Toronto: Harcourt, 2001) 5 at 9.

[13]Nacro Youth Crime, *supra* note 7 at 2.

[14]Youth Justice Board Preliminary Report, *supra* note 5 at 8.

[15]M. Lofty, "Restorative Justice and Youth Offending Teams" (Crime and Disorder Seminar, 24 January 2001, Bramshill, England).

[16]*Ibid.*

[17]C. Pollard, "Policing and Young People" (remarks to the First Annual Youth Justice Conference, 9–10 November 2000, Maldon, Essex).

[18]J. Graham, "Juvenile Crime and Justice in England and Wales" in N. Bala, J. Hornick, H. Snyder & J. Paetsch, eds., *Juvenile Justice Systems: An International Comparison of Problems and Solutions* (Toronto: Thompson Educational Publishing, 2002) 67 at 99.

[19]*Ibid.* at 99–100. They can also be made against parents of a youth made the subject of "a child safety order, an antisocial behaviour order, or a sex offender order." *Ibid.* at 100.

[20]*Ibid.*

[21]*Ibid.* at 102.

[22]*Ibid.* at 103. Rand is described here as being a "non-profit institution that advises on various aspects of public policy in the US."

[23]C. Love, "Family Group Conferencing: Cultural Origins, Sharing and Appropriation—A Maori Reflection" in G. Burford and J. Hudson, eds., *Family Group Conferencing: New Directions in Community-Centred Child and Family Practice* (New York: Aldine de Gruyter, 2000) at 24.

[24]*Ibid.*

[25]*Ibid.* at 25.

[26]1989 No. 24.

[27]M. Levine, "The Family Group Conference in the New Zealand Children, Young Persons and Their Families Act of 1989: Review and Evaluation" (2000) 18 Behav. Sci. Law 517 at 517.

[28]J. Consedine, *Restorative Justice: Healing the Effects of Crime* (New Zealand: Ploughshares Publications, 1995) at 89.

[29]*Ibid.*

[30]*Ibid.* at 104.

[31]A. Morris & G. Maxwell, "Re-Forming Juvenile Justice: The New Zealand Experiment" in R. Smandych, ed., *Youth Justice: History Legislation, and Reform* (Toronto: Harcourt, 2001) 215 at 216–17.

[32]M. Brown, "Background Paper on New Zealand Youth Justice Process" (paper presented at the International Bar Association Judges' Forum section on General Practice, Edinburgh, 10–13 June 1995), online: International Institute for Restorative Practices <http://www.restorativepractices.org/Pages/NZ.html>.

[33]*Ibid.*

[34]M. Levine, *supra* note 27 at 520.

[35]*Ibid.*

[36]*Ibid.* at 530.

[37]Morris and Maxwell, *supra* note 31 at 219.

[38]Levine, *supra* note 27 at 550.

[39]*Ibid.*

[40]J. Tauri, "Family Group Conferencing: A Case Study of the Indigenisation of New Zealand's Justice System" 10:20 Current Issues in Criminal Justice 168 at 176–77.

[41]J. Tauri, "Explaining Recent Innovations in New Zealand's Criminal Justice System: Empowering Maori or Biculturalising the State" (1999) 32:2 Austl. Crim. & N.Z.J. 153 at 160.

[42]Love, *supra* note 23 at 26.

[43]*Ibid.*

[44]*Ibid.*

[45]*Ibid.* at 26–28.

[46]G. Maxwell and A. Morris, "Juvenile Crime and Justice in New Zealand" in N. Bala, J. Hornick, H. Snyder & J. Paetsch, eds., *Juvenile Justice Systems: An International Comparison of Problems and Solutions* (Toronto: Thompson Educational Publishing, 2002) 189 at 212.

[47]*Ibid.*

[48]*Ibid.* at 216.

[49]*Ibid.* at 215.

[50]*Ibid.* at 216.

[51]These statistics are online: Australian Institute of Criminology <http://www.aic.gov.au/>.

[52]J. Consedine, *supra* note 28 at 113.

[53]*Ibid.* These quotations represent J. Consedine's summary of Professor Crawford's view.

[54]H. McRae, G. Nettheim, L. Beacroft & L. McNamara, *Indigenous Legal Issues* (Sydney: LBC Information Services, 1997) at 343.

[55]J. Consedine, *supra* note 28 at 118.

[56]*Ibid.*

[57]*Ibid.* at 118–19.

[58]R. Homel, R. Lincoln & B. Herd, "Risk and Resilience: Crime and Violence Prevention in Aboriginal Communities" (1999) 32:2 Austl. Crim. & N.Z.J. 182 at 182–84.

[59]*Ibid.* at 185–91.

[60]R. White. "Indigenous Youth and Offensive Spaces" (April 1999) 18:2 Social Alternatives at 39.

[61]A. Freiberg, "Three Strikes and You're Out—It's Not Cricket: Colonization and Resistance in Australian Sentencing" in M. Tonry & R. Frase, eds., *Sentencing and Sanctions in Western Countries* (New York: Oxford University Press, 2001) 29 at 52.

[62]J. Braithwaite, *Crime, Shame and Reintegration* (Cambridge University Press, 1989) at 54–68.

[63]J. Braithwaite, "Democracy, Community and Problem Solving" in G. Burford and J. Hudson, eds., *Family Group Conferencing: New Directions in Community-Centred Child and Family Practice,* 31.

[64]*Ibid.,* 33.

[65]Law Reform Commission of New South Wales, *Sentencing: Aboriginal Offenders* (Sydney: 2000) 96.

[66]*Ibid.* at paragraph 1.33.

[67]G. Palk, H. Hayes & T. Prenzler, *Restorative Justice and Community Conferencing: Summary of Findings from a Pilot Study* (Restorative Justice and Community Conferencing, November 1998) 138 at 142.

[68]T. O'Connell, "From Wagga Wagga to Minnesota" (paper presented at the First North Ameri-

can Conference on Conferencing, 6–8 August 1998, Minneapolis, MN), online: International Institute for Restorative Practices <http://www.restorativepractices.org/Pages/nacc_oco.html>

[69]H. Blagg, "A Just Measure of Shame? Aboriginal Youth and Conferencing in Australia" in R. Smandych, ed., *Youth Justice: History, Legislation, and Reform* (Toronto: Harcourt, 2001) 225 at 226.

[70]*Ibid.*

[71]J. Braitwaite, "Conferencing and Plurality: Reply to Blagg" (Autumn 1997) 37:4 British Journal of Criminology 502 at 503.

[72]K. Daly, "Conferencing in Australia and New Zealand: Variations, Research Findings, and Prospects" in A. Morris & G. Maxwell, eds., *Restorative Justice for Juveniles: Conferencing, Mediation and Circles* (London: Hart Publishing, 2001) 59 at 64.

[73]*Ibid.*

[74]Palk, *supra* note 67 at 142.

[75]J. Wundersitz, "Aboriginal Youth and the South Australian Juvenile Justice System: Has Anything Changed?" in C. Alder, ed., *Juvenile Crime and Juvenile Justice: Toward 2000 and Beyond* (Canberra: Australian Institute of Criminology, 1998) 32 at 35.

[76]H. Strang, *Restorative Justice Programs in Australia: A Report to the Criminology Research Council* (March 2001), online: Criminology Research Council <http://www.aic.gov.au/crc/reports/strang/> at 12.

[77]Daly, *supra* note 72 at 74–81.

[78]*Ibid.* at 76–77.

[79]*Ibid.* at 77–79.

[80]Wundersitz, *supra* note 75 at 42.

[81]*Juvenile Justice Act 1992* including amendments up to Act no. 59 of 2002.

[82]Palk, *supra* note 67 at 142.

[83]*Ibid.*

[84]*Ibid.* at 144.

[85]*Ibid.* at 152.

[86]I. O'Connor, K. Daly & L. Hinds, "Juvenile Crime and Justice in Australia" in N. Bala, J. Hornick, H. Snyder & J. Paetsch, eds., *Juvenile Justice Systems: An International Comparison of Problems and Solutions* (Toronto: Thompson Educational Publishing, 2002) 221 at 231.

[87]South Australia *Young Offenders Act* no. 57 of 1993.

[88]*Supra* note 86 at 231–32.

[89]D. Miers, *An International Review of Restorative Justice* (London: British Home Office, 2001) at 5.

[90]*Ibid.* at 7–38.

[91]Declaration of Basic Principles on the Use of Restorative Justice Programmes in Criminal Matters, UNCCPCJ, 11th Sess. (2002), section 6.

[92]Daly, *supra* note 72 at 59.

[93]*Ibid.* at 61.

Chapter 6

[1]C. Cooper and J. Chatterjee, "Punishment at the Turn of the Century: The RCMP Perspective" (paper presented to conference entitled Changing Punishment at the Turn of the Century: Finding a Common Ground, Saskatoon, 26–29 September 1999) at 1.

[2]As quoted in D. Cayley, "To Hurt or to Heal" *Ideas* (CBC Radio transcript, 2000) at 31.

[3]*Ibid.* at 33.

[4]J. Gouk, "A New Approach to the Punishment of Crime in Canada" (paper presented to conference entitled Changing Punishment at the Turn of the Century: Finding a Common Ground, Saskatoon, 26–29 September 1999) at 1.

[5]*Ibid.*

[6]"Prevention and Children: Offender Profiles" National Crime Prevention Council, at 3,

online: <http://www.acbr.com/fas/offpro_e.htm>.

[7]Interview with B.W. (19 December 2002) White Buffalo Youth Lodge.

[8]D. Jones-Brown & Z. Weston Henriques, "Promises and Pitfalls of Mentoring as a Juvenile Justice Strategy" in R. Smandych, ed., *Youth Crime: Varieties, Theories and Prevention* (Toronto: Harcourt, 2001) 292 at 295.

[9]*Ibid.*

[10]D. Cornell, "What Works in Youth Violence Prevention" in R. Smandych, ed., *Youth Crime: Varieties, Theories and Prevention* (Toronto: Harcourt, 2001) 273 at 283.

[11]D. MacKenzie, A. Gover, G. Armstrong & O. Mitchell, "A National Study Comparing the Environments of Boot Camps with Traditional Facilities for Juvenile Offenders" (August 2001), online: National Criminal Justice Reference Centre <http://www.ncjrs.org/txtfiles1/nij/187680.txt>.

[12]L. Woodbury, "Boot Camps" (August, 2001) 84 Woodbury Reports Archives: Opinion & Essays, online: <http://www.strugglingteens.com/archives/2001/8/oe02.html>.

[13]N. Hendley, "The Shine Is off Boot Camps" (1 January 2000) *Eye Weekly,* online: Eye Weekly <http://www.eye.net/eye/issue/issue_01.20.00/news/bootcamp.html>.

[14]*Ibid.*

[15]Ontario Government, press release "Ontario's First Young Offender Boot Camp a Success" (24 March 2001).

[16]A. Doob et al. (May 2001) 4:1 Criminological Highlights, Centre of Criminology, University of Toronto.

[17]K. O'Connor, "Youth Work Camps Get the Boot" *Saskatoon Star Phoenix* (1 February 2002).

[18]J. Blum & Y. Woodlee, "Trying to Give Kids a Good Scare" *Washington Post* (3 June 2001) C01.

[19]A. Petrosino & C. Turpin-Petrosino, "'Scared Straight' and other Prison Tour Programs for Preventing Juvenile Delinquency" (protocol for a Cochrane Review) (2000) 4 The Cochrane Library, Oxford: Update Software.

[20]S. Aos, P. Phipps, R. Barnoski & R. Lieb, *The Comparative Costs and Benefits of Programs to Reduce Crime* (Washington State Institute for Public Policy, May 2001) at 18. The Washington State Institute for Public Policy studied the effectiveness of "Scared Straight," a program where youth who seem to be in danger of beginning a long dismal journey into crime are taken to a prison where prisoners tell them how bad life can be if they carry on. The "Scared Straight" programs (eight were studied) were cheap to run, about $50 per person. However they increased crime substantially, 13 percent. The bottom line analysis was after taking into account their future crimes, etc., the program lost $24,531 per participant.

[21]*Ibid.*

[22]Interview with Justice Murray Sinclair (21 February 2002) Winnipeg, Manitoba.

[23]Interview with Harry Morin (19 October 1994) Sandy Bay, Saskatchewan.

[24]*Tribal Justice: A New Beginning* (Whitehorse, 1991) [unpublished] at 7.

[25]Felicia Daunt, *Briarpatch* 27:9 (November 1998).

[26]M. Brokenleg, "Reclaiming Youth at Risk" (lecture, 28 August 2000, Regina, Saskatchewan).

[27]B. Clark, P. O'Reilly & T. Fleming, "From Care to Punishment" in *Youth Injustice: Canadian Perspectives* (Canadian Scholars Press Inc.,1993) at 189. The quote is at 194–95.

[28]A summary of P. Smith, C. Goggin & P. Gendreau, *The Effects of Prison Sentences and Intermediate Sanctions on Recidivism: General Effects and Individual Differences* (Ottawa: Solicitor General Canada, 2002, User Report 2002–01) stated: "...further analysis of the incarceration studies found that longer sentences were associated with higher recidivism rates. Sentences of more than 2 years has an average increase in recidivism of seven percent." *Research Summary: Corrections Research and Development*, 7:3 (May 2002).

[29]Washington State study, *supra* note 20 at 21.

[30]"This Morning" (CBC Radio, 26 May 1998).

[31]Brokenleg, *supra* note 26.

[32]R. Curwin & A. Mendler, *Discipline with Dignity* (Virginia: Association for Supervision and Curriculum Development, 1998) at 65.

[33]This sentence combines the works used by these authors in headings on pages 66–69.

[34]J. Bonta, "Offender Rehabilitation: From Research to Practice" (Association of Parole Authorities International Conference, 2000).

[35]B. Schissel, *Blaming Children: Youth Crime, Moral Panics and the Politics of Hate* (Halifax: Fernwood Publishing, 1997) at 10.

[36]B. Schissel, "Youth Crime, Moral Panics, and the News: The Conspiracy against the Marginalised in Canada" in R. Smandych, ed., *Youth Justice: History Education and Reform* (Toronto: Harcourt, 2001) 84 at 85.

[37]A. Doob, "Transforming the Punishment Environment: Understanding Public Views of What Should Be Accomplished at Sentencing" (July 2000) Can. J. Crim. 323 at 327.

[38]*Ibid.*

[39]*Ibid.* at 332.

[40]*Ibid.* at 331.

[41]*Ibid.* at 332.

[42]*Ibid.* at 335.

[43]J. Roberts & A. Doob, "News Media Influences on Public Views of Sentencing" (1990) 14:5 Law and Human Behavior 451 at 453.

[44]*Ibid.* at 457 & 458.

[45]*Ibid.* at 462–65.

[46]Public meeting, Melfort United Church (April 2001).

[47]J. Roberts & A. Doob, "Sentencing and Public Opinion: Taking False Shadows for True Substances" (1989) 27:3 Osgoode Hall L.J. 491 at 502.

[48]Canadian Press, "Courts too Lenient on Criminals: Poll" *Saskatoon Star Phoenix* (12 August 2002).

[49]FSIN and the Courts, meeting in Saskatoon, October 2000.

[50]"Transforming the Punishment Environment: Understanding Public Views of What Should Be Accomplished at Sentencing" (July 2000) Can. J. Crim. 323.

[51]*Ibid.* at 328–29.

[52]*Ibid.*

[53]*R. v. L.E.K.* [2000] S.J. No. 844 (QL).

[54]*Ibid.* at paragraph 25.

[55]D. Cayley, "To Hurt or to Heal" *Ideas* (CBC Radio transcript, 2000) at 2.

[56]*Ibid.*

[57]*Ibid.* at 4.

Chapter 7

[1]Church Council on Justice and Corrections, *Restorative Justice Reflection Sheet #1: Restorative Justice, What Are We Talking About?* (Ottawa: undated) at 1.

[2]S. Sharpe, "Restorative Justice: A Vision for Healing and Change" (Mediation and Restorative Justice Centre: Edmonton, 1998) at 7.

[3]G. Brazemore, "The Fork in the Road to Juvenile Court Reform" (July 1999) 564 Annals of the American Academy of Political and Social Science 81.

[4](1990) 1 O.R. (3d) 247, [1990] O.J. No. 2343 (QL).

[5]*Ibid.* at 11 (QL).

[6](Ottawa, 1997).

[7]*Ibid.* at 27.

[8]*McDougall, supra* note 4 at 12 (QL).

[9]This conference was held in Ottawa, 2–4 November 2001.

[10]G. Brazemore & M. Umbreit, "Rethinking the Sanctioning Function in Juvenile Court: Retributive or Restorative Responses to Youth Crime" in R. Smandych, ed., *Youth Justice: History Education and Reform* (Toronto: Harcourt, 2001) at 196.

[11]*Ibid.* at 198.

[12]*Ibid.* at 199–200.

[13]As mentioned earlier, U.S. youth custody statistics are suspect, mainly because of the significant number of American young people transferred to adult court that, if incarcerated, do not show up in the youth custody statistics. This leads to the likely conclusion that U.S. figures greatly understate the number of young people incarcerated.

[14](1992), 71 C.C.C.(3d) 347. This decision discussed the process of circle sentencing which allowed local community members and victims to join active consideration of offender sentences.

[15]*Ibid.* at 357.

[16]Interview with Associate Chief Judge Murray Sinclair (1995) 1:4 *Family Violence Research Centre Bulletin* at 5.

[17]Brazemore & Umbreit, *supra* note 10 at 201.

[18]A. Doob, "Transforming the Punishment Environment: Understanding Public Views of What Should Be Accomplished at Sentencing" (July 2000) Can. J. Crim. 323 at 328 and 338.

[19]D. Cayley, "To Hurt or to Heal" *Ideas* (CBC Radio transcript, 2000) at 3.

[20]R. Ross, "Victims and Criminal Justice: Exploring the Disconnect" (Oct. 2002) 46 Crim. L.Q. 483–502.

[21]*Ibid.* at 3–4.

[22]G. Brazemore & C. Griffiths, "Conferences, Circles, Boards, and Mediations: The "New Wave" of Community Justice Decision Making" (June 1997) 61:2 Federal Probation 25.

[23]D. van Ness, A. Morris & G. Maxwell, "Introducing Restorative Justice" in A. Morris & G. Maxwell, eds., *Restorative Justice for Juveniles: Conferencing, Mediation & Circles* (Oregon: Hart Publishing, 2001) 3 at 7.

[24]*Ibid.*

[25]*Ibid.*

[26]Brazemore & Griffiths, *supra* note 22.

[27]M. Levine, "The Family Group Conference in the New Zealand Children, Young Persons and Their Families Act of 1989: Review and Evaluation" (2000) 18 Behav. Sci. Law 517 at 517.

[28]*Ibid.* at 520.

[29]R. Green, *Justice in Aboriginal Communities: Sentencing Alternatives* (Saskatoon: Purich Publishing, 1998) at 68.

[30]*Ibid.* at 69.

[31]G. Brazemore & M. Umbriet, *A Comparison of Four Restorative Conferencing Models* (Washington: U.S. Department of Justice, Office of Juvenile Justice and Delinquency Prevention, Juvenile Justice Bulletin, February 2001) at 3.

[32]*Ibid.*

[33]G. Brazemore & C. Griffiths, *supra* note 22.

[34]Brazemore and Umbreit, *supra* note 31.

[35]D. Karp, "Harm and Repair: Observing Restorative Justice in Vermont" (2001) 18:4 Justice Quarterly 727–57 at 727–30.

[36]Cayley, *supra* note 19 at 10.

[37]*R. v. Thomas* (November 2000), Nipawin (Sask. Prov. Ct.)

[38]Restorative justice conference, *supra* note 9.

[39]Interview with M. Sinclair (21 February 2002) Winnipeg, Manitoba.

[40]Cayley, *supra* note 19 at 85.

[41]Interview (7 August 2001) Kenora, Ontario.

[42]R. Ross, *supra* note 20.

[43]Cayley, *supra* note 19 at 10.

[44]This comment is taken from Principal Youth Court Judge Michael Brown (of New Zealand), "Background Paper on New Zealand Youth Justice Process" (presented at the International Bar Association Judges' Forum section on General Practice, Edinburgh, 10–13 June 1995), online: International Institute for Restorative Practices <http://www.restorativepractices.org/Pages/NZ.html>.

[45]Brazemore & Griffiths, *supra* note 22.

[46]*Ibid.*

[47]Church council reflection sheet, *supra* note 1 at 2.

[48]H. Zehr, *Taking Victims and their Advocates Seriously: The Listening Project, 1999,* as cited in "Restorative Justice Week 2000 Basic Resource Kit: Harmony and Healing, Broken Wings Take New Flight" (Ottawa: Correctional Service of Canada, 2000) at 7.

[49]R. Ross, *supra* note 20.

[50]K.R. Peterson. *The Justice House—Report of the Special Advisor on Gender Equality* (Yellowknife, Canada: Department of Justice, Government of the Northwest Territories, 1992) at 75.

[51]Brazemore & Griffiths, *supra* note 22.

[52]E. LaRocque, "Re-examining Culturally Appropriate Models in Criminal Justice Applications" in Michael Asch, ed., *Aboriginal and Treaty Rights in Canada: Essays on Law, Equity and Respect for Difference* (Vancouver: University of British Columbia Press, 1998) 75–96 at 86. For a detailed discussion of domestic violence in Aboriginal communities see A. McGillivray & B. Comaskey, *Black Eyes All the Time: Intimate Violence, Aboriginal Women, and the Justice System* (Toronto: University of Toronto Press, 1999).

[53]F. Cullen, B. Fulton, S. Levrant & J. Wozniak, "Reconsidering Restorative Justice: The Corruption of Benevolence Revisited?" (Jan 99) 45:1 Crime & Delinquency 3 (25 pp).

[54]*Ibid.*

[55]*Ibid.*

[56]*Ibid.*

[57]D. Garland, *The Culture of Control: Crime and Social Order in Contemporary Society* (Oxford: Oxford University Press, 2001) at 143.

[58]Brazemore & Griffiths, *supra* note 22.

[59]Green, *supra* note 29 at 122.

[60]M. Levine, "The Family Group Conference in the New Zealand Children, Young Persons and Their Families Act of 1989: Review and Evaluation" (2000) 18 Behav. Sci. Law 517 at 522.

[61](1993) 114 Sask. R. 2, [1994] 1 C.N.L.R. 150 (Sask. Q.B.).

[62]Online: Aboriginal Legal Services of Toronto <http://www.aboriginallegal.ca/council.php>.

[63]Interview with Justice Murray Sinclair (21 February 2002).

[64]*Ibid.*

[65]The reference to intimacy and its possible connection with spirituality was identified during a meeting with author and prosecutor Rupert Ross in August 2002 at Kenora, ON.

[66]D. Breton & S. Lehman, *The Mystic Heart of Justice: Restoring Wholeness in a Broken World* (Pennsylvania: Chrisalis Books, 2001). Quotations in this sentence are taken from the book's inside cover.

[67]*Ibid.*

[68]Interview with Doug Borch (11 December 2000) Calgary, Alberta.

[69]Online: Calgary Community Conferencing <http://calgarycommunityconferencing.com. previewmysite.com/about_us.php>.

[70]*Ibid.*

[71]*Ibid.*

[72]*Ibid.*

[73]*Ibid.*

[74]Online: Calgary Community Conferencing, "Research and Eval – Participant Satisfaction" <http://www.calgaryconferencing.com/r_and_e/satisfaction.html>.

[75]Borch, *supra* note 68.

[76]Interview with Daphne Buffet (13 December 2000) Calgary, Alberta.

[77]Borch, *supra* note 68.

[78]*Ibid.*

[79]*Ibid.*

[80]Borch, *supra* note 68.

[81]See R. Green, *Justice in Aboriginal Communities: Sentencing Alternatives* (Saskatoon: Purich Publishing, 1998) at 80–82.

[82]Borch, *supra* note 68.

[83][2000] A.J. No. 988 (QL), 2000 ABPC 125, (2000) 90 Alta. L.R. (3d) 185, (2000) 270 A.R. 312 (Alta. Prov. Ct, Yth. Div.).

[84]At paragraph 60.

[85]At paragraph 100.

[86]*Ibid.*

[87]*Ibid.*

[88]At paragraphs 101 & 102.

[89]CCC's web site <http://calgarycommunityconferencing.com/index.php> contains citations to other cases involving this program.

Chapter 8

[1]Canadian Centre for Justice Statistics, Youth Court Survey, 2000–2001. The rates were obtained from the graph provided by this centre. Prince Edward Island is the lowest at 17/1,000.

[2]*Ibid.*

[3]These statistics were provided by Professor Jean Trepanier of the Université de Montreal (21 October 2002).

[4]22:6 Juristat crime statistics.

[5]*House of Commons Debates* (25 September 2000).

[6]Interview with Clement Laporte (23 October 2002) Montreal, Quebec

[7]Interview with Serge Charbonneau (21 October 2002) Montreal, Quebec.

[8]Interview with Serge Charbonneau (22 October 2002) Montreal, Quebec. First Nations in Quebec do not fall within these OJAs but rather operate separately through their own justice committees (telephone interview the Serge Charbonneau, 18 June 2003).

[9]Interview with Michel Côté (23 October 2002).

[10]*Ibid.*

[11]*Ibid.*

[12]Trajet Jeunesse booklet (Montreal, undated).

[13]Charbonneau, *supra* note 7.

[14]Côté, *supra* note 9.

[15]*Ibid.*

[16]Trepanier, *supra* note 3.

[17]Trepanier, *supra* note 3, and Charbonneau, *supra* note 7.Other provinces also have a significant number of cases diverted from the youth court system. In particular, Saskatchewan and Alberta have rates much higher than the national average. Cherly Engler and Shannon Crowe, "Alternative Measures in Canada, 1998–99" 20 Juristat 6 at 6.

[18]R.S.Q. P-34.

[19]Trepanier, *supra* note 3.

[20]*Ibid.*

[21]Manitoba also set the upper limit at eighteen. See T. Leonard, R. Smandych & S. Brickey, "Changes in the Youth Justice System" in J. Winterdyck, ed., *Issues and Perspectives on Young Offenders in Canada* (Toronto: HBJ-Holt, 1996) 119–41 at 128. Professor Trepanier noted British Columbia and Newfoundland increased the ceiling, but only to seventeen years (thereby including sixteen year olds).

[22]Trepanier, *supra* note 3.

[23]E-mail from Professor Jean Trepanier (5 November 2002).

[24]*Ibid.*

[25]M. Le Blanc, *Rehabilitation of Young Offenders in Quebec: 30 Years of Empirical Research and Professional Interventions* (19 September 2002) [unpublished, Toronto: National Judicial Institute Youth Justice Educational Program].

[26]Interview with Jean Trepanier.

[27]Laporte interview, *supra* note 6.

[28]Interview with Judge Ann-Marie Jones (24 October 2002) Montreal, Quebec.

[29]This is found in subsections 3(b)(iv) and (v).

[30]R.T. Can 1992 No. 3.

[31]R.T. Can 1976 No. 47.

[32]Renvoi relatif au projet de loi C-7 sur le système de justice pénale pour les adolescents [2003] J.Q. (QL) No. 2850 (Qué. CA). Quotations are taken from the English translation of this decision.

[33]Sections 62, 63, 64(1) and (5), 70, 72(1) and (2), and 73(1) of the *YCJA*.

[34]*Supra* note 32 at paragraph 286 of translation.

[35]Sections 75 and 110(2)(b).

[36]*Supra* note 32 at paragraph 290 of translation.

[37]C. Gillis & R. Benzie, "Ontario Fights Youth-Crime Changes: Ottawa to Soften New Act" *National Post (6 May 2003)*.

[38]R. Benzie, "Youths Will Get Away with Murder: Sterling" *National Post* (9 May 2003).

[39]L. Fowler, *Adults as Role Models and Mentors for Youth* (Columbus: Ohio State University Fact Sheet, FLM-FS-2-00, Family and Consumer Sciences), online <http://ohioline.osu.edu/flm00/fs02.html>.

[40]J. Grossman & E. Garry, *Mentoring—A Proven Delinquency Prevention Strategy*, Juvenile Justice Bulletin (Washington, D.C.: Office of Juvenile Justice and Delinquency Prevention). The account of this study was quoted from D. Cornell, "What Works in Youth Violence Protection" in R. Smandych, ed., *Youth Crime: Varieties, Theories and Prevention* (Toronto: Harcourt Canada, 2001) 273 at 274.

[41]"Quantum Opportunities Program Center for Human Resources," Brandeis University report, n.d., at 4.

[42]S. Aos, P. Phipps, R. Barnoski & R. Lieb, *The Comparative Costs and Benefits of Programs to Reduce Crime* (Washington State Institute for Public Policy, May 2001) at 14. It should be noted that the Institute used a conservative approach to financial estimates (at page 3) and that they did not estimate benefits such as youth obtaining employment or finishing school (at page 2).

[43]Rand Corp., prepared for University of California, Berkley by the James Irvine Foundation (April 1996).

[44](April 2000) 154 Archives of Pediatric and Adolescent Medicine 327 at 331, American Medical Assocation.

[45]Aos et al., *supra* note 42 at 15 and 21.

[46]Interview with R.T. (19 December 2002) Saskatoon, Saskatchewan

[47]Project funding proposal for CHUMS (6 June 2002).

[48]Manitoba Aboriginal Role Model Profile 4, Manitoba Education and Training and Youth (February 2001).

[49]Interview with Clayton Sandy (16 May 2002) Winnipeg, Manitoba.

[50]Online: MAYCAC <http://www.maycac.com/intro.html>.

[51]Role model profile, *supra* note 48.

[52]*Ibid.*

[53]*Ibid.*

[54]*Ibid.*

[55]Sandy, *supra* note 49.

[56]MAYCAC, *supra* note 50.

[57]Sandy, *supra* note 49.

[58]*Aboriginal Gang Initiative: Mending the Sacred Hoop* (Ottawa: Correctional Service of Canada, undated pamphlet).

[59]Interview with Clayton Sandy (19 February 2002).

[60]This is the second WHEREAS in the Preamble.

[61][2002] Y.J. No. 49 (Yukon Ter. Ct.).

[62]At paragraph 129. Also see M. Schactor. "When Accountability Fails" (Summer 2001) 2 *Isuma* magazine, Canadian Journal of Policy Research at 134. Mr. Schactor of the Institute of Governance in Ottawa argued at page 135 that democracy is best served by both vertical accountability (i.e., voters holding their government accountable at election day) but also horizontal accountability (i.e., where such bodies as the auditor general or the privacy commissioner report to the public directly).

[63]Section 3(1)(c)(iii).

[64]Online: Campaign 2000 <http://www.campaign2000.ca/rc/00/>.

[65]"'Persistent poverty' crippling Canadian children" CBC News Online (4 November 2002).

[66]*Supra* note 61 at paragraphs 139 and 140.

[67](Jan 98) 44:1 Crime & Delinquency 89.

[68]H. Foxcroft, "A solution that benefits everybody" *The Independent* (24 September 2002) at 5.

[69]In section 3(1)(a)(i).

[70]P. Chartrand & W. Whitecloud. *Aboriginal Implementation Commission: Final Report and Recommendations* (Winnipeg: Statutory Publications Office, 2001) at 135.

[71]*Ibid.*

[72]*Ibid.* at 137.

[73]Interview with B.W. (19 December 2002) White Buffalo Youth Lodge, Saskatchewan.

[74]"Kids First: Nipawin" (pamphlet obtained at Northeast Regional Forum on School PLUS, Melfort, 3 December 2002).

[75][1999] Y.J. No. 119 (Yukon Territorial Court).

[76]*Ibid.* in paragraph 66.

[77]*Securing Saskatchewan's Future: Ensuring the Well-being and Success of Saskatchewan's Children and Youth*, Provincial Response [of the Government of Saskatchewan] to the Role of the School Task Force Final Report (Regina, 2002) at 3.

[78]*Ibid.*

[79]In section 19(1).

[80]In subsections 18(2)(iii) & (iv).

[81]J. VanDenBerg, *Wraparound Planning: Training and Presentation Materials*, online <http://cecp.air.org/wraparound/intro.html>.

[82]*Ibid.*

[83]*Ibid.*

[84]E. Morley & S.B. Rossman, "Helping At-Risk Youth, Lessons from Community-Based Initiatives," online: The Urban Institute <http://www.urban.org/family/helpyouth.html>.

[85][2000] S.J. No. 844 (QL).

[86]Aos et al., *supra* note 42 at 21.

[87]AMA, *supra* note 44.

[88]The summary and quotes in this paragraph come from *M.N.J., supra* note 61 at paragraphs 35 and 36.

[89]*Ibid.* at paragraph 61.

[90]*Ibid.* at paragraph 161.

[91]J. Sekulich, "Making It Work: Integrated Services" (materials from Sixth National Congress on Rural Education, Saskatoon, 1 April 2001).

[92]*Ibid.*

[93][2002] O.J. No. 4497 Toronto Registry No. YW000914 (Ontario Court of Justice).

[94]*Ibid.* at paragraph 10.

[95]M. Rutter. "Protective Factors in Children's Responses to Stress and Disadvantage" in M.W. Kent & J.E. Rolf, eds., *Primary Prevention of Psychopathology* (Lebanon, NH: University Press of New England, 1979) at 49–74.

[96]N. Garmezy, "Children in Poverty: Resilience Despite Risk" 56 Psychiatry at 128.

[97]*Ibid.* at 127.

[98]Susan B. Fine, "Resilience and Human Adaptability: Who Rises Above Adversity?" Eleanor Clarke Slagle Lecture (June 1991) 45:6 American Journal of Occupational Therapy at 496.

[99]J. White, "Getting the Word Out... Promoting Resiliency in Children As a Youth Suicide Prevention Strategy," a paper presented at the Sixth Annual Canadian Association for Suicide Prevention (11–14 October 1995) at 5.

[100]Fine, *supra* note 98 at 473.

[101]S. Baron & L. Kennedy, "Deterrence and Homeless Male Street Youths" (January 1998) Can. J. Crim. at 27.

[102]Dr. P. Steinhauer, "Methods for Developing Resiliency in Children from Disadvantaged Populations" (for the National Forum on Health, 31 March 1996).

[103]Fine, *supra* note 98 at 501.

[104]In section 3(1)(c)(iii).

[105]P. Greenwood, K. Model, C. Rydell & J. Chiesa, *Diverting Children from a Life of Crime: Measuring Costs and Benefits* (Rand Corporation, 1996). Delinquency in this report refers to criminal behaviour.

[106]White, *supra* note 99 at 3.

[107]J. Bonta, "Offender Rehabilitation: From Research to Practice" (Association of Parole Authorities International Conference, Ottawa, 2000).

[108]*Ibid.* at 6.

[109]*Ibid.*

[110]Fine, *supra* note 98 at 500.

[111](Ottawa, 3–4 November 2001).

[112]*Supra* note 61 at paragraph 135.

[113]Accounts of Jerome Miller come mainly from J. Miller, *Last One Over the Wall* (Columbus, Ohio: Ohio State University Press, 1991). Mr. Miller's career was also discussed in some detail in D. Cayley, "Prison and Its Alternatives" *Ideas* (CBC Radio transcript, 17–28 June 1996).

[114]J. Miller, *Last One Over the Wall* (Columbus, Ohio: Ohio State University Press, 1991) at 220. The Harvard study was S. Gould, "Jerome Miller and the Department of Youth Services" (Cambridge: Kennedy School of Government, Harvard University, case #c-114-76-101A and B).

[115]J. Miller, *Last One Over the Wall* (Columbus, Ohio: Ohio State University Press, 1991) at 222.

[116]*Ibid.* at 34.

[117]*Ibid.*

[118]*Ibid.*

[119]*Ibid.* at 35.

[120]*Ibid.*

[121]*Ibid.* at 223.

[122]Interview with Katherine Grier (20 December 2002) Saskatoon, Saskatchewan.

[123]Interview with Mike Dunphy (25 November 2002) Saskatoon, Saskatchewan.

[124]*Honourable Mention*, 19 June 2002, online: Department of Justice Canada <http://canada.justice.gc.ca/en/ps/yj/awards/hko.html>.

[125]*Ibid.*

[126]N. Herland, "Operation Help: Saskatoon Police Try a New Approach to Get Teen Hookers off the Street" (CBC Saskatchewan, 27 November 2002), online: <http://www.sask.cbc.ca/archives/operationhelp/index.html>.

[127]Justice Canada, *supra* note 124.

[128]*Ibid.*

[129]Herland, *supra* note 126.

[130]*Ibid.*

[131]Interview with Tim Tarala (19 December 2002) Tisdale, Saskatchewan.

[132]*Ibid.*

[133]*Ibid.*

[134]*Ibid.*

[135]"Student Support Centre Grand Opening" *Tisdale Recorder* (4 December 2002) at 1.

[136]T. Shire, "Minister of Education Presides Over Opening of Tisdale's Student Support Cen-

tre" *Ensign,* Faster Than Light Communications, Tisdale (28 November 2002), online: <http://ensign.ftlcomm.com/education/partners/storefront/grandOpening/op>.

[137]T. Shire, "Bike Repair Shop and Student Support Centre" *Ensign,* Faster Than Light Communications, Tisdale (13 May 2002), online: <http://ensign.ftlcomm.com>.

[138]T. Shire, "Tisdale School Division Signs Partner Deal with RM of Tisdale, Credit Union and Metis Nation" *Ensign,* Faster Than Light Communications, Tisdale (22 October 2002), online: <http://ensign.ftlcomm.com/education/partners/storefront/signing.html>.

[139]Tarala, *supra* note 131.

[140]*Tisdale Recorder, supra* note 135 at 10.

[141]Tarala, *supra* note 131.

[142]T. Shire, "Minister of Education Presides over Opening of Tisdale's Student Support Centre" *Ensign,* Faster Than Light Communications, Tisdale (28 November 2002), online: <http://ensign.ftlcomm.com>.

[143]*Tisdale Recorder, supra* note 135 at 10.

[144]*Ibid.*

[145]Telephone interview with K. Homeniuk (31 December 2002).

[146]Tarala, *supra* note 131.

Chapter 9

[1](1991), 4 O.R. (3d) 203, [1991] O.J. No. 1382, 1991 CarswellOnt 107 (Ont. Prov. Div.).

[2]Part I of Schedule B to the *Canada Act 1982,* c. 11 (U.K.).

[3]*R. v. E.T.F.,* [2002] O.J. No. 4497 (QL) (Ont. Ct. Jus.) at paragraphs 13 and 14.

[4]See generally B. Coloroso, *Kids Are Worth It: Giving Your Child the Gift of Inner Discipline* (Penguin Books: Middlesex, 2001). At page 5 of this book, the author said: "A Lebanese citizen, weary of continuous shelling in his homeland told a New York Times correspondent: 'There will be peace when we love our children more than we hate our enemies.' If we are going to say our kids are worth it, we must be willing to put our money where our mouth is. We must be willing to put our child-rearing practices there as well."

[5]Crime Prevention Council of Canada. *The Dollars and Sense of Comprehensive Crime Prevention Strategy for Canada* (January 1997).

[6]Interview with S.N. (18 December 2002) Saskatoon, Saskatchewan.

[7]Christie, *Crime Control as Industry: Towards Gulags Western Style,* 3d ed. (London: Routledge, 2000) at 108.

[8]Interview with R.T. (19 December 2002) Saskatoon, Saskatchewan.

[9]L. Joseph, opening address at File Hills Qu'Appelle Tribal Council Justice Conference (26 April 1999) Regina, Saskatchewan.

[10][2002] O.J. No. 4497. Toronto Registry No. YW000914 (Ontario Court of Justice).

[11]Section 39(5) of the *YCJA.*

[12]G. Hamel, "10 Rules for Making Billion Dollar Business Ideas Bubble Up From Below" (12 June 2000).

[13]Quoted in Solicitor General of Canada Aboriginal Peoples Collection, online: Solicitor General of Canada, Conquest by Law <http://www.sgc.gc.ca/publications/abor_policing/Conquest_by_Law_e.asp> at 136. Original manuscript published by Random House in 1950.

[14]C. Wilson, *The Outsider,* 3d ed. (Pan Books, 1970), 33.

[15]Interview with S.N. (18 December 2002) Saskatoon, Saskatchewan.

[16]Interview with Max Dressler (18 November 2002) Regina, Saskatchewan.

[17]Interview with T.W. (19 December 2002) White Buffalo Youth Lodge.

[18]Interview with T.W. (December 2002).

[19]W. Hubbell, "Light From Darkness" (August 1997) *George* magazine, online <ncia.igc.org/george.html>.

[20]Government of Canada. "Knowledge Matters: Skills and Learning for Canadians" Canada's Innovation Strategy, online: Canada's Innovation Strategy <innovationstrategy.gc.ca>.

Index

262